PORTFOLIO
THE CONSOLIDATORS

Prince Mathews Thomas wanted to be a newspaper man, but then grew up to realize that journalism is not about delivering papers, but the news itself. Mentored by K. Thomas Oommen, the iconic teacher, Prince started off with the *Week*, and later worked in *Business Standard*, the *Economic Times*, Dow Jones Newswires and *Forbes India*. A Chevening Scholar, the author is currently the senior deputy editor at *The Hindu Business Line*. Prince is otherwise a confused Indian, having lived in Bokaro, Hyderabad, Delhi, Mumbai and Chennai. His roots are in Kerala.

PRAISE FOR THE BOOK

'Prince has used storytelling as an able tool to tell us why second-generation entrepreneurs are integral to the survival of business families. The stories of these seven entrepreneurs are a guide to how business families can scale, build systems and survive beyond generations'—Ram Charan, adviser to boards, CEOs, Oberoi Realty; member of several boards and co-author of the bestselling *Execution*

'These seven entrepreneurs show that a family business is much the same as any business. Essentially, one has to carry all interested parties/stakeholders with one set of values and operating principles. It is also essential to have a strong connect with the type and nature of the business. The seven entrepreneurs profiled here did this with élan and against a lot of odds. This book is a valuable read for any entrepreneur'—Analjit Singh, founder and chairman emeritus, Max Group

'Against popular belief, it's not easy being a second-generation entrepreneur. Often, as these seven profiles will tell, it's the second generation that brings in scale, sets up processes and systems; and in due course creates an institution out of a family business. Each of these seven entrepreneurs has taken his and her family business to newer, greater heights. These are compelling stories, each a lesson for other aspiring entrepreneurs'—Harsh Mariwala, chairman, Marico Ltd

THE

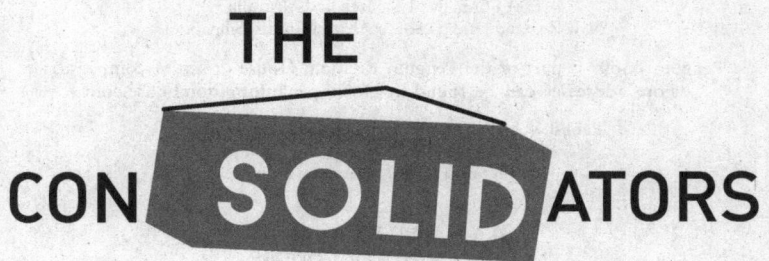

CON SOLID ATORS

PRINCE MATHEWS THOMAS

PORTFOLIO
PENGUIN

An imprint of Penguin Random House

PORTFOLIO

USA | Canada | UK | Ireland | Australia
New Zealand | India | South Africa | China | Singapore

Penguin Books is part of the Penguin Random House group of companies
whose addresses can be found at global.penguinrandomhouse.com

Published by Penguin Random House India Pvt. Ltd
4th Floor, Capital Tower 1, MG Road,
Gurugram 122 002, Haryana, India

First published in Portfolio by Penguin Random House India 2017

ISBN 9780143429302

Typeset in Adobe Jenson Pro by Manipal Digital Systems, Manipal

Printed at Repro India Limited

www.penguin.co.in

This is a legitimate digitally printed version of the book and therefore might not
have certain extra finishing on the cover.

For Papa and Mummy

Contents

Introduction

Which is tougher—to start a business or to grow it? The obvious answer is to set up a business, especially when the stakes are against you. And that is why most of the stories of corporate triumphs have been about the founders, and they deserve to be feted. For instance, look at the story of Dilip Shanghvi, the founder of Sun Pharmaceuticals. He started manufacturing drugs in 1982, with an investment of Rs 10,000. Today, Dilip is only second to Mukesh Ambani on the Forbes India Rich List. In 2016, *Forbes India* said he was worth $16.9 billion.

At the same time, does it mean it is easy to be a second-generation entrepreneur? After all, one is born with a silver spoon. But the answer would be a resounding 'heck, no!' from each of the seven entrepreneurs profiled in the book. Yes, they might be born with a silver spoon, but they had to make sure they didn't lose it.

Take a look at the career of one of the seven—Vikas Oberoi. He was a teenager when his father, Ranvir Oberoi, sold off the family's trading business to venture into real estate full-time. Ranvir was eager to turn his passion for real estate into a successful business.

'When you look at first-generation entrepreneurs, they have more hunger and desire than we, the second generation, have. They in a way have a cross to carry [as they have founded a company] . . . We have to find our own cross. That's a big difference,' says Vikas.

But the business transition that his father had initiated didn't turn out to be successful. By the time Vikas got about constructing his first project, before he turned nineteen, Oberoi Constructions was burdened by debt, and delayed projects had harmed its reputation.

Fortunately, irrespective of the fate of the business, Vikas found his cross. As a teenager, he was intrigued by the stories his father would narrate about real estate deals or about a particular design of a fountain. Even as he finished his school and joined a college in Mumbai, Vikas got more and more involved in the family business. It was his first project, which he completed before its schedule, that steadied Oberoi Constructions and put it on a path to recovery.

Vikas is one of the few successes among second-generation entrepreneurs. Not many find their cross. Most get caught between managing their inheritance and their zeal to prove themselves; they set up businesses that fail to make an impact. The rot sets in and by the time the third generation steps in, the business collapses.

One of the most high-profile business families that has seen its fortune vanish is the Sungrace-Mafatlal family. The fall began in the second generation when 'a series of wrong judgements, tactical mistakes and the inability to ride out a textile recession led to the downfall of a once-prosperous clutch of companies.'[1]

---

[1] Shyamal Majumdar, 'Love, Sex-change and Dhokha', *Business Standard*, 10 September 2011, http://www.business-standard.com/article/beyond-business/love-sex-change-and-dhokha-111091000005_1.html.

The third generation's tenure has been underlined by litigations. Many of the family's companies are in red and its remaining jewels have got too many claimants.

Few family businesses survive beyond the third generation. The *Forbes* magazine makes a startling statement. 'Less than one-third of family businesses survive the transition from first to second generation ownership. Another 50 per cent don't survive the transition from second to third generation.'[2]

Internationally, some of the most famous families have lost control of their businesses, including the Barings family whose bank collapsed in 1995, and the Cadbury family which saw its ownership diluting over the years until Kraft took over the reins in 2010.

Is it because only a few from the following generations have a passion to grow the business? Vikas thinks so. 'A common theme between the people who are successful is that they have a passion. I think we need to find our motivation and our motivation lies in our passion in what we do. And if you are passionate about what you are doing, then you end up being successful,' adds the chairman and managing director of Oberoi Realty (rechristened from Oberoi Constructions).

'Oberoi Realty is the second most valued real estate company in India. He is the least leveraged real estate developer that I know of,' says Deepak Parekh, chairman of Housing Development Finance Corporation, country's leading housing finance company.

---

[2] Aileron, 'The Facts of Family Business,' *Forbes*, 31 July 2013, https://www.forbes.com/sites/aileron/2013/07/31/the-facts-of-family-business/#207baea09884.

It was passion for the business that took Vikas to Harvard Business School for the Owners and Presidents management course. He passed out in 1999, along with Ajay Bijli, chairman and managing director of PVR, and Priya Paul, chairperson of Park Hotels.

Making It Count

Most of India's biggest companies are run by families, handing them down the generations. Take the Forbes India Rich List. Only two among the ten richest businessmen on the list are self-made. All the others, including Mukesh Ambani, Azim Premji and Kumar Mangalam Birla come from business families.

While some of the frontline entrepreneurs belong to the second generation of their families (like Ambani and Premji), others are from the third (Adi Godrej), or even further spread out in the family tree (Kumar Mangalam Birla is from the sixth generation of the venerable family).

In many cases, the second generation has been the pivot in building the business. There have been quite a few success stories, including that of Azim Premji and L.N. Mittal. Premji was just twenty-one years old when he took over the family business after his father's demise. The family was manufacturing cooking oil and laundry soaps. In the 1980s, Premji diversified into IT and, well, as they say, the rest is history. Premji is known as the czar of the Indian IT industry.

Mittal's father had a steel business, headquartered in Kolkata. He sent his eldest son to Indonesia to run a unit. From the South-east Asian country, Mittal started an acquisition spree that culminated with Arcelor in 2006, making him the owner of the world's biggest steel company.

The seven second-generation entrepreneurs in this book— Ajay Bijli, Abhishek Khaitan, Priya Paul, Rituraj Sinha, Vikas Oberoi, T.S. Kalyanaraman and Mithun Chittilappilly— have inspirational stories and career graphs. There are a few similarities between this set of successful seven, and Premji and Mittal.

Like Premji, Priya Paul, chairperson of Park Hotels, had to take charge of the company at a young age. Her father, Surrendra Paul, was assassinated and Priya stepped up to manage the family business. She was twenty-three years old.

Abhishek Khaitan, managing director of Radico Khaitan, also joined the family business during dire times. Rampur Distillery, which was managed by his father, Lalit Khaitan, was at the risk of closing down under a mountain of debt. The situation was made worse when the distillery lost its biggest client. Abhishek was just out of engineering college and recently engaged!

Mittal's passion for the steel industry mirrors the fervour Vikas Oberoi and Ajay Bijli have for their businesses. The first time Ajay told his father, Kishan Mohan, about refurbishing Priya, the single-screen theatre that the family owned, the reaction was, 'Have you lost your mind?' It was very similar to what Vikas' father would tell him every time the youngster wanted to buy more land. Ajay is today the biggest cinema exhibitor in the country, and Vikas the second-most valuable real estate developer.

It's also about having stars in your eyes. Look at these numbers. When Rituraj Sinha, the group chief operating officer of SIS India joined the family business, the company had a revenue of Rs 23 crore. Today it's Rs 5,000 crore.

Similarly, V-Guard was a successful, but content company when Mithun Chittilappilly returned from Australia after completing his management studies. The company, which his father Kochouseph Chittilappilly had founded, was little known outside Kerala and more than 50 per cent of its revenues and 90 per cent of its operating profit came from one product—stabilizers. Today, V-Guard has a handful of hot-selling products (share of the stabilizers is just a little above 20 per cent) and is present pan-India. Its stock was recently rated an 'outperformer'. And to think that V-Guard's IPO in 2008 was a near failure.

Talking about scale, look at what T.S. Kalyanaraman has built. The soft-spoken entrepreneur had intended to open two gold jewellery shops in Thrissur, one each for his two sons. It was similar to what his father had done—built one textile shop each for Kalyanaraman and his brothers. But since its first shop in 1993, Kalyan Jewellers has grown into a Rs 10,000-crore company with 106 outlets in India and overseas.

Apart from their individual brilliance, the success of these seven entrepreneurs also marks the emergence of new India, which was born after the 1991 reforms. Each of the second-generation entrepreneur featured in this book was quick in spotting the opportunity that came with higher aspirations and booming consumerism in India post the 1991 reforms. In executing that opportunity, each one of them showed grit, ambition and tenacity. That is what entrepreneurship is about.

1

Ajay Bijli

It was a warm, sunny day in mid-2012 when Renuka Ramnath, founder of the private equity firm, Multiples Equity, landed in Delhi. She was on a two-day business trip from Mumbai. As she switched on her mobile phone, Renuka was startled to find dozens of missed calls and messages from Ajay Bijli, owner of PVR, the cinema exhibition company.

Their association went back nearly ten years. In 2003, Renuka, who then headed ICICI Bank's private equity arm, ICICI Ventures, had invested Rs 38 crore in PVR. An ICICI Bank veteran, Renuka had set up the private equity business for the lender, and her first investment had been the cinema company. Though ICICI Ventures exited PVR in 2007 after making four times the return on its investment and Renuka herself quit the firm in 2009, she and Ajay remained in constant touch.

When ICICI Ventures invested in PVR, Ajay promised Renuka he would keep her in the loop on everything that went on at the exhibition company. 'If there is any bad news, you will give it to me first,' Renuka had specifically told Ajay. 'Good news will always find its way to reach me.' So even after ICICI Ventures exited PVR, Ajay frequently called Renuka to pick her brains or to just share an update on his company.

But now, as she walked towards the airport exit for her car, Renuka knew that this was unusual. Ajay would have called her office and they would have told him she was travelling to Delhi. He would now be waiting for her call. When she called him back, Ajay answered immediately and said, 'Renuka, I need to meet you very urgently.' But Renuka was headed for a meeting and her schedule was packed for the rest of the day. The two then agreed to meet the next morning for breakfast.

'We met at a hotel, and I thought the meeting would last for an hour or so, but it went on for four hours,' says Renuka.

Ajay had come with an exciting proposal. Cinemax, the theatre-chain owned by Mumbai-based real estate developer Rasesh Kanakia, was up for sale. 'I have been working on this for so many years, but Rasesh *pakad main nahin aa raha tha* . . . now that he has put the company on the block, should I buy it?' asked Ajay

It looked like an exciting opportunity, and Renuka was encouraging. 'This is a once-in-a-lifetime opportunity. You should buy it,' she told Ajay. But this couldn't be an emotional decision. The maths had to be worked out. Renuka asked Ajay for some time for her team to go through the numbers and check if the deal would make sense for PVR. 'I am going back to Mumbai and will put my ace team on this. Let them look at this dispassionately. Prima facie, it looks like we shouldn't miss this,' were her parting words to Ajay.

Renuka's team worked on the numbers for two days. They had free access to data on PVR's business, including its box-office collections, footfall and per-screen performance. These parameters were important to ascertain if PVR had the wherewithal to acquire Cinemax and if the acquisition would work overall.

The team submitted its report, and Renuka immediately called Ajay. 'Ajay, the team is also saying that you should do it. So please go ahead.' Ajay was relieved. The Cinemax acquisition was important for him.

Ajay Bijli started the multiplex craze in the country in 1997 when he opened the four-screen cinema, PVR Anupam, in Delhi. Of late, however, his company seemed to have lost some steam. Big Cinemas, owned by the Anil Dhirubhai Ambani Group (ADAG), had 250 screens in India and nearly 500 worldwide. Another Mumbai peer, INOX, had nearly 260 screens, consolidating its position at the top of the industry after acquiring Fame India in 2010. PVR had only 213 screens.

The financial market too had sensed that PVR was now falling behind in the competition for scale. The PVR scrip was stagnating at around the Rs 200 mark. The fact that the group had lost money in its production business under the banner of PVR Pictures didn't help. Ajay had diversified into movie production in 2006 and had hoped that the diversification would help integrate the exhibition business. Content, or movies, is king in the exhibition business, and Ajay hoped that by producing feature films, he could get a control over content.

Though the start was promising—PVR Pictures' first two productions, *Taare Zameen Par* and *Jaane Tu Ya Jaane Na*, were huge hits—most of the subsequent movies, including *Kheley Hum Jee Jaan Se* and *Teen Thay Bhai* failed at the box office. In the 2010–11 fiscal year, PVR Pictures reported losses of

Rs 20 crore. As PVR shares slid on the stock exchanges (the share price even went below the Rs 200 mark in early 2011), brokerage house analysts questioned the diversification and wondered if Ajay was losing focus from the exhibition business.

Soon enough, in July 2011, PVR Pictures announced its exit from the production business. The diversification had failed. Instead, the subsidiary of PVR would now focus only on distribution of movies.

Now with Cinemax, Ajay had the opportunity he was looking for. The acquisition would bring scale to PVR, helping it regain its numero uno position in the industry. It would also signal that Ajay was more serious and passionate about the exhibition business than he had ever been.

But he couldn't pull it off alone. For one, Big Cinemas, INOX and Cinepolis, the Mexican cinema chain, were also interested in signing a deal with Cinemax. INOX and Big Cinemas had squared off in a race earlier to buy Fame in 2010. R-Cap, an ADAG company, had launched a hostile bid on Fame with an offer that was higher than INOX's. But Fame's promoter, Shravan Shroff, had eventually sided with INOX, which was led by Delhi-based billionaire-entrepreneur Devendra Jain.

While for Big Cinemas and INOX, the Cinemax deal would cement their position in the industry, for Cinepolis a possible acquisition would pave a path to its Indian dreams. Cinepolis was the world's fourth largest cinema chain, and had entered the Indian market in 2008 hoping to emerge among the frontrunners. Cinemax was that opportunity.

To stave off this formidable competition, Ajay needed financial support. Cinemax was 85 per cent the size of PVR. And to top it all, the Kanakias held nearly 70 per cent of the company's equity. Anyone acquiring that stake would also have to contend with having to make an open offer, which would be triggered once the share sale crossed 25 per cent of the company's equity.

That is why help from Renuka, who was the first to show confidence in Ajay and PVR through the ICICI Ventures investment in 2003, was critical for the second-generation entrepreneur. Renuka, who had also set up the investment banking and e-commerce businesses at ICICI Bank, had considerable experience in mergers and acquisitions. This was critical for Ajay, as Cinemax would be his first acquisition.

Secondly, Renuka also brought with her financial might. By the time she left ICICI Ventures, the firm was managing funds of over $2 billion. And now at Multiples, she had raised $405 million in its maiden fund. Ajay needed that financial backing to bag Cinemax.

That was why when Renuka now asked Ajay to go ahead with the acquisition, the PVR CEO shot back, 'What do you mean go ahead? I can't buy without you. You have to help me.'

Renuka agreed. Though the two did not talk about what Multiples' specific financial commitment would be, Renuka was now part of the deal-making process—first as a friend of Ajay's and now as a financial backer. In Mumbai, she figured out who was intermediating on behalf of Rasesh Kanakia. She called the intermediary and said, 'Ajay is quite keen to buy the asset. Is your client in a mood to make a deal?' adding, 'Ajay wants to have a meeting and wants me to come too. But I don't have time to waste. So if your client is in the mood, then I will come.'

When the intermediary asked for ten minutes to talk to his client and get back to her, Renuka said, 'Let me know. I'm at home and until you call me I won't leave my house because I want to know if I am going to my office or coming to your client's office.' In Mumbai, notorious for its traffic snarls, one had to be careful in planning one's schedules. The intermediary called back in less than ten minutes. 'Yes, the client is in the mood to do the deal. You can come.'

The meeting was held in the intermediary's office in Bandra-Kurla Complex, a commercial neighbourhood in Mumbai where many financial institutions and companies are clustered. Ajay and his brother, Sanjeev Kumar, were accompanied by Renuka and another senior executive from Multiples. On his part, Rasesh was pleased to see Renuka. As much as he admired Ajay and PVR, he knew that a deal of this size would be a strain on PVR's books, and Ajay might have to cough up the money himself. What if Ajay is forced to dilute his stake in PVR beyond his comfort level and then develops cold feet? But with the support of Renuka, the prospects for a successful deal looked better. Multiples would not just fund the acquisition, but Renuka would also help Ajay tie up the debt that would be needed. 'I'm comforted by the fact that there is money on the table,' he told Renuka.

As the five-hour meeting came to an end, there was just one more thing to do. Ajay and Renuka needed to seal the deal to ensure that Rasesh wouldn't take the offer from them and then scout the market for better bids. Renuka asked Rasesh and Ajay to sign on a simple document as a token of their agreement to do the deal.

But the Cinemax promoter demurred. Rasesh said his lawyer didn't allow him to sign on any paper as Cinemax was a listed company and he would have to inform the stock exchanges about it. Even PVR, which had its IPO in 2006, would have to make an announcement. It would be too risky for them, Rasesh said. He hadn't done his due diligence on the acquisition yet and wasn't 100 per cent sure. 'We have only confirmed our intention to do the deal,' he said.

When Ajay and Renuka raised fears that PVR's competition, or the market, might get to know that a deal had been made, Rasesh replied that he would continue the facade of scouting for a buyer. 'But you have to trust me that if you produce the money, I will do the deal,' he assured them.

Renuka was still not convinced. There had to be some sort of document or proof of the talks they had just concluded. One could never anticipate what the next day would bring. She asked Ajay how much money he had in his wallet. Ajay opened his wallet and took out a solitary note of Rs 1000. He handed over the note to Rasesh and the exchange was photographed. And that was it. A deal of nearly Rs 550 crore was agreed upon after exchanging a Rs 1000 note!

'It was madness, the following days,' said Renuka. 'All of us were so nervous. We would wonder what would happen to PVR's stock price, or whether we were doing the right thing. And, until the last minute, we were counting the number of shares that needed to be bought or arranging the money for it. There was tension right up to the end.' Renuka also had to finalize the deal between Multiples and PVR.

PVR announced the acquisition of Cinemax on 22 November 2012. A press release said one of PVR's subsidiaries would acquire the 69.27 per cent stake that the promoters held in Cinemax, at Rs 203.65 per share, making the deal worth Rs 395 crore. Additionally, there would be an open offer for another 26 per cent stake, taking the total deal to Rs 543 crore.

'This is an important transaction for us as it takes us to the market leadership position . . . Cinemax has a premium portfolio of multiplex screens across India and has been a market leader in western India,' said Ajay.

The acquisition expanded PVR's reach to 351 screens across eighty-five locations, with a total capacity of 84,190 seats. PVR's revenues ballooned to Rs 1,270 crore in 2012, from Rs 669 crore the year before. The company had taken quite a lead over its nearest competitor, INOX. The deal had also filled a significant gap—Mumbai and the rest of the western market—in PVR's screen network. As a Delhi-based company, PVR was the dominant player in its home market. Now, with Cinemax, it would own forty-five screens in fourteen locations in and around Mumbai.

PVR also announced a preferential issue of 1,06,25,205 shares at a price of Rs 245 apiece, amounting to Rs 260 crore, to its promoters—existing investor L Capital and new private equity investor, Multiples Alternate Asset Management (Multiples)—to partly fund the acquisition.[1] Multiples had put in Rs 153 crore for a 15.8 per cent stake in PVR, marking Renuka's second innings as a business associate of Ajay's.

The investment by her firm was also remarkable for the way it was finalized. It is common for two sides to bargain and haggle for a price that suits their interests best, but both Ajay and Renuka refrained from doing anything like that. While Renuka never inquired about the price at which he was going to

---

[1] Vidhi Choudhary and Aminah Sheikh, 'PVR to Buy Majority Stake in Cinemax', Livemint.com, 30 November 2012, http://www.livemint.com/Companies/DCzBfBsQYG8Hl3HBs5K00M/PVR-to-buy-majority-stake-in-Cinemax.html.

offer PVR shares to Multiples, Ajay offered her a deal that was
fair on all counts. 'It was all trust based. I had to simply trust
that he would be fair to me because I had been fair to him . . .
he could have turned around and said Rs 275, and what could
have I done? The share price was then Rs 225. So he too did
something fair. He locked our deal at Rs 245, which was at a
Rs 20 premium to the market price,' said Renuka. When the
PVR-Cinemax deal was announced in 2012, PVR's scrip raced
to Rs 325 a share. Within moments, Multiples had made a
handsome return on its investment in PVR. In another two
years, PVR's share price would increase by 178 per cent, during
which time the Sensex grew by only 39 per cent.

The Cinemax deal was a huge milestone for Ajay Bijli. 'I
would say that between the acquisitions of Cinemax and DT
Cinema (which PVR acquired later in 2015), a lot had changed
(in him). The confidence with which he pursued DT . . . if there
had been a little bit of fluttering on his part during the Cinemax
deal, that was gone now,' says Renuka. 'The two transactions
helped him grow his leadership style . . . how quickly he could
put in a team to integrate cinemas and show results within a
year. That's absolutely remarkable, and that too without
compromising the brand,' she added.

The focus on brand was something that marked Ajay's
career, from its start.

The Making of Priya

Basant Lok is a buzzing neighbourhood in south Delhi's Vasant
Vihar. Its market complex, popularly known as Priya's, has been
a favourite hangout for generations of Delhiites. Apart from the

offices of big corporate names such as Hero, there are scores
of popular outlets in the market. These range from food joints
and restaurants (including the likes of KFC and McDonald's,
which in 1996 opened its first outlet in India here in Priya's) and
white goods stores (Sony), to innumerable book shops and top
clothing brand stores.

But the neighbourhood is best known for Priya, the single-
screen theatre from which the market complex gets its name.
The theatre lies at the heart of this melting pot. It attracts
hordes of cinema-goers every day from the nearby residential
areas (and also from Jawaharlal Nehru University), and many
more who come from far-off areas of the capital, attracted by the
reputation that the cinema and the neighbourhood have built
over the years.

But nearly forty years ago, when Kishan Mohan Bijli, Ajay's
father, bought the theatre in 1978, Basant Lok was a sleepy area.
There were few shops around it, except for Modern Bazaar, the
supermarket that had moved to the neighbourhood just two years
earlier. It was not as if Kishan Mohan, who ran Amritsar Transport
Company (ATC), saw any business opportunity in Priya. In fact,
he had bought Priya more out of a sense of social service.

Kishan Mohan ran the trucking business from his office in
Old Delhi. In 1964, he had migrated to Delhi from Amritsar,
where his father had set up the business. Popularly known as Bijli
Pehalwan, his father was a popular figure in Amritsar, having
helped a lot of people during the Partition. Now Kishan Mohan
was continuing the family tradition—both professionally and
socially.

'He was about six-foot-two with a great personality. Even
as he expanded ATC, his stature grew socially. People used to

talk about his foresightedness,' says Sanjay Khanna, a nephew
of Kishan Mohan's. 'People used to say that his instinct was so
strong that if someone entered his room, Mr Bijli could sense
what the guy had come for,' says Sanjay. The legend goes that
once Kishan Mohan went to a casino in London in slippers and
was allowed in because the management thought he was an
Indian prince.

While ATC was immensely successful, Kishan Mohan
over the years gained a reputation for being an arbitrator. Such
was the effectiveness of his decisions that, as the tale goes, even
courts would agree with him. 'He was sharp. People would
come to him with all kinds of disputes—property, divorce . . .'
remembers Sanjay.

Adds Ajay: 'All Delhi families have a story to tell about
dad. People regarded him well and respected his judgements.
He never liked to see brothers fighting and he could somehow
produce an agreement that would meet everyone's demand.'

But in one case, even the seasoned Kishan Mohan couldn't
get the opposing sides to agree. This case was about a single-
screen theatre owned by six or seven partners, who were not
interested in it after running it for a few years. But they couldn't
agree on what to do with it. 'And then my father, according to
the story that I hear from my mother, offered to buy the theatre
and solve their problem,' says Ajay.

For Kishan Mohan though, the cinema held no interest.
He was busy expanding the truck business, which in its heyday
was said to be one of the biggest in the country. But Ajay was
interested in Priya.

'I never knew I would develop an affinity towards it. I was
very fond of cinema, especially sitting in the box (the balcony).'

Along with his friends, or with his younger brother, Sanjeev, Ajay would visit regularly to watch films, often sitting through all four shows of the day, especially if it was a movie by director Prakash Mehra or featured stars like Amitabh Bachchan or Vinod Mehra. He would also watch Bruce Lee movies.

It was the whole experience that he enjoyed. The excitement of getting into the auditorium, with food in hand, and getting transported into another world. If not watching the movies, he would spend hours in the projector room, fascinated by the whole process of film screening.

His love for movies and Priya only grew with age. Ajay studied in Modern School. 'He was always very good at everything and set the bar very high,' says Sanjeev, who is three years younger than Ajay. Cricket, basketball, badminton . . . the list was long. 'He would take up something and excel in it. He never took up a sport just for recreation. It was the same with studies,' says Sanjeev, who benefited from having a popular older brother at school.

Modern School had a separate building for students in the junior section (classes six to eight). Students making the transition to senior school had to wear a white shirt instead of a blue shirt. An 'old tradition' of the school involved older students throwing ink on the hapless younger ones. But Sanjeev escaped the ragging as he was Ajay Bijli's brother. 'He would protect me,' says Sanjeev.

At home, the brothers lived in comfort. Kishan Mohan had a taste for the good life and was fond of Mercedes cars. He was a collector and would buy whatever came up for sale at the State Trading Corporation. And he had a good collection of cars. 'He influenced me as far as travel and cars are concerned. He would always say that if you are travelling, then travel well. That has stayed with me,' Ajay told *Forbes India* in an interview.[2] The family would travel first class during international holidays.

An indulgent father, Kishan Mohan once had his employee go to a shop owner late in the night to request him to open his outlet only because a young Ajay wanted a particular toy 'right now'! Later on, as Ajay got into Hindu College to do commerce (after he had unsuccessfully tried for entry to Sri Ram College of Commerce and St. Stephen's College) he wanted a car of his own. 'So dad bought me a Volvo. Immediately after that I wanted a Honda; that too he gave me. Then when I got married, he gave me a Mercedes. So there was incremental improvement in the cars I got,' says Ajay.

If one thought that a pampered young Ajay might grow up to be a spoiled youth, it was not so. The sports all-rounder was once an obese kid who was spurred to change his food habits after an acquaintance teased him about his weight. At Hindu College, where he had got a seat because of his exploits on the basketball court, Ajay wanted to prove that he could excel in studies too. 'I topped my class all the three years [of graduation]. I was very keen to show I was not just a sports case,' says Ajay.

After completing college in 1988, Ajay wanted to go abroad for further studies. But Kishan Mohan put his foot down. 'Anything else is fine, but don't go abroad,' he told his older son. Ajay joined the truck business.

ATC, the truck business, had a turnover of about Rs 20 crore a year and was like any other medium-scale family business.

---

[2] Ashish K. Mishra, 'Ajay Bijli's Pursuit of Simple Luxury', *Forbes India*, 9 October 2013, http://www.forbesindia.com/article/best-things-money-can-buy/ajay-bijlis-pursuit-of-simple-luxury/36263/1.

The management was done by family loyalists. There were few processes or systems in place. Ajay tried to make some changes, but with limited success. The business was about transporting goods from one place to another. Customers could book a whole truck or a part of it, and according to the package they chose, the goods would be either sent directly to their destination or could be picked up from a warehouse.

Ajay focused on customer service. He tried to introduce systems and processes to ensure that delivery deadlines were met. But these were concepts the old-timers didn't understand well. While Kishan Mohan was encouraging, Ajay was struggling to find his passion in the business. Kishan Mohan's associates had warned him that Ajay didn't look as if he was cut for the trucking company. 'He studied in Modern and in Hindu. His friends are different,' a close relative told Kishan Mohan, who, for a while, even thought about opening a jewellery shop for Ajay in Connaught Place, Delhi's well-known shopping district.

The youngster himself found his mind wandering from ATC. Every morning he would walk about a kilometre to reach ATC's office in Chandni Chowk (as there was no place to park his car near the office). The dust, the crowds, the noise from the street and the smell of the spices from the shops around would get to him. There was no way that ATC's office could be shifted out from there. 'I used to keep getting a cold all the time . . . walking down to the office I would keep asking myself—is this what I am supposed to do?'

In April 1990, Ajay got married to his school sweetheart, Selina Kothari, who belonged to a family of doctors. Her father was an acclaimed psychiatrist and her mother a well-known gynaecologist. The family also had a famous entrepreneur—Balvant Parekh, who had founded Pidilite, maker of Fevicol.

For their honeymoon, Ajay and Selina went to Orlando and spent their time at the Walt Disney World Resort. While the trip accounted for some very enjoyable days for the young couple, for Ajay it was also a turning point. In Orlando, he saw a multiplex for the first time. It was like a Eureka moment, and Ajay suddenly knew what he wanted to do in life. The childhood fascination for cinema and love for movies could become a lifelong calling.

'I became restless after seeing the multiplex. I thought, we have this cinema back home, why can't we do something similar?'

The couple got back to Delhi in June, and Ajay, all charged up, went straightaway to his father. 'Dad,' said Ajay, 'Let me renovate Priya.' For a while, Kishan Mohan thought his son was joking. Priya was now a rundown cinema. Apart from running Bollywood movies, it was now also known for showing soft porn movies. And, it hardly made any business sense. Entertainment tax was at 60 per cent, and to make matters worse there was a cap on how high owners could price tickets. Everyone in the family, including Kishan Mohan, had lost interest in the cinema hall.

But Ajay was adamant. Though he didn't do any number crunching, he was convinced there was a business in running a cinema that showed the latest Hollywood blockbusters. He chose English films because that would make Priya stand out from the rest of the theatres in the capital. Only Chanakya, another iconic cinema situated in Delhi's Chanakyapuri, was showing English movies at the time. Also, there was an ongoing feud between Hindi movie distributors and cinema owners over

profit sharing and minimum guarantee. That was a risk that
Ajay, who was looking to rebuild Priya, didn't want to take.

Even as he was trying to convince his father, Ajay started
checking out the competition. He would attend shows at
Chanakya to understand how the whole experience went. 'It
was an iconic building and had passionate owners. But I found
that the facilities were just okay. While the air conditioning was
okay, the seating and sound systems were not very good. Still,
people were coming in hordes. *Pretty Woman* [the Hollywood
blockbuster starring Richard Gere and Julia Roberts] was
playing, and it ran for almost twenty-five weeks. I thought the
owners were taking the consumers for granted,' says Ajay.

An associate suggested he take a look at Sterling Cinema,
one of Mumbai's distinctive theatres, owned by the Tata
Group. It had opened in 1969 with *Doctor Dolittle*, a Hollywood
musical.[3] Sterling was the first cinema in the country to have
a Dolby sound system and Xenon projectors. The cinema also
pioneered the food and beverage concept in cinemas and was the
first to offer caramel popcorn to customers.

'When I saw Sterling, my heart was beating at some pace.
"Wow, a cinema can be like this too," I told myself. It had
efficient AC, clean floors and Dolby systems,' says Ajay.

He returned to Delhi surer than ever about his plans. Ajay
shared the Sterling experience with his father and explained
to him the new technologies he had seen. When his dad again
said, 'What's wrong with you? This will cost Rs 20–30 lakh,
and it's not going to make any sense,' Ajay was adamant.
'Whatever happens, *aap mujhe sirf Dolby karva do* [you just get

3 Wikipedia.com, https://en.wikipedia.org/wiki/Sterling_Cineplex.

me Dolby]. I won't spend much on the theatre. I will improve the AC and clean up the place,' he said. Kishan Mohan, ever the indulgent father, gave in. Though he didn't set a specific budget, he cautioned Ajay about spending too much. Otherwise there would not be any return from the investment, he warned. Kishan Mohan hoped that the experience, even if it amounted to failure, would be a good lesson and make Ajay turn back to the family business, or get into something more traditional.

Ajay got to work and was helped by Sanjeev, Selina and his friends, who included architects. The idea was to make Priya look colourful and vibrant. They peeled the old paint off its walls, painting them fuchsia and teal. They put up some artwork. One of the doors had a blow-up of a picture of Marilyn Monroe and another had the image of Marlon Brando—both Hollywood legends.

Ajay also had to ensure a constant supply of good English movies. He started making the rounds of the India offices of Hollywood studios, which were located in Mumbai. He would sit in the visiting room of Warner Brothers for hours for an appointment. And then there was a stroke of luck. 'This is where providence comes in. I didn't know that they were also looking for more good cinemas,' says Ajay.

The distributors thought it was not enough to have just one theatre in Delhi for English movies. Consumers were feeling the need for more. At the same time, it took a lot of convincing from Ajay for distributors to agree to show their films at Priya.

Priya was very well located, with a catchment of affluent customers in south Delhi. 'There was a hunger for clean cinemas and good films,' says Sanjeev. The distributors asked Ajay to fit Dolby in Priya. 'Every time I would go to Mumbai to meet them, they would give me posters of movies, and I would carry them back to Delhi. I got posters of *Tango and Cash*, *Ghost* and *Three Men and a Baby*. I used to put them up in Priya with Selina's help,' said Ajay.

Priya was ready and so was the content. The cinema reopened in 1991. It was a slow beginning, but customers did begin to take notice of the changes at Priya. Though occupancy was low and there was never a full house, people started saying that Priya was now cleaner, with better facilities. Ajay started putting up ads to woo customers as competition between Priya and Chanakya gathered pace. Now English releases were divided between the two cinemas.

Ajay wanted to get a full house and prove to his father that Priya could be a profitable business. He went back to the distributors with the idea of a movie festival at Priya. The distributors agreed. Priya held festivals, themed 'Heroes of Hollywood', 'Romantics of Hollywood', 'Comedies of Hollywood,' and so on. The idea clicked, and Priya had its first full house in 1992.

'Earlier, it would rarely break even, and now for the first time it was making money. We realized there is a business here,' says Sanjeev. The high point was when Kishan Mohan visited Priya for an Arnold Schwarzenegger movie. 'He was very happy,' says Ajay.

Then, tragedy struck. Kishan Mohan suffered a heart attack and passed away while he was being taken to the hospital, which they could not reach in time because of a traffic jam.

The patriarch's demise was a shock to the family. For twenty-five-year-old Ajay, it was the moment when, 'I grew from a boy into a man. After dad passed away, I was in the doldrums.'

He now had to divide his time between Priya and ATC. In the morning he would head to the ATC office and in the evening go to Priya. 'I tried to do both. But service standards at Priya went down. The food suffered. I was concerned about how I would deal with this . . . and I didn't want to let ATC down either.'

Even as he was bringing back some semblance of normalcy in the two businesses, another tragedy struck two years later. In 1994, there was a massive fire in ATC's godown, destroying goods worth crores of rupees. 'Luckily there were no fatalities. Whatever liquidity we had in the banks, we used that to pay the customers who had lost their goods in the fire.'

It was not that Ajay was liable to pay all the customers, who were also responsible for insuring their own goods. But Ajay decided to compensate them for reasons of goodwill. 'I asked my mom, and she said that dad or granddad would have given [the money] as we were the custodian of the goods.'

The fire increased Ajay's disillusionment with ATC. As he had done before, he went to his mother again for guidance. 'She asked me what I wanted to do. I said I wanted to go back to the cinemas. I just felt that this was what I wanted to do.' Fortunately, by then the entertainment tax had gone down and ticket prices had been decontrolled by 80 per cent. Cinema owners still needed to keep 20 per cent of the seats priced at Rs 5 a seat.

His mother agreed. Her brother, H.L. Khanna, who had been a close associate of Kishan Mohan, took over the daily affairs of ATC.

Ajay got back to Priya full-time. A friend at Warner Brothers talked about the popularity of multiplexes, and Ajay's thoughts went back to the multiplex he had seen in Orlando.

'Why don't you check with Village Roadshow? It's an Australian company and they are expanding in Asia. They recently opened in Singapore, and maybe they would be interested in India,' the friend said.

Ajay was hooked. He flew to Singapore and met Village Roadshow's head in Asia. The two got along well and did some number-crunching on the scope for a multiplex in India. 'And it was making sense even with the tax, as volumes were high,' says Ajay. When the Village Roadshow head inquired about a site for the multiplex, especially one that didn't have high rentals, Ajay invited him to India and see the market for himself.

Ajay took his guest to Priya. By 1996, Priya had cemented its position as the favourite cinema for anyone who wanted to watch English movies in Delhi. It was now constantly running at 85 per cent occupancy. Priya's success rubbed off on its neighbourhood.

'Priya was next to my house. After Ajay took over, a lot of development happened around it,' said Amit Burman, Ajay's close friend and a director in Dabur, the FMCG company promoted by the Burman family. 'It was visionary to create things around Priya. You come for entertainment, and after watching a movie you have other things to do around Priya. It had become a centre for entertainment and F&B [food and beverage],' said Burman, who is also on the board of PVR. Ajay had personally met the promoters of many companies, including Pizza Hut, to open their outlets in the neighbourhood.

Looking at Priya and the neighbourhood, the Village Roadshow official remarked, 'You have already got the location.' But Ajay's face fell. He said, 'This is not the location. I can't kill Priya. My business will collapse, and my revenues will go for a toss. This is all I have got.' Ajay didn't want to fix something that was not broken.

Though there was no site, the two men decided to form a joint venture. The two signed on the dotted line in 1995, and Priya Village Roadshow, or PVR, was born.

As luck would have it, Ajay got to know that an opportunity had come up in the form of Anupam cinema in Saket, another neighbourhood in south Delhi. Ajay was glad as he understood the south Delhi market, which would be good for English movies. He still didn't want to rely on Hindi movies.

When he visited Anupam, *Raziya Sultan*, the Dharmendra and Hema Malini-starrer was running. Inside the auditorium, the quality of the screen was so bad it was difficult to identify the two stars. Though his colleagues at PVR were disappointed, Ajay couldn't have been happier. He was smiling ear-to-ear. As they wondered why Ajay was smiling, he remarked, 'It's so bad. Now I can do whatever I want to make the cinema good. If it were good, I wouldn't have the space to make the changes.' Also, as the property was doing poorly, he had good bargaining power to negotiate for rentals.

He met Gopal Ansal, the owner. Gopal offered a fifteen-year lease and in return asked Ajay to underwrite whatever he was getting from the cinema. Ajay promptly signed up and informed his partners at Village Roadshow that PVR finally had a site for a multiplex.

The Australian company sent its people to work on the property. But it was not easy. It was the first multiplex in Delhi and in the country, and building by-laws had to be amended. Until now a cinema had a single box office, one auditorium and one projection room. But now at Anupam, Ajay was planning four screens, and each screen would need a separate auditorium and projector. Along with the entrepreneur, the Delhi authorities too went into top gear as they had to now rewrite regulations on requirements such as fire exits.

It took the teams at PVR and Village Roadshow fourteen months to complete the renovation of Anupam. The country's first multiplex opened in 1997. But opening it was not enough. As the concept was new, Ajay needed to educate his customers about it. 'As people didn't know about a multiplex, my first campaign was to define a multiplex for them. We put up hoardings. They explained that the multiplex was like four cinemas under one roof, or like so many shows a day.'

At Rs 75 a head, the tickets rates were the highest that Delhiites had seen. Some asked whether they could see all four movies at the multiplex on one ticket. There was computerized ticketing, and the tickets for each screen were of a different colour. Wooed, first by the curiosity of a multiplex, and then by the most good-looking theatre they had ever seen, consumers started coming in droves.

The first week saw Ajay standing by the gates welcoming people. When he was still around in the fourth week, his hotelier friend Arun Khanna, who had come to see a show, remarked, 'Ajay, you are still standing here! Buddy, it's a success. You don't have to stand here any more. Get a manager for this, and make more multiplexes.'

Ajay replied, 'Yes, I should do that.'

* * *

By the late 1990s, the seeds of a mall revolution had been sowed. The country's first malls had come up in Mumbai, Chennai, and in Delhi, where Ansal Plaza opened in 1999. By then, Ajay had completed the Owner/President Management Program at Harvard, after close friend and Bharti Enterprises chairman, Sunil Mittal, advised him to. The two had become friends over bowling at Delhi's Qutub Hotel.

The programme made sense to Ajay as he had hit upon an idea in multiplexes and wanted to scale it up. Also, he had always had the desire to study further. So he spoke to his partners at Village Roadshow and enrolled for the programme, for which he would be away for three weeks annually over three years.

After Anupam, PVR converted more single-screen cinemas into multiplexes. Sonia became PVR Vikaspuri and Payal was renamed PVR Naraina. But the business was not growing at the pace that Ajay had wished for from the joint venture. Village Roadshow seemed to be busier in other parts of Asia, including in Bangkok and Kuala Lumpur. For India, they had given the reins to Ajay. But the Indian businessman himself was looking for ideas. The Harvard course was of help.

'I was keen to learn about scaling, putting in place systems and processes. I wanted to build an organization. When I went to Harvard, I was charged up,' says Ajay. He did case studies on organizations such as Wal Mart and Dunkin Donuts, who had built world-class set-ups that were continually scaling their businesses. 'The case studies really opened my mind. I would even call up my team from Boston telling them we should do this and that.'

Now back in Delhi, Ajay refurbished Priya in 2000. By then PVR had twelve screens in four theatres. Ajay then went on a project-signing spree to make the most of the unfolding mall revolution. He selected malls with good locations and catchment areas. Within a couple of years, PVR had signed up for fifty more projects entailing an investment of Rs 100 crore.

But a setback came in the form of the 9/11 attacks in 2001. Shaken by the global impact of the terrorist attacks in the US, Village Roadshow curtailed its expansion plans, including in India. It wanted to exit the venture with Ajay. Now not only did Ajay have to fund his expansion plan, he also had to get the money to buy Village Roadshow's 40 per cent stake in PVR. Ajay requested his partners for time, to which they agreed.

That was when Sunil Mittal, who by now was riding a telecom wave in the country, advised Ajay to look for private equity investment. It was then that Ajay met Renuka Ramnath. Talks led to ICICI Venture's Rs 38 crore investment in PVR. Ajay put in money and took loans to raise a total of Rs 80 crore. The rest of the money would come from PVR's internal accruals.

Backed by money, Ajay expanded beyond Delhi to Bengaluru, Hyderabad and Mumbai. In Bengaluru and Hyderabad, he was the first to set up a multiplex, and in Mumbai he was the second.

By now, competition had appeared in the form of INOX in 1999, and Big Cinemas in 2001. With billionaire-promoters, who had much deeper pockets than him, venturing into the industry, Ajay had to ensure that along with the scale, PVR's brand positioning also had to be unbeatable.

That's why he doesn't leave any aspect of a cinema to chance. 'I felt Indians take movies more seriously than anyone else. That should be respected. Going to the movie is like an event, and one has to plan it—what to do before and after the movie, car parking, traffic . . . so we have to appreciate their choice. They could have just gone shopping or eating.

'So I felt that the moment they come to a box office— whether a standalone one or one in a mall—they should look at the building and say, "Wow, I am glad am here." From the moment they buy a ticket and enter the foyer, they must be in a world of make-believe. We create a world of movies, filled with posters of actors, movies, famous dialogues . . .

'I can't control the content but the patron's journey to the screen, even when the slides or the commercials are going on, should have them say, "Wow, nice carpet, nice seats, nice AC."

'That is why one PVR cinema doesn't look like another. If the cinema in Baroda reflects the local Gujarati culture, then the one in Chennai speaks another language. We respond to the city, the competitive environment around, and then decide what to do to be different,' says Ajay.

This concept has become second nature to the people at PVR. Ajay doesn't work with one architect, but with many of them to get in as many diverse ideas and potentialities as possible. 'I give them the PVR mission and let them interpret it themselves.'

Obsessed that his brand should be uncompromising in quality, Ajay likes to get into the details. There have been instances where he has asked for the whole restroom of a cinema to be redone. 'He gives the same attention to the cleanliness of washrooms that he does to the installation of the latest technology in his multiplexes,' says Kamal Gianchandani, CEO of PVR Pictures and chief of business planning and strategy at PVR.

That is why Ajay doesn't mind spending whatever it takes to make PVR cinemas stand out. He has spent more than Rs 10 crore on a single screen when the industry average was around Rs 4 crore. PVR also has different products to cater to a diverse set of customers. PVR's top product is the Director's Cut cinema in Vasant Kunj's Ambience Mall, which offers plush seats, dine-in facilities (including Sushi from an acclaimed Japanese chef) and other goodies and services. Tickets here can cost Rs 2000 for a show, about seven times more than a regular ticket.

At present, a little over 5 per cent of the company's revenue comes from its luxury brands, including Director's Cut. The plan is to increase this share to 30 per cent. The focus on luxury has helped PVR improve its margins. Its EBITDA (earnings before interest, taxes, depreciation and amortization) per screen of 6.5 per cent is unmatched in the industry.

This focus has also helped PVR attract brands to advertise on its screens. Gautam Dutta, the CEO of PVR Cinemas, who has been pushing the vertical, told me in 2016 that on-screen advertising generated over Rs 200 crore in revenue for PVR in 2015-16, the most for any exhibition company in the country. 'We have 75 million discerning customers who visit our cinemas every year. Along with that, we take our insight in the premium segment to our advertisers,' says Dutta. The three German luxury car brands—Audi, BMW and Mercedes—advertised with PVR in the 2015 festival season.[4]

---

[4] Prince Mathews Thomas, 'Popcorn Luxe', *The Hindu Business Line*, 20 October 2016, http://www.thehindubusinessline.com/specials/luxe/popcorn-luxe/article9240484.ece.

Ajay also places equal importance on training his people, especially those at the cinemas. 'A good-looking cinema will not last long if the people who are running it have an unpleasant attitude. It's unavoidable that sometimes seats and carpets will be torn. But your customer service can compensate for the deficiency. At the same time, no matter how good the food or the seat or the AC, if your attitude is poor then people won't like it. Look at British Airways. Their customer service is a function of the mood of the attendant,' says Ajay. He talks about the customer service at his favourite hotel, Four Seasons, when once, without being asked, a staff member cleaned and polished his shoes.

PVR employees are trained for behavioural etiquette, and those at the F&B outlets are given specialized training on the food on the menu. The company also conducts 'third party mystery audits' to keep a check on customer service. This particularly helped in turning around a property in Baroda that was on the verge of shut down.[5]

To keep an eye and an ear on the ground, Ajay encourages customers to write to him about their experience in PVR. In 2013, he got an email complaint from a customer, sent at 10 p.m. The customer was at the PVR multiplex in Bengaluru's Orion Mall and had found popcorn strewn on his seat. Ajay immediately replied and saw to it that the seat was cleaned. And he didn't stop at that. As Dutta told me in 2014,[6] 'The next day,

---

[5] Abhilasha Ojha, 'Measuring Training Effectiveness', *Business Standard*, 17 December 2012, http://www.business-standard.com/article/specials/measuringtraining-effectiveness-112121700157_1.html.

[6] Prince Mathews Thomas, 'How PVR Fast-tracked Growth with a Master Acquisition', *Forbes India*, 28 October 2014, http://www.forbesindia.com/article/boardroom/how-pvrfasttracked-growth-with-a-master-acquisition/38901/1.

I held a video conference with the manager to find out what went wrong. Six screens in the cinema were programmed to start new shows between 9.50 p.m. and 10.05 p.m. With just twelve cleaners on the job, there was not enough time for them to work efficiently. We changed the timing of the shows so that the auditoriums could be cleaned properly.'

The focus on brand and customer service is driven by systems and processes and a steady senior leadership. Ajay was among the first in the industry to invest in an online e-ticket system that reduced manpower costs, improved margins and gathered important data on PVR customers. As said earlier, more than 75 million people visit PVR cinemas across the country. Ajay now wants to use the data to customize PVR's offerings, including food and movies, to people's tastes. To manage its workforce payroll, its scheduling (which was earlier manual) and its auditing of workforce data, PVR invested in a workforce management software provided by Kronos Corporation, a US-based multinational.

Most of PVR's senior leadership has worked in the company for over ten years. 'As much as Ajay's passion for PVR is contagious—and he likes to get into the details—he also gives space to people to do their work and trusts their decisions. You also get a sense of ownership,' says Kamal, who was a founder-member of PVR Pictures, having joined the company in 2002. In 2006, he left to join Reliance Entertainment, only to be wooed back by Ajay four years later.

'It also makes a difference that he is a great example of how to balance work and life,' adds Kamal. Ajay leaves office by 4 p.m. to escape the notorious peak office-hour traffic in Gurgaon, where PVR is headquartered, and then follows up on mails and makes calls and conducts video conferences from his home in Vasant Vihar. 'I have an office at home for this purpose. That is one privilege I have given myself,' says Ajay, about leaving office early.

Last year he and his family, including his mother and brother Sanjeev, moved into their new house from their ancestral home in Rohtak Road. Ever the perfectionist, it took Ajay over fifteen years to build the new house. More than sixty architects worked on it, and the two-storeyed structure was razed four times before Ajay was satisfied.

His zeal for fitness has rubbed off on others around him too. While brother Sanjeev jokes that one is scared of eating a bar of chocolate in front of Ajay, everyone accepts that grooming and fitness is an important part of being an agile leader. Once a marathoner, Ajay's fitness has also evolved. He now does more CrossFit workouts than running. Also the top management, including Ajay and Sanjeev, has lunch together at the Gurgaon office, with the menu monitored by Ajay. 'It is normal human nature that if you take care of yourself, people will look up to you. There is no downside or harm in taking care of yourself,' says Ajay.

Another passion for PVR's chairman and managing director has been singing. Ajay, who in 2013 sang a Bollywood number for designer Suneet Varma's fashion show, has squeezed in time for voice training three or four times a week. 'One of my dreams is to one day have a small band and do some serious work that befits my age . . . like Sting and [Phil] Collins.'

* * *

Processes, systems, a senior management consisting of seasoned professionals and work-life balance now allow Ajay to choose his focus areas. He doesn't have a formal division of responsibilities with Sanjeev, who is the joint managing director. 'We felt it's better and easier that we both know what we are doing and are on the same page. It doesn't make sense that I keep doing something and later he doesn't like it, and vice versa,' says Sanjeev. Many a time, they manage a vertical together. So while Ajay engages with high-profile mall developers in the metros, Sanjeev takes care of the partners in smaller cities such as Lucknow. 'We are now in fifty locations, so it is difficult for just one of us to manage everything,' says Sanjeev.

Over the years, Ajay has built fruitful partnerships with the big names in the real estate sector. These include Vikas Oberoi of Oberoi Realty in Mumbai and Irfan Razack of the Bengaluru-based Prestige Group.

I had a chat with Irfan in 2014 and he said,[7] 'Starting from [Bengaluru's] Forum Mall in 2003, Ajay has been our favourite exhibitor. He understands the product. As a partner, he meets timelines.' Ajay and Irfan were partnering in new mall projects in Bengaluru, Mangalore, Hyderabad and Kochi. 'Ajay has the first right of refusal for all my mall projects,' said Irfan.

When in Gurgaon, the two brothers often attend review meetings together, starting the day with a twenty-minute meeting to set the agenda. At the same time there are aspects

[7] Prince Mathews Thomas, 'How PVR Fast-tracked Growth with a Master Acquisition, *Forbes India*, 28 October 2014, http://www. forbesindia.com/article/boardroom/how-pvrfasttracked-growth-with-a-master-acquisition/38901/1.

of the business that one focuses on more than the other. While Sanjeev looks at IT and PVR Pictures, the distribution arm, almost single-handedly and fills in for Ajay whenever needed, Ajay oversees BluO, the entertainment arm that majors in bowling alleys. On 8 August, PVR announced the sale of BluO to Smaash Entertainment for Rs 86 crore. PVR owned 51 per cent stake in the company. PVR Pictures is now a Rs 100-crore business and BluO has a positive EBITDA.

Ajay loves to get off the routine treadmill of work and get his feet wet, especially when it comes to big projects like integrating Cinemax into PVR and redoing its screens, as he did with Pacific Mall in Subhash Nagar in west Delhi.

Early on, Ajay had an eye on the mall as it clicked all the boxes from an exhibitor's point of view—location, developer and development. But Cinemax had managed to seal the deal with Pacific Mall. Now, after acquiring Cinemax, Ajay could finally put his stamp on the screens here. Not that they were doing badly. The cinema at Pacific Mall was netting Rs 8 crore a year, the biggest box office for Cinemax, despite the presence of Satyam and Wave Cinemas in the neighbourhood. But Ajay knew more could be done.

When I visited Pacific Mall in mid-2014, more than a year after the Cinemax acquisition, the cinema there had undergone a sea change. Only the roof and tiles of the multiplex remained from its past. Everything else, including the box office and food counters, had been changed.

The place was bright with a collage of DVD movie covers on the walls. Though Ajay had increased the ticket prices by 10 per cent to bring this cinema on par with the rest of the PVR cinemas, the property in Pacific Mall continued to do well. From

April to July that year, the cinema at the mall saw its revenues grow by 5.2 per cent. On the other hand, the company claimed that the revenues of the nearby Satyam and Wave screens fell by 0.6 per cent and 4.6 per cent respectively.

Cinemax's 138 screens have been integrated with those of PVR.

But it's not just one-way traffic. PVR has been open about embracing Cinemax's best practices, including its F&B strategy. Until now PVR had been itself handling the food counters at the cinemas. But Cinemax would rent out the space to vendors. PVR tweaked its strategy, looking at Cinemax's success, and is now adopting the model across its properties. At present, F&B contributes 26 per cent of the total revenues.

Ajay also focuses on inorganic growth at PVR. After buying Cinemax, Ajay toyed with the idea of buying Fun Cinemas and Satyam Cineplexes (not to be confused with the Chennai-based Sathyam Cinemas). But INOX acquired Satyam for Rs 182 crore, strengthening its position in the Delhi market, which is otherwise dominated by PVR.

Ajay hated losing out on Satyam, which had thirty-eight screens including three marquee ones in Delhi. But if he had acquired Satyam, he would have had a tough time convincing the Competition Commission of India (CCI) that the deal wouldn't lead to a monopoly-kind of situation. He decided to opt out of the race. He needed to save money and also his bargaining chip with the CCI.

A year later, Cinepolis acquired Fun Cinemas, owned by Subhash Chandra, in January 2015, making it the third largest cinema chain in the country after PVR and INOX.

But Ajay was waiting more eagerly for DT Cinemas to be put on the block. DT was owned by DLF, the country's biggest real estate company, which was looking to sell a non-core business to pare down its debts. Ajay had made an earlier attempt to acquire DT in 2009, but the deal had fallen through. Since then, he had always been on the lookout for the opportunity of a second attempt.

In 2015, with DT again on the block, Ajay called out to Renuka for help in sealing the deal. Ajay called her on the morning of the day the bids had to be placed. 'I know they won't agree to anything less than Rs 500 crore . . . I am thinking of bidding Rs 520 crore,' he told Renuka. It was a successful bid. On 9 June 2015, PVR announced the acquisition of DT Cinemas' thirty-nine screens (with a capacity of about 9000 seats) for Rs 500 crore. In 2009, the same offer had been reportedly valued at Rs 50 crore.

Less than a week later, PVR announced that its promoters had diluted a 10.7 per cent stake to Multiples Alternate Asset Management for Rs 350 crore. Once again, Renuka had played a critical role in sealing a deal for Ajay.

But it would take the entrepreneur more than a year to complete the deal. Aware that the deal would give PVR a monopoly-like domination in certain markets of Delhi-NCR, including Noida, Gurgaon and south Delhi, the CCI asked for a response from a varied set of stakeholders—distributors, licensing authorities, single-screen owners and other multiplex players such as INOX and Cinepolis—on the deal. The CCI sent a notice to PVR asking for explanations, and this was followed by a series of presentations and meetings, many of which were led by Ajay himself.

In July 2016, more than thirteen months after the deal was first announced, CCI finally cleared the deal. But with changes. While PVR would have to now freeze its work in Gurgaon and Noida for three years, it could no longer buy or add any screens in south Delhi for five years. The overall deal was now valued at Rs 450 crore and thirty-two screens. DT Cinemas would later sell the rest of the screens to Cinepolis.

The deals have only whetted Ajay's appetite. As Sanjeev says, 'We have tasted blood.' The two have also drawn up a roadmap for aggressive organic growth. 'Now we get flustered if there is no new opening in a month.' The roadmap has a target of 1000 screens. There is also the international market; Ajay has specific plans for Sri Lanka and London.

With PVR now looking to stretch its lead at the top of the industry to an unassailable distance, Ajay has also put in place a professional head at ATC, which now has 1000 employees and sixty branches across the country. His uncle, H.L. Khanna, has retired and Ajay has brought in a professional CEO to bring in systems and processes in the transport company.

The second-generation entrepreneur also reached another milestone in February 2017. He turned fifty. He brought in the New Year of this landmark year in Dubai, surrounded by family and friends (who included actors Aamir Khan and Shah Rukh Khan). Just like his Bollywood friends, Ajay Bijli was also a superstar now. The small boy who would spend a whole day in the projector room of a local cinema was now the unmatched superstar of India's exhibition industry.

* * *

My Learnings

+ Do a professional course.

  I was keen to learn about scaling, putting in place systems and processes. I wanted to build an organization. When I went there [Harvard] I was charged up.

+ Respect customers.

  I felt Indians take movies more seriously than anyone else. This should be respected. Going to a movie is like an event and one has to plan it—what to do before and after the movie, car parking, traffic . . . so we have to appreciate their choice. They could have just gone shopping or eating.

+ Take care of your health.

  It is normal human nature that if you take care of yourself, people will look up to you. There is no downside or harm in taking care of yourself.

+ Go for inorganic growth.

  This is an important transaction [acquisition of Cinemax] for us as it takes us to the market leadership position . . . Cinemax has a premium portfolio of the multiplex screen across India and has been a market leader in western India.

+ Let passion drive you.

  I never knew I would develop an affinity towards it. I was very fond of cinema, especially sitting in the box [the balcony].

2

Abhishek Khaitan

'I'm screwed,' Abhishek Khaitan told his friend Shrawan Binani.

Shrawan looked at his best friend sitting next to him. He had never seen Abhishek this dejected. The two had been friends since they were fifteen, when they had met at a club in New Friend's Colony in south Delhi. Shrawan, who used to play badminton, wanted to learn snooker. But the bigger boys would bully him, and he would be defeated easily by them. Looking for someone his age to play with, Shrawan came across Abhishek, who too was searching for a partner to learn the sport with.

Since then the two had been almost inseparable. Other than the time they spent in school—Abhishek was in Modern School and Shrawan in Birla Vidya Niketan—they were mostly together. One would call up to make sure the other was at the club for a game of snooker.

Later, as the friendship blossomed, Abhishek invited Shrawan over to his home and introduced him to his parents—Lalit Khaitan, promoter of Rampur Distillery and Kiran Khaitan. When Shrawan topped his class, Lalit called up his father and said, 'I'm glad that my son has friends like Shrawan.'

After his schooling Abhishek went to Bengaluru to study engineering. The two friends kept in touch. Whenever Abhishek came home for the holidays, he would immediately call up Shrawan and announce, 'I'm back!', and the two would chalk out plans for the next ten days.

* * *

Now Abhishek had completed his engineering and was back. But the twenty-four-year-old had not returned to happy circumstances. Shrawan could only empathize with his friend.

It was 1995. The Khaitan family, consisting of G.N. Khaitan and his five sons, including Lalit, had just gone in for a division of the family assets. Based in Kolkata, the Khaitans were a well-known name among the Marwari business community. While one part of the larger Khaitan family consisted of lawyers and chartered accountants, the other half consisted of businessmen. G.N. Khaitan had dabbled in several businesses, and at the time of the division, the family had interests in fertilizers, real estate, construction and liquor.

The division of the family assets, which included the Rampur distillery and the fertilizer units run by Lalit's younger brothers, might have ended amicably. But there were tensions and disagreements over who would get what. In the end, Lalit received ownership of the distillery unit in Rampur, which was the biggest asset of all and had revenues of Rs 70 crore a year. But by the time Abhishek completed his higher studies, the distillery was running up losses of about Rs 10 crore a year.

Rampur distillery was producing ENA (extra neutral alcohol) that was supplied to alcohol companies.

Not only that, one condition for ownership of the distillery, which accounted for 70 per cent of the combined revenues of all the family companies, was the assumption of its liabilities of over Rs 40 crore. This debt only worsened the company's precarious financial health.

To make matters worse, Rampur distillery had also just lost its biggest client, Shaw Wallace. This Manu Chhabria company was its biggest bottling client. But Shaw Wallace had recently bought a distiller in Uttar Pradesh (UP) and no longer needed the services of its older supplier.

In a last-ditch effort to keep Rampur afloat, Abhishek accompanied his father to meet Vijay Mallya, the high-profile owner of United Spirits Limited (USL). Mallya, who had taken over the reins at USL at a young age after his father, Vittal Mallya, passed away, was fast gaining the reputation of a fierce competitor to Shaw Wallace, and his USL was steadily making its way up the pecking order in the Indian liquor industry.

Father and son were hoping to present a business proposition that would make sense to Mallya, and provide a lifeline to their company. But this was not to be. While the Khaitans were hoping to get a contract from Mallya to supply him alcohol, Mallya—always looking for a good deal—offered to pick up equity in Rampur Distillery in return for the contract. Lalit, who had revived Rampur with his grit and sweat, wasn't agreeable to this.

He seemed to have reached a dead end in his endeavour to save the distillery. Abhishek was also at his wits' end. The sorry state of the company had put to death a wish he had been harbouring, adding to his despair and frustration. He had always wanted to go for higher studies and was hoping to follow up his engineering degree with an MBA from the US. But such was the environment at home and the company that when his parents asked him to be at home to help out, he couldn't say no.

There was one more thing.

In 1996, his parents got him engaged to Deepshikha Somany, daughter of Vikram Somany, promoter of Cera Sanitaryware, a fast-emerging company from Kolkata. Abhishek wanted some time to himself before tying the knot, but again bowed to his parents' wishes. And what with the situation at home, Abhishek didn't feel it was right to open that bottle of champagne to celebrate his engagement as he wanted to.

So here he was, the scion of the Khaitan family, his studies truncated, engaged to be married much earlier than he would have liked, witness to a family division, and now supposed to help save a company that his father had nurtured, but was now close to collapse.

'Our back was against the wall. *Par marna hain to ijjat se marenge* [if we have to die, let's die honourably],' said Abhishek. He had an idea that could break or make Rampur Distillery. It was an ambition that he had nursed since he saw Deepak Roy launch Gilbey's Green Label. Abhishek was then studying in Bengaluru. He was mesmerized by the look of the bottle and the marketing campaign around its launch. 'I don't want to be a bottler,' he had told himself then. His vision for Rampur Distillery was clear. He wanted to take the company, which until now had been producing a bulk commodity, higher up the value chain and launch brands.

But did he have it in him to pull off the idea, especially when almost all the veterans in the company were against his plan?

* * *

The process of division of the family assets had begun when Abhishek was in his third year of engineering. G.N. Khaitan, his grandfather, was adamant that the family assets should be divided while he was still alive. It was a sane decision, given the number of ugly divisions and break-ups India Inc has seen after the passing away of a patriarch.

As the talks between the brothers panned out through the year, Abhishek stood by the side of his father. He was there as an observer. Not once did he voice his opinion on any matter when his father conversed with his uncles. It was only when they were back home that he would confer with his father and go through the details of the discussions.

There were disagreements and disputes. But in the end the separation was amicable. For a while after the separation— for almost three years—there were 'cold vibes' between the brothers. But by the turn of the millennium, the brothers came around and the whole family holidayed overseas together for fifty days.

But before all this, Abhishek had to help save the company.

* * *

Lalit and Abhishek were glad to get ownership of Rampur Distillery. But there was hardly any time to be lost if they had to save their baby. Their visit to Mallya hadn't resulted in any lifeline for the company. 'We will do it in our own way,' father and son said to each other.

That's when Abhishek told his father about the idea he had had after the launch of Gilbey's Green Label in India: 'We knew how to make the best spirit. We knew the art of bottling. We were bottlers for Shaw Wallace. The only thing we lacked was the marketing and distribution network. That we could create,' said Abhishek. Lalit was convinced, and backed his son.

The veterans in the company had doubts, and many of their questions were legitimate. The industry was crowded, especially the whisky market which the Khaitans had selected for their brand launch. Whisky had the biggest share in the spirits market in India and, for that same reason, was the most competitive too.

Other than the international players such as IDV and Seagram, there was a host of domestic players including USL, Shaw Wallace, Mohan Meakins and Jagatjit Industries. It was mostly a volumes game, and the margins were slim. But, as Abhishek says, the myth was that more Scotch was consumed in India than in Scotland, and everyone wanted a pie of this market.

This was precisely the reason why the old-timers at Rampur Distillery were unsure about the new venture. 'Ours is a commodity, sell it and you will get money. What is the need to sell brands? Not worth it,' Abhishek was frequently told when he made presentations to explain why the company needed to change its business from a high volumes-low margin model to lower volumes-high margin one. The only way to make the transition was to introduce brands.

Their doubts were not unfounded. Says Shailesh Khaitan, Lalit's youngest brother: 'It is very difficult to establish a brand. First of all, branding is an expensive proposition and you need to consider too many factors. The competition is huge. So even if you put in Rs 100 crore, the brand might not click. It has to be backed by quality. So many things have to go hand-in-hand. The death rate of brands would be about 90 per cent.'

So fragile was its condition that Rampur Distillery couldn't afford a failure. But Abhishek was sure he was on the right track, and he had the backing of his father. Lalit Khaitan had been to Harvard for a short course called OPM (Owner/President Management). 'They taught me that at the bottom of the pyramid was commodity and on the top were brands. I told Abhishek to go ahead.'

Once he got the green signal from his father, Abhishek wanted to do everything differently at the company. First, he did some mass hiring to create teams to handle sales and marketing, functions that the company hadn't focused on earlier. He recruited about 100 people. Their average age was twenty-three, and Abhishek had personally selected each of them. 'I realized that if we hired someone who was around thirty-five, he would take the beaten path. We needed fresh thinking.'

Next, Abhishek needed a wide network of manufacturing units across the country to feed the distribution network. That was a tough task. The liquor industry in India is unique. Each state is a different market with its own separate tax structures. A centralized production unit would add to the costs every time the product would move from one state to another. Instead, Abhishek needed a bottling facility in each state he was targeting.

'I begged eight to ten bottlers to work for us. Everyone asked for a minimum guarantee.' But the Khaitan scion was not in a position to give them even a single rupee. 'I said I was not running away. Just start with us.' He was eventually able to convince them. And then the team at Rampur started developing the product.

Even as the production team got busy, Abhishek roped in an agency for the marketing campaign. First, they had to come up with a name for the product. Though the agency came up with about seventy names over a few days' time, Abhishek had an early favourite—'8PM'. It had an instant connect. Like most revellers, Abhishek used to hit the pubs at around 8 p.m. It was that time of the day when people would start gathering for a night out. And, most importantly, the name would cut across language barriers.

Abhishek also spent time and resources in packaging the bottle. As with Gilbey's Green Label, he used a guala cap for the bottle, giving it that premium look. Guala caps gave a different look to a bottle, and also prevented its refilling or tampering.

Things were looking good, but there was something that was troubling Abhishek. And then he had this dream: 'I had a dream that there was something missing. I thought that I was targeting a customer who was aspirational. But was my product aspirational?' The dream triggered the idea of blending the whisky with Scotch to make it a standout product in the market.

But the problem was that a lot of bottling had already been done. Would this late brainwave be worth the losses it would entail? Lalit again backed his son's idea, even though it meant pushing back the launch by two months.

The product was almost ready when there came up another challenge. 'We couldn't say, here is 8PM whisky by Rampur Distillery. It would sound like a product from a shop in Karol Bagh,' said Abhishek. The company needed to be rechristened. Abhishek led a campaign to change the name of the company. There was resistance from the old boys, who had an emotional connect with the Rampur tag. Most of them were from the production side and had spent considerable time at the facility in UP.

It took Abhishek four days and a lot of stretching of his presentation and persuasion skills to bring around the old boys. And it was decided to rename the company, taking the first two letters from each word of its earlier name, Rampur Distillery, to Radico Khaitan.

There is an interesting story on the marketing campaign for 8PM. Abhishek loved three ad campaigns—Cadbury's (the one where the girl enters the ground dancing), Ericsson's (in which an elderly gentleman in a restaurant thinks that the woman at the next table is talking to him) and the evergreen ones of Fevikwik. 'So, I asked around who made these ads. And the answer was Prasoon Pandey,' says Abhishek.

The two met, and Prasoon promised to do the ad campaign for 8PM. This was before the government banned liquor companies from advertising. A month later, when Prasoon presented his script for the ad, Abhishek was a little bewildered. There was no glamour, sex or women. And it was in black and white. How would it work?

But Abhishek didn't have the time to dawdle. If Prasoon thinks it will work, then let's go with it, he told his colleagues.

The ad film soon followed, and was presented to the company's senior management. After the screening, everyone in the room fell silent for a while. The seniors then asked Abhishek what the ad meant. They could not understand anything, they said. Abhishek was filled with dismay. *'Meri to phat lee,'* he says. The campaign had cost Radico Rs 1.5 crore, at a time when it was in deep losses.

But they were so hard pressed for time that there was no choice but to go ahead with the ad. For five days after it was aired for the first time, Abhishek kept calling up his friends and relatives to ask if they had seen it. None had. His heart began to sink when, suddenly, the tide changed. He started getting calls, and people congratulated him for a 'fabulous ad'.

It looked like Prasoon had delivered a hit, as he had promised. It also helped that it was 1999 and the country was high on patriotism, what with the Kargil war and the cricket World Cup of that year. The ad did well to evoke this feeling. It had senior army officers from India and Pakistan squaring off at the border. The two sides first engage in showing off each other's arsenal. But when the Indian officer opens a bottle of 8PM, his Pakistani counterpart's resolve breaks and the two share a drink on the sly.

Like the ad, sales of 8PM too started off slow. The liquor was first launched in Delhi, and later in Karnataka, Kerala and Tamil Nadu. But once it picked up, there was no looking back. 8PM became the first brand in the country to hit the one million cases mark within a year of its launch. A report in *The Hindu-Business Line* said:

> The 'exhilarating' growth of 8PM comes at a time when the overall domestic liquor sale is bogged down by the recessionary feel. The brand . . . has virtually stormed the key liquor markets in the North, especially Uttar Pradesh and Punjab.
>
> In these two States alone, the brand sale accounts for about 1.3 lakh cases a month. 8PM has also extended its

aggression down South—in Andhra Pradesh—where it is a force to reckon with.[1]

There were reports about how the success of 8PM put to rest the plans of rival companies, none of whom expected Radico Khaitan to deliver a hit. The same report cited above said:

> In fact, its rocketing sales have impacted rival regular whisky brands, especially Bagpiper from the Herbertsons' stable. The brand also scuttled McDowell & Co's recent plans to revive some of its lacklustre regular whisky brands. The domestic regular whisky segment is pegged at around 20 million cases annually.

Most importantly for Abhishek, Lalit and the rest of the management at the company, the success of 8PM saved their boat from drowning. Such was the pace of 8PM's sales that Radico's revenues were increasing by 100 per cent quarter after quarter. Within two years, the company that was short of Rs 100 crore in revenues had raced on to cross the Rs 300-crore revenue mark.

'The whisky helped improve the image of the company. We started doing exports, which kept increasing. When things start improving, everything else starts falling into place. That is how the beginning was made,' says Abhishek.

* * *

---

[1] Boby Kurian, 'Radico's 8PM Rides High in Hope of Selling 3 Million Cases', *The Hindu Business Line*, 09 August 2001, http://www. thehindubusinessline.com/catalyst/2001/08/09/stories/1909m052.htm.

But if the young man thought that his, and Radico Khaitan's, problems were over, he was sorely mistaken. Even after pulling off a spectacular success with 8PM, two years later Abhishek was facing a fresh crisis in the company. Many of the employees whom he had painstakingly recruited a couple of years ago left the company en masse in 2000 and joined the competition.

Amar Sinha, who was president of the joint venture Abhishek had floated with Whyte & Mackay and had earlier played a crucial role in the launch of 8PM, left Radico and joined Shaw Wallace. Chhabria—who had the reputation of being a 'corporate raider' and had taken over Shaw Wallace and Falcon Tyres, among other companies—poached, along with Sinha, all the zonal managers and the finance team from Radico Khaitan. 'He paid them three times what I was paying. I couldn't do anything about it. Shaw Wallace was Shaw Wallace. I was left all alone,' said Abhishek.

Interestingly, a story on Rediff[2].com, dated 27 September 2003, suggests that Sinha left because of 'some friction' with Abhishek. The report said Sinha was in the middle of launching a premium whisky and had even prepared a blueprint for a foray into beer under the brand name X, but it didn't see the light of day.

The reasons for the mass desertion are unclear. Nevertheless, Abhishek was left with 170 salesmen reporting directly to him. It took him over a year to stabilize operations again, but by then he was almost a wreck. The 27-year-old had put on weight, had no time for sports or leisure, and suffered from high blood pressure.

Radico Khaitan continued to do well nonetheless. It was growing by over 30 per cent year on year. Abhishek had hired

---

[2] 'Amar Sinha: A Spirited Leader', Rediff.com, 27 September 2003, http://www.rediff.com/money/2003/sep/27profile.htm.

Raju Vaziraney to head marketing; Vaziraney would go on to become the chief operating officer and head of Radico's joint venture with Diageo. Together they launched the Old Admiral brandy in Kerala in late 2002.

Brandy is the third largest selling spirit in the country after whisky and rum, and is particularly popular in the southern states of Kerala and Tamil Nadu. USL's Honey Bee and McDowell's No. 1—both millionaire brands—dominated the segment. Abhishek executed a strategy similar to the one he had for 8PM. He placed his product at a competitive price point, at the same time giving it a premium look. Within months the new product had made its mark in the market. And of March 2003, it even sold more than Honey Bee in Kerala. Soon, Old Admiral was crossing the million cases mark, and by 2010, would be selling about 2.7 million cases a year.

But as Old Admiral was being launched, there was one more churn at the top. The COO, V.K. Arora, resigned. 'Mr Khaitan said these developments would have no impact on the growth of the company,'[3] The Hindu Business Line reported in December 2002.

The twin successes of 8PM and Old Admiral had by now earned Radico and Abhishek the respect of the industry. By 2003–2005, the liquor industry in the country was undergoing a fundamental change. Vijay Mallya's USL, after acquiring Shaw Wallace in 2005, had cemented its place at the top of the industry. USL was well on its way to becoming the world's largest liquor selling company.

---

[3] Boby Kurian, 'Radico Uncorks Old Admiral for Southern Brandy Market', *The Hindu Business Line*, 14 December 2002, http://www. thehindubus ine s s l i n e . com/2002/12/14/stories/2002121401830600.htm.

But as Nikhil Vora, managing director at IDFC Securities, told me in 2011, 'What is the point of calling yourself the largest in the world if you don't have the profits to show for it.' By 2010, the French company Pernod Ricard, with its focus on premiumization, would become the most profitable liquor company in India with a profit of Rs 500 crore (while USL's bottom line was Rs 403 crore). Most importantly, Pernod was making this profit on sales of just 20 million cases, a little less than one-fifth of what USL sold.

'We realized that going forward we had to go premium. That was the only way for us. It would be painful and expensive, but in the long run that would make us survive,' says Abhishek. So the focus at Radico from then on was not on volumes, which 8PM, Old Admiral and Contessa Rum were bringing in, but on margins. The focus was on margin per case of liquor sold. 8PM was operating in a segment that was facing price pressure; costs were increasing and Radico was struggling to generate positive cash flows. For any company, margins are important for survival, and Radico was no exception.

'We need to launch a new brand, but in a segment that is untapped,' Abhishek had told Radico Khaitan's then marketing head (now president, sales and marketing) Rahul Gagerna.

The Eureka moment came in 2004 in a bar in Las Vegas, where the two were taking a break from a twelve-city financial roadshow for attracting foreign institutional investors (FIIs). Having a drink and looking around, he realized that most of the people around were drinking vodka. And Grey Goose was the most popular brand.

Launched by Sidney Frank in 1996, the brand had taken the liquor market in the US by storm despite its premium tag.

The packaging was again a differentiator, and Grey Goose came in a distinctive smoked glass bottle featuring French geese in flight. Within a year of its launch, more than 1.5 million cases of Grey Goose were sold in the US alone. Sidney sold the brand to Bacardi in 2004, for a cool $2.2 billion.

The popularity of the brand sparked an idea for Abhishek. 'We did some research and realized that vodka was bigger than whisky worldwide and was becoming more popular, especially among youngsters and women. It was already the biggest spirit in the US,' says Gagerna.

The demographic trend in India was also showing a definite change in the consumer profile. More women were now entering the market, and they preferred vodka to any other spirit. And youngsters, conscious of brands, were willing to dole out money for a smooth drink.

Still, entering the vodka segment was not easy. The making of a new vodka brand took Abhishek and his team two years. For one, the naysayers in Radico still questioned the rationale for launching a vodka brand in a country that boasted of mostly whisky lovers. The veterans, including his father, asked many questions. 'I didn't answer any of their questions and didn't even make any presentations. I told them I had a gut feeling that this would succeed. This was one brand that was launched out of passion,' says Abhishek.

Much of the time during the run-up to the launch was spent on two important aspects of the new brand, which was christened Magic Moments. First—its blend. It took a long time for the team at Radico to perfect the blend. They imported grain spirits from France especially for the purpose. Second, instead of labelling the bottle the traditional way,

Abhishek used a different type of 'direct printing' for the bottle.

Gagerna made several trips to Germany in 2004 and 2005 to buy the printing technology. 'We used to travel to Germany as if we were going to Mumbai. Within a year or so, I must have been to the country about fifteen times,' said Gagerna. Once they got hold of the technology, Abhishek invested Rs 150 crore in the screen printing machine. It could print six colours in one shot and fifty bottles in a minute. Today the company has ten of these German machines.

Though the printing made the bottle look transparent, giving the product a premium appearance, there were problems. 'The different look immediately evoked protests from Radico Khaitan's former joint venture partner, Bacardi. The international company, famous for its white rum, alleged that Magic Moments's packaging closely resembled the packaging of its own Grey Goose vodka brand. But the scrap didn't escalate, and it was resolved "amicably",' says an industry source.[4]

Abhishek took the risk of pricing the product a little higher than the closest competition, White Mischief, the brand owned by Shaw Wallace (now with USL, after it acquired the Manu Chhabria company). Internally, the pricing wisdom was questioned. 'Why start a new price point?' Abhishek was asked. But he was clear. If White Mischief was earning 0.2X, then Magic Moments was going to be in a segment that would earn X, he had decided.

---

[4] Prince Mathews Thomas, 'Radico Khaitan Is on a High', *Forbes India*, 24 July 2013, http://www.forbesindia.com/article/boardroom/radico-khaitan-ison-a-high/35651/1.

Also, at a strategic level, the company had decided it was no longer going to chase volumes and the focus would be on cash flows. It was going to be a painful process, and it was extremely tough to create a brand in this segment. But Abhishek's team decided to press on.

When Magic Moments was finally launched in late 2005, there was additional pressure on Abhishek. Three more vodka brands hit the market around the same time—Diageo's Shark Tooth, Pernod Ricard's Fuel and USL's Red Romanov. Though Shark Tooth and Fuel didn't fare well, Red Romanov would go on to become the market leader in the low-price segment.

Abhishek pushed his team by challenging them. He egged them on, saying they'd celebrate with champagne if they managed to sell 60,000 cases of Magic Moments every month. To meet the challenge, the team roped in Bollywood superstar Hrithik Roshan as brand ambassador (of course, Hrithik was not endorsing the vodka but music CDs under the same brand name, one of the ways that liquor companies have found to circumvent the government's ban on liquor advertising).

Later, Radico Khaitan launched Magic Moments in six flavours, including chocolate and lemon. The pricing was also tweaked, taking the brand higher on the premium scale and closer to Smirnoff. This strategy also helped Radico up the price of Magic Moments's original classic flavour.

After all this effort, it was not surprising when the 'magic' moment came in May 2008, when sales of the vodka crossed 64,000 cases a month. Abhishek kept his word. 'I remember his mother was unwell. But he still came to a nightclub in GK 1 (in south Delhi) and opened that champagne bottle,' says Gagerna.

In two years, Magic Moments had a market share of over 60 per cent in the prestige segment in vodka. Other brands in the segment, which is just below the premium section, included Shark Tooth and Class 21. Sales of Magic Moments Vodka kept increasing and at present, it has a near monopoly in the segment, with nearly 90 per cent market share. Magic Moments now has a 50 per cent market share of the entire vodka market in India, across price segments. 'No other liquor brand in any segment, and in any market, has been able to do this,' says Abhishek.

The success of its vodka did wonders for Radico Khaitan's financial health. 'This is making the difference. When I sell one case of Magic Moments, it is equal to eight cases of 8PM,' says Abhishek.

The brokerage firms noticed the change in Radico's fortunes. The 2016 report of HDFC Securities on Radico Khaitan noted that premium brands now accounted for nearly 21 per cent of the company's volumes, compared to the 18 per cent a year earlier. This helped as the company increased its net profits by 17.8 per cent despite a fall of 5.2 per cent in sales. The report said, 'With the changing demographics and the company's focus on premium brands, we expect margins of the company to improve going forward.'

Radico's improved bottom line has helped Abhishek reduce the company's debt and interest payments, in line with his vision to make Radico a zero-debt company.

The success of Magic Moments gave him the confidence to launch more brands in the premium range. Radico has, in the past few years, launched Verve vodka, Morpheus brandy (which has a 70 per cent market share in its category) and Rampur in the premium and super premium segments. There is also Magic

Moments Electra, a ready-to-drink product that was priced 30 per cent higher than Bacardi, says Abhishek. 'While Bacardi reduced its prices, we stuck to our strategy,' he adds.

Rampur, the single malt launched in 2016, is perhaps the boldest statement the entrepreneur could make. Priced at about $70 a bottle, the brand has fetched 'great response' after its international-only launch last year, says Abhishek. It is now available in fifteen countries, including the US. 'We are sold out. Recently, it entered the duty-free market in India. For us, Rampur is not for money, but for pride,' he adds.

* * *

In many ways, the situation that Abhishek found himself in upon returning home from his studies in Bengaluru was similar to what his father Lalit had faced many years ago. The senior Khaitan too had harboured dreams of higher studies. 'In those days there were two choices for us—law or chartered accountancy. I wanted to do law,' he says.

The larger Khaitan families had quite a few eminent lawyers, including Devi Prasad Khaitan, founder of Khaitan & Co, the country's third largest law firm, which completed a century of practice in 2010. Devi Prasad was part of the drafting committee that prepared the Constitution of India.

But being the oldest among his brothers and cousins, Lalit was asked by his father and uncle to study commerce at St. Xavier's College in Kolkata, and at the same time join the family business. So after completing his classes for the day, Lalit would head to the bakery or the restaurant near Park Street that the family owned.

And then he was married at nineteen.

This—joining the family business and marrying early—was the norm in Marwari families. It was a tradition that had stood the test of time.

Many among the following generations of the family became leading lawyers, cementing the legacy of the Khaitan family in the country's legal fraternity. A few of the Khaitans chose to do business and ventured into several industries—education, tea, batteries, cinema, restaurants, fertilizers and chemicals. Lalit's father, G.N. Khaitan, also chose to do business.

Along with his brother, G.N. dabbled in several businesses—furniture, soap making, bakery, restaurants and a general provisions store. 'We were a joint family. We were nine children living under the same roof [we were four brothers and a sister, and uncle had a daughter and three sons]. Everything was done jointly, everything was shared. And we would all even sleep together in the same room. We didn't have much money and were just a little above middle-class, or an upper middle-class family,' says Lalit.

His father, called Gajju or Gajanand by his friends, was a well-known personality in Kolkata's vibrant social circle. He had headed several institutions, including business bodies such as the Bharat Chamber of Commerce, Export Council of Engineering, and other organizations like the Indian Red Cross Society, and some popular clubs like Rajasthan Club and Bengal Rowing Club.

'He used to be known for his bow tie. He never wore a regular tie in his life. He was very well connected, even in Bollywood. Once, he arranged a cricket match in Kolkata that had most of the biggest Bollywood names, including Raj

Kapoor, attending. Shailesh Khaitan, my youngest brother, remembers the actor telling my father, "Khaitan sahib, you have got the whole of Bollywood here. If the plane crashes, Bollywood is dead".'

Actor Pran, the legendary villain of Indian cinema, and often more popular than the heroes, was a close friend. 'He would often drop by at our house in Kolkata. Once he was visiting after *Zanjeer* (a film that famously starred Amitabh Bachchan and Jaya Bhaduri) had released. I remarked that Amitabh had done a great job. Pran retorted, "What did he do? I did everything!"'

The sons learnt a lot from their fathers—especially, they learnt Gajanand's sincerity at work. Once his third son, Gangesh, had sat down for lunch when he got a call from his bank for an urgent meeting. Those were the times when customers chased banks and not the other way around, as it is now. When Gangesh said he would meet the bankers after lunch, Gajanand asked him to leave immediately for the meeting and leave his lunch for later. Two hours later, when Gangesh returned to resume his meal, his father joined him at the table—Gajanand had not eaten either. 'He would always say that work was more important than anything else,' says Shailesh.

'He also inculcated in us the diary system. He would note down in his diary anything that needed to be followed up. Every morning he would take out his diary and, referring to his notes, would start calling up people, inquiring if the expected work had been done. If it wasn't, he would give the person at the other end three more days and make a note of it. We could be sure of getting that call three days later, and to save ourselves further embarrassment, we would make sure our work was done,' says Shailesh.

Shailesh now follows the diary system: 'Because of that, I feel relaxed and my mind is fresh. Without my diary, I would be zero.'

'Lalit Bhaiya,' Shailesh adds, 'is also very well connected, like our father, and is active across several platforms.'

* * *

Gajanand's eldest son was a 'fairly good student'. After studying at Kolkata's Hindi High School, he went on to study at Mayo College in Ajmer, where the well-heeled sent their children, for four years, from 1955 to 1958. The oldest public boarding school in the country is named after a former viceroy of India and, as it is even now, was seen as accessible to only a select few. While the government had abolished royalty, the young princes from the royal houses of Patiala, Tripura and Jodhpur still moved around in grandeur in the school. 'I could feel the distance between them and us, the ordinary people,' said Lalit.

Back then, the family, though comfortably off, couldn't afford luxury. 'I would cherish every pair of new shoes or trousers that I got. Eating in five-star hotels was a rarity. But once in a while when we were taken to a fine dining restaurant, it would be a memorable experience,' says Lalit.

The young Lalit was ambitious and wanted to study further, much like his cousins in the larger family, which by now had quite a few lawyers and chartered accountants of repute. Lalit wanted to study law. He could finish classes by nine in the morning and then join his father and uncle in one of the family businesses, as they had wanted him to. But they didn't agree to this. 'You will be too tired to concentrate on work. You are the eldest of the children [the next oldest cousin was nine years younger than him] and have to take some responsibility,' he would be told by his father or his uncle. They managed to convince him to drop the idea. So Lalit went to St. Xavier's College to study commerce, and, as earlier mentioned, helped at the family bakery and restaurant.

But the passion to do something different remained. After his marriage at nineteen, he convinced his father that it was time for the family business to diversify and possibly look outside Kolkata. Around that time, they got information that a distillery in Rampur, an industrial town in Uttar Pradesh known for its sugar industry, was up for sale.

Liquor was a taboo in Marwari families, who were mostly teetotallers and vegetarians. But Gajanand still seemed interested, especially now that he was being egged on by his eldest son. Expert advice came from his teeing partner, Kushal Singh, who was working in Shaw Wallace. Gajanand asked him about the distillery. Kushal asked him to go ahead and predicted that Rampur would be a good buy.

The distillery belonged to Vishnu Hari Dalmia, who wanted to sell off the sick unit. To strike the deal, Lalit, accompanied by a cousin, went to meet Vishnu Hari. 'The interesting part is that nowadays, when you look to acquire something, there are the likes of E&Y and McKinsey who advise you. In those days, there was nobody. We didn't even know what a distillery looked like,' said Lalit. He was simply following his gut.

While Vishnu Hari quoted a sum of Rs 18 lakh, Lalit offered Rs 16 lakh. And Rs 16 lakh it was. Within a week the company had a new board of directors, and a cheque was handed over to Vishnu Hari. Rampur Distillery now belonged to the Khaitan family.

'This was how we purchased the distillery. When I visited Rampur, it was the first time I was seeing a distillery,' says Lalit. It was now up to him to make something out of a concern they had no idea about.

The facility, which had run into losses, was lying closed. One of the oldest distilleries in the country, it had been set up in 1943 to produce extra neutral alcohol and to supply bulk alcohol, like a commodity, to liquor companies across the country.

Back home in Kolkata, not many were confident that young Lalit, with little knowledge of the business, could pull it off. The taboo also meant that many in the family were unhappy about the diversification. 'When you told someone that you were in the liquor business you were discounted. The perception was that, "*Badhmash aadmi hain*. You are not in the right kind of business".' There were a few liquor companies at the time, like Mohan Meakin, Jagatjit and USL, but they were not very big. Wallace was there too. They had a few brands.

'In those days drinking was looked down upon. Anyone who drank alcohol was a bad man. And there was no question about women drinking. But gradually the perception changed. Now, of course, no party can last unless there is alcohol,' says Lalit.

But back in the 1970s, though Lalit had been to parties where liquor was served, he didn't know what it tasted like. That was why when he entered the distillery for the first time, he had no idea that the pit in front of him had molasses, which is used to make alcohol. He stepped right ahead and fell head first into the pit. 'The molasses was covered with dust and I just fell, walking as if into a mirage. That is why I keep telling my people that my understanding of molasses is better than anyone else's. Even if you are technically qualified, I know molasses better!'

Lalit was only joking, because since that first day he went on to rebuild the facility with such aplomb that years later he became known as a specialist in alcohol production.

Eager to get his hands dirty, Lalit shifted to Rampur from Kolkata with his wife Kiran and two daughters, Smita and Shailja. The family stayed in Rampur for a year. It was a life without any comforts. They had shifted in June when the summer was at its peak. The house rarely got piped water and, forget about air conditioning, most of the time there would be no power to even run the fans. Lalit and his family had to take to sleeping outside in the open air.

Kiran had no help at home. She would take the rickshaw to the markets to buy vegetables and other home essentials. The saving grace was a gardener who would sometimes cook for them.

Life was equally challenging at the company. 'There was nothing there. I had to do everything, right from purchasing the materials to getting a team to man the production,' says Lalit. A sick company, Rampur Distillery had no working capital. But despite the tough times and little money, Lalit was adamant he would not accept any financial help from the family. 'I wanted to grow and develop Rampur myself.'

He took a loan to buy molasses and restarted the facility. The same Kushal Singh who had advised Lalit and his father to buy the distillery joined the team in Rampur, taking premature retirement from Shaw Wallace. 'Gradually, we understood the business, which grew and stabilized,' says Lalit.

The Dalmias had launched a brand, Contessa Rum, that was supplied to the armed forces through the CSD (Canteen Stores Department) network. But when Lalit took over, the brand was selling just about 2000 cases a month. Lalit formed a team that took over the brand and re-established contacts with the CSD network to increase sales.

Rampur Distillery made slow but steady progress. It started doing well and made its first profits. Even as Lalit made visits to the offices of liquor companies to get orders (Kushal managed to get the alcohol supply contract with Shaw Wallace, which proved to be an important lifeline), he also developed Rampur's business in country liquor.

Indian made Indian liquor (IMIL) currently makes for about 35 per cent of the Indian spirits market. Back then, in the 1970s and 1980s, its share was even bigger. Lalit spotted a great opportunity to increase Rampur Distillery's sales volumes by tapping into this opportunity. Over the years, Rampur's country liquor brands such as Masti, Jhoom and, more recently, Miss Jalwal, have become immensely popular in the Uttar Pradesh market. In 2012, the company was selling three million cases of country liquor in UP alone.

'The country liquor brands were good and quite popular. But here the margins are low. You can't survive just on country liquor,' says Lalit. At present the share of country liquor in Radico's revenue is insignificant, but when Rampur was looking to stabilize, this additional stream of revenues helped.

Rampur Distillery had, by the 1980s, hit the ground running, and soon became the biggest business in the G.N. Khaitan fold. 'It was a brilliant experience. I loved all the challenges along the way. There is great satisfaction in rising from the bottom,' says Lalit. Rampur Distillery's profits would rise to more than Rs 10 crore and its top-line to within touching distance of Rs 100 crore by the mid-1990s.

The company's growth left a big impression on Lalit's son. From the time he was in school, and even before he had entered his teens, Abhishek was sure of what he wanted to become when he grew up. At school, teachers would often ask students this inevitable question, as to what they wanted to become. Most of them would give predictable answers—doctor, engineer, scientist . . . 'But I was clear that I wanted to be in business, and that too in the liquor industry. It has been a passion since then,' says Abhishek.

* * *

The youngest of three children, Abhishek was different from his siblings. There is an anecdote that the family often narrates for a good laugh, and which also underlines Abhishek's personality.

It was when the children were in school. Shailja, three years older to Abhishek, was always a nervous wreck during the week of exams. Often she would complain of a stomach ache and cry her way to school. Her brother, on the other hand, always played it cool. The night before exams, while the others would be busy revising their lessons, Abhishek would watch a movie.

This one time, though, when it was exam time, Abhishek asked his sister to watch a movie too, telling her she could relax and have a clear mind for her exams the next day. Shailja followed his advice. And she failed that exam. Abhishek, as usual, was among the top three in his class. During his tenth standard board exams, Abhishek was very much the cool, colourful chap, going for a Samantha Fox concert in Delhi a day before he was to sit for one of the papers.

At school, he was notorious for his back-bencher antics. But the teachers would seldom punish him because he was also among the toppers.

He was in the ninth standard when his father asked him to study hard enough to be the topper. He did, and stood first in his class. But he told his father, 'Dad, you wanted me to come first. I have come first. But coming first is different from being second or third. If it's about the second or third place, I get time to do other things I'm interested in. So please let me be like this.' Lalit agreed, and replied, 'See, I don't expect you to look for a job somewhere else. So you go on with your extra-curricular activities. I will be happy if you are in the top three.'

Even as he excelled in academics, Abhishek also took part in sports. In high school he was the school prefect. 'I liked being the prefect. One of the reasons was I could use it as an excuse to be out of the class,' he says, with a smile. His friends were like him—good in studies but equally interested in activities outside the class. But the class toppers were not his friends, as he found them too serious. 'I was colourful,' says Abhishek, of his life in school.

Mathematics was his favourite subject, and most of the time he would end up scoring full marks in it. In the tenth board exams, Abhishek got 99.5 per cent marks, topping the country in physics, chemistry and mathematics. But he hated science, as it was 'too technical' for him.

After his boards, Abhishek was hoping to take commerce as his subject, as he eventually wanted to do chartered accountancy, given his penchant for numbers. But his parents weren't amused. 'First, you will have to complete a degree in three years. And CA will take another four years, at least. You will be wasting too

many years,' he was told. 'Instead, go for an engineering course
and then do your MBA if you want. It will help you save at
least a year.' And that was what he did. After his tenth boards,
Abhishek selected science. He didn't enjoy it but still managed
to top his class.

At home, his parents kept the environment as 'normal' as
possible. There were no luxuries. The family lived in a rented
house till Abhishek turned eighteen, when a house was built in
New Friends Colony in south Delhi. The family had earlier lived
in Maharani Bagh, then in Chirag Delhi, afterwards moving to
a rented house in New Friends Colony. Abhishek would take
the bus to school. The bus stop was close by—a twenty-minute
walk or a ten-minute bicycle ride from his house.

The Khaitans loved to travel. They would often visit the
hill stations close to Delhi, staying in not-so-luxurious hotels
that would cost Rs 25-50 a night. There were overseas trips too,
including one to Switzerland. But, unable to afford the expensive
Swiss hotels, the family used to stay in dormitories. Their visits
to other places in Europe would sometimes see them finding
space in monasteries, where washrooms would be a four-minute
walk away, not a pleasant situation in the winter.

Lalit would take out time to spend it with his wife and
children, even cutting down on his socializing for this. One
activity was especially sacrosanct. Almost every day, he would
take Kiran on a drive to the international airport. 'It would take
about an hour-and-a-half. My mother used to love long drives,'
says Abhishek.

Abhishek was extremely close to his mother, Kiran, who
died in 2011. For him, she was god, says his uncle, Shailesh.
Every day, especially after he joined his father in the business,

Abhishek would have hour-long conversations with her before he retired to bed. And, when he shifted to Bengaluru for his engineering in BMS College, Kiran would visit him to make sure he was taking care of himself as he was staying alone in a flat on Bengaluru's Cunningham Road.

* * *

After school, when he realized that his CA dreams would have to be extinguished, Abhishek opted to do engineering in Bengaluru. 'IIT was too serious for me,' he says. There was a specific reason for choosing India's IT capital for his engineering studies. For someone who had developed an early passion for the liquor industry, Abhishek wanted to get a taste of Bengaluru's pub culture. 'It was the pub city. The amount I learnt about drinks and consumers in Bengaluru, I wouldn't have anywhere else,' he says.

However, he had to complete his studies first. Engineering was a nightmare; there were twenty subjects to be studied, and the exams, though conducted only once a year, would pan out over fifty days. Abhishek again made his mark in class, and was one of the only two students who didn't have any arrears at the end of four years. He was even among the rank holders in the university. It didn't come easily, and called for many an all-nighter on his part.

Staying away from home for the first time also taught the youngster valuable life lessons. The independence of staying alone came with the responsibility of managing one's own affairs. On a monthly budget, he learnt to ration supplies. Still there would be months when he ran short of money and had to drop fruit from his diet or was forced to stop eating out for a while.

There were also those little learning experiences, such as the time when he was a little high while returning from a pub in his 118NE car and had a very close shave with another vehicle. Life became a little more precious after that.

Once in a while, it helped to have parents who could afford a little luxury. So when a friend rammed his 118NE beyond repair, Abhishek spent a month without a car. A few calls home and 'pulling a long face' resulted in a Maruti Esteem, in which he zoomed around in a Bengaluru that hadn't yet become infamous for its traffic snarls.

But the biggest lesson he learnt, the one that would decide the direction his career would take, was, quite fittingly, at one of the pubs of Bengaluru. It was 1994, and Abhishek was in his second year of college. On one of his many visits to a nearby pub he came across a newly launched whisky. It was Gilbey's Green Label, launched by IDV, the Indian arm of UDV. Launched specifically for the Indian market, it was a runaway hit.

Gilbey's Green Label had managed to do something unique in the very competitive Indian whisky market. As it is even today, whisky dominated the Indian liquor market, with a 65 per cent share. But it was a segment dominated by some big names, including Diplomat, Aristocrat, Bagpiper's and Officer's Choice. But Deepak Roy, who was heading IDV, had different plans.

Most of these brands operated in the budget segment—Rs 170 to Rs 245 a bottle. Deepak's latest introduction was priced at Rs 185. So the price was not much of a differentiator, and the product competed directly with USL's Bagpiper and Diplomat. But Deepak did something with Gilbey's Green Label that the others hadn't with their whiskies. He gave the bottle a premium look. It sported a guala cap (a tamper-proof cap usually used by the more expensive brands). This look helped; the customers thought that they were paying Rs 185 for a product that looked as if it cost Rs 220–250.

The strategy worked. In no time, Roy sold one million cases of Gilbey's Green Label. Later, leveraging on the market the brand had created, Roy launched the premium version of Gilbey's Green Label, called Gilbey Solitaire.

'I had followed the launch, and how Gilbey's became a rage, very closely. Personally, Green Label was not my brand. I was more into Peter Scot and sometimes McDowell, or Black and White or Black Dog,' says Abhishek. 'But I loved the packaging and the look and feel of the brand, Gilbey's Green Label, and how it had been positioned as an international brand.'

The new brand's success had enlightened the youngster, and it dawned on him that the possibilities in the sector were immense. He knew what was needed to be done at Rampur Distillery to take it to the next level.

* * *

It has been more than twenty years since Abhishek joined Rampur Distillery. There have been stiff challenges and a few failures, including some high-profile joint ventures with multinational liquor companies that didn't work out as expected. The JVs were a sign of an entrepreneur at the helm of a company that was still on the learning curve and had a fear of the unknown. Radico didn't have a premium brand at that time. The team was unsure if it could pull off the launch of a high-brow brand all by itself. Some of the brands launched under the JVs, including Masterstroke premium whisky, in partnership with Diageo, failed to get going.

But when one meets Abhishek at Radico's corporate office in Delhi's Mohan Co-operative Industrial Area, it appears as if the doubts that assailed the young entrepreneur and the fledgling company two decades ago have vanished. Puffing on his cigarette in a room which has a dominantly white décor, with M.F. Hussain's paintings and photographs signed by celebrities on the walls, Abhishek sounds as passionate about his business as he was two decades ago.

'I have not diversified even once. People ask me to get into beer. But I'm clear. Money is limited, so put money in what you know. Look at the houses that have run into trouble,' he says, throwing a not-so-subtle hint at his infamous industry peer now in exile overseas.

He would be keen to consolidate Radico Khaitan's perch at the top of the Indian liquor industry—it is the biggest domestic player in the market now. While it has tough competition in the form of two big MNCs—Diageo and Pernod Ricard—with deep pockets, Abhishek is backing himself to keep chipping away at the domestic market. 'In five years, close to 110 million Indians will enter the legal drinking age. That is a huge market waiting for us,' he says.

The managing director would like to believe that he has created an organization that will make the most of this opportunity. His leadership team now includes heads of the domestic and export businesses at the company (Radico brands

are now available in sixty countries); production (the facilities
are now spread across India) is under the able hands of the
veteran K.P. Singh.

Operationally, Abhishek is learning to detach himself
from the day-to-day affairs of his company. And he strongly
believes that if he has to be in office for more than four hours,
something is not right. 'I like to delegate work. In my entire
life I have never signed a cheque,' he says. That indeed could
be an achievement, as in most traditional Marwari businesses,
cheques and vouchers are still under the control of the
promoter—family members.

It is not clear if it is his father from whom he has picked up
the art of delegation. But Lalit was the one in the family who
first started thinking a little differently from the traditional
methods of management. And that has helped him create a
balance when it comes to dividing the business responsibilities
between himself and his son. When Abhishek joined the
business, the two would depend on each other when it came
to decision making. They would go together for meetings, and
Lalit would give his son enough time and space to present his
viewpoint. 'As a father I have never imposed myself. When
he was eighteen, I told him he was my partner. Even our
shareholding is equal,' says Lalit.

While the system has worked over the years, Lalit has
passed on the baton. A few years ago he told his son to take
over. While earlier, the final decision would be Lalit's, now it
is Abhishek's. 'I give my suggestions, but leave the decisions to
him,' says Lalit.

And he underlines Abhishek's performance: 'People who
are brilliant are not always successful. They think others are

fools. I was not sure how successful Abhishek would be. But he has made it. He has been extremely good at his work and is now acknowledged as a successful person.'

Relatives say that father and son have become closer after the demise of Kiran Khaitan. Abhishek and his family live with Lalit in their New Friends Colony mansion.

Over the years, the larger Khaitan family—Lalit's four brothers—have shifted to Delhi. The disagreements that had cropped up during the separation of family assets have been buried. 'The entire joint family now holidays together once a year. And separately, three generations of Khaitans now get together once in two years,' says Shailesh Khaitan.

Abhishek, who is the eldest of the grandchildren, has taken an initiative to keep in touch with his cousins. He and his four male cousins—each now running his own business—meet every month. The first two or three hours are a serious affair, so anyone coming late, even by ten minutes, has to pay a fine of Rs 15,000. What they discuss or share is confidential, but these meetings are followed by drinks and dinner. These get-togethers have helped create a bond among the cousins. 'It is a great way to advise each other, leverage each other's networks and come up with ideas,' says Shailesh. His son Utsav is part of this exclusive group.

Abhishek is equally passionate about his friends, especially the close-knit circle that includes Shrawan. 'We share a lot, including matters that we might not talk about to our wives,' says Shrawan. Soon after Abhishek came back from Bengaluru to help his father in the business, Shrawan left for the US to do his MBA. Once back, he found a different Abhishek, one who had crossed a milestone. 'Boss, you are now a successful businessman,' Shrawan had told Abhishek.

'We grew up together. From the moment of our meeting after my return, I started seeing him in another light. I now started looking up to him,' says Shrawan, whose family owns the chain of shops, Himalaya Opticals.

Looking to expand the business, Shrawan was tempted to go the private equity way, after having being approached by several PE players who were offering good valuations. But confused about what to do, Shrawan approached Abhishek for advice. 'You don't require the money. You are growing organically, don't worry about that. And as for money, it will come,' Abhishek told his friend.

Shrawan paid heed to that advice, and is glad about it. Since then, Himalaya Opticals has grown from about thirty stores to nearly ninety-five stores. 'I'm glad I didn't take the PE offers. Otherwise, I might have been one of the Lilliputs,' says Shrawan, referring to the kids-wear retailer whose PE-backed search for fast growth turned awry. Abhishek too has used his friends as a sounding board when decisions became tricky.

Abhishek turns his back to potential buyers eyeing stakes in Radico Khaitan. 'What will I do with the money? I have a lifestyle that I have dreamed of. What more should I aspire for,' he tells his friends.

Instead, he wants to keep driving Radico Khaitan to greater heights. And his eyes are on international shores. 'I like what other firms, such as Dabur and Marico, have done overseas. I see Radico doing something similar. I want Radico to become a formidable MNC in the liquor industry,' he says.

* * *

My Learnings

♦ Go up the value chain to increase margins.

I don't want to be a bottler.

♦ Focus on hiring not just the best, but the relevant talent.

I realized that if we hired someone who was around thirty-five, he would go the beaten way. We needed fresh thinking.

♦ Go the extra mile, don't give up when it's a matter of survival.

I begged eight to ten bottlers to work for us. Everyone asked for a minimum guarantee . . . I said I was not running away. Just start with us. [He was able to convince them. And then the team at Rampur started developing the product.]

♦ One's name is sometimes as important as the product itself. Be open to change, and move away from the legacy.

[The product was almost ready.] But we couldn't say, here is 8PM whisky by Rampur Distillery. It would sound like a product from a shop in Karol Bagh.

♦ No change comes without pain. Be ready for the long haul. Shun shortcuts.

We realized that going forward, we had to go premium. That was the only way for us. It would be painful and expensive, but in the long run that would make us survive.

+ Specialization is the key. Diversification shouldn't come at the price of specialization.

I have not diversified even once. People ask me to get into beer. But I'm clear. Money is limited, so put money in what you know. Look at the houses that have run into trouble.

+ As you grow in scale, learn to delegate. All the decision making can't be done by you alone.

I like to delegate work. In my whole life I have never signed a cheque.

3

Mithun Chittilappilly

Mithun Chittilappilly was at the Nedumbassery airport in Kochi, waiting for his flight to Mumbai. It was a Monday. He would be spending the rest of the week meeting investors, trying to convince them to put money in the upcoming initial public offering (IPO) of V Guard. The company had been founded by his father Kochouseph Chittilappilly, in 1977. It was the end of 2007 now, and Mithun was hoping to raise Rs 65 crore to fund the company's expansion.

As his flight was announced and he proceeded to the boarding gates, the twenty-seven-year-old didn't have a good feeling about the five days ahead. This was going to be his third week of the drill—flying to Mumbai on a Monday and spending the rest of the week doing the roadshow. The response had been tepid, at best; and it didn't look as if the tide was going to change.

It was not as if V Guard, which is ubiquitous in the state for its stabilizers, was not doing well. In fact, it was one of the few success stories of entrepreneurship from Kerala, a state more known for its communist leaders and their inclination for industrial strikes. V Guard had revenues of about Rs 200 crore and was profitable. Its return on capital employed (ROCE) was high, and it had a monopoly in its flagship product—stabilizers. And its logo, the kangaroo, was among the most recognizable in the state.

However, in the financial capital of Mumbai, home to India Inc's biggest names, bankers and brokerage firm owners started finding holes in V Guard's business model. For starters, few potential investors had heard about V Guard, the exceptions being those who had lived in or hailed from south India. The company was a small fish outside the Kerala market, about one-tenth the size of competitors such as Havells or Finolex. The bankers and brokers also contended that even though V Guard had other products like cable wires, it was basically a one-product company. More than 50 per cent of its revenues and 90 per cent of its operating profit came from stabilizers.

'And what is the scope of stabilizers in the future as the electricity situation in India improves? Your product will go out of the market in five years and you will shut down,' said one of the bankers to Mithun. Earlier, when power fluctuations were the norm in Kerala, people simply had to have stabilizers to protect their fridges and televisions. However, even though the quality of power there has now improved, stabilizers continue to be popular in the state.

Many of the bigger bankers refused to even consider the IPO as it was too small for them. 'We were a small-cap company. The entire market cap was estimated to be Rs 240 crore, and we wanted to raise Rs 65 crore. So it was a small IPO. Investment bankers refused to consider the IPO. The larger ones said they don't do IPOs of less than Rs 200–300 crore,' says Mithun.

The IPO market was almost at its peak and the market was booming.

Initially, it was Kochouseph taking the lead at the roadshows, but within a week's time the V Guard founder got tired of the questions being thrown his way. He knew his younger son had a thing for numbers. 'You do the roadshows in Mumbai. I will see what I can do from Kerala,' he told his son.

This week, Mithun was accompanied by his chief financial officer. As he had feared, this trip to Mumbai too appeared to be going the way of his earlier trips. Pessimism about V Guard's IPO had only increased, what with financial markets in India and overseas tanking after the subprime crisis in the US. In one of the meetings, a senior investor asked Mithun, 'Are you nuts to consider an IPO now?'

'I was demoralized,' says Mithun, of the days spent in Mumbai making the rounds of banks and brokerages.

* * *

The young man had not anticipated this situation when he joined V Guard as executive director in June 2006. He was back after a fruitful MBA from Melbourne, Australia.

Before leaving for Australia he had been a bit unsure about working in India, especially in Kerala. But his years in Australia completely changed his outlook, kindling in him an enthusiasm for his own country. One of his teachers in Melbourne had told him, 'If I were you, I would be in India and join the family business. The country is booming. These are the golden decades for India to grow. Australia is reaching maturity, and growth prospects are limited.'

For someone who was a little disillusioned by the chaos of India, this was a moment of awakening. Another factor that ensured his return was a hint from his older brother, Arun Chittilappilly, that he was needed back home. Though Kochouseph was open to the idea of Mithun working in Australia for a couple of years before returning home, Mithun realized it was time that he returned even sooner. Arun had joined the family business in 2002 and had taken over the controls at Wonderla—the entertainment park business that Kochouseph had founded in 2000. This water amusement park (earlier called Veega Land) in Kochi is immensely popular in Kerala. A second one was opened in Bengaluru in 2000, and a third in Hyderabad, in 2016. Now an extra pair of hands was needed at V Guard.

Mithun spent the first few months after his return to Kochi dividing his time between V Guard and Wonderla. There were plans to open a new theme park in Mumbai, and Mithun got involved in that. But land acquisition problems delayed the project, which was eventually dropped.

Around the same time, Kochouseph got the idea of raising money after his acquaintance Navas Meeran successfully raised $10 million for his Eastern Condiments by selling a minority stake in it to private equity firm, New Vernon. Kochouseph approached the same consultant who had arranged the deal for Navas. But after chats with a few PEs, the Malayalee entrepreneur learned that most of the investors were looking at a five-year window for exit, after getting returns from their investment. He wasn't amused. 'How can I ensure them an exit in five years?' That was when C.J. George, the founder of broking firm Geojit BNP Paribas and someone he respected, suggested that Kochouseph could instead go for an IPO.

When the roadshows didn't turn out as well as expected, Kochouseph used his contacts in the Kerala industry and among Malayalees in the rest of the country and overseas to make sure that the IPO was subscribed fully. He worked his contacts and got the State Bank of India, South Indian Bank, Federal Bank and Sundaram Finance to participate in the IPO. The V Guard founder even travelled to the Middle East to work his influence among the Malayalee community there.

He and Mithun were sure that the retail part of the IPO would be subscribed. IPOs were becoming a popular route for promoters to raise money by diluting their stakes in their companies. There was enough appetite among the investors in Kerala and among the Malayalees abroad to raise Rs 35 crore, about half of the IPO size. The rest, they hoped, would be bought by the institutions. To ensure the IPO's success, the price was brought down to Rs 82 a share, from the earlier suggestions of Rs 100 a share and then Rs 90 a share.

The run-up to the listing wasn't great. According to the rules, at least 90 per cent of the offering has to be subscribed for the listing to go through. Wockhardt Hospitals had to withdraw its IPO after only 18 per cent of its issue was subscribed. Emaar MGF, the real estate firm, was another company whose IPO met a similar fate. Even after its issue price was slashed, the IPO got a poor response, and the company had to withdraw it.

The IPO failure of companies that were bigger and better known than V Guard prompted its bankers to ask for a postponement of the issue. But Kochouseph had made up his mind, and he wanted the listing to go through as was planned.

V Guard was listed on the Bombay Stock Exchange on 18 February 2008. Family members and senior executives of the company were present at the exchange as Kochouseph rang the bell. The scrip was listed at Rs 84, Rs 2 higher than the issue price. The issue itself was subscribed 2.45 times, which means it fetched applications for 2.45 shares for every share on offer.

But bad news followed immediately. Some of the institutional investors sold their stake on the first day of the company's listing. A senior executive from one of the financial institutions that had invested in the IPO told Mithun, 'I bought the issue because I was pressured to. But am selling on the first day itself.' From its first week of listing, the V Guard scrip took the southward route, losing 3–4 per cent every week. Within a year it was in danger of touching sub-Rs 40 levels.

The plunging share price even marred Mithun's big day. He got married on 25 January 2009. It was a Sunday. Two days earlier, on Friday, the V Guard scrip was quoting at Rs 44. 'I remember that when I got married, V-Guard owned land that was valued higher than its market capitalization.'

Over the next three years though, V Guard did well, increasing revenues and building scale. But those institutional investors who still held its shares were waiting to exit the company. They were not sure about the long-term viability of V Guard's business. By April 2010, when the scrip touched the Rs 100 mark for the first time, riding the company's improved financials, each of the institutional investors who had bought V Guard shares in the IPO exited the company. None of them, it seemed, trusted the company to continue to do well, and preferred to exit at what appeared to be a high for its shares.

Mithun has been in touch with a few of them since the IPO days. He told one of them, 'If you guys don't want to take the risk, then you will not get the returns.' Had the institutional investors stuck to their V Guard shares, they would have made a return of twenty times their investment within five years. At present, the shares, which were split in 2016 (from Rs 10 to Rs 1 per share) are now quoting above the Rs 200 (or Rs 2,000 by pre-split face value) mark. The promoters split their company stock so that more shares would be available to investors, making the company more attractive to them.

'The IPO changed me. It changed V Guard,' says Mithun.

* * *

However, back in Kochi after the issue in 2008, Mithun was smarting. And so was the rest of the leadership at V Guard. It was clear to the top team that the company could no longer afford to grow at 10–15 per cent per annum. To have any hopes of pushing its scrip past the Rs 100 mark, the original price of the issue, the company had to bring in the numbers—grow fast, increase its revenues and expand its margins by expanding its markets and introducing more products. The team felt they owed the investors that much. But for that V Guard would have to reinvent itself.

There was one thing that was going for V Guard, which was its research and development (R&D) department, thanks to the legacy of Kochouseph.

Growing up in the Parappur suburb of Thrissur, the V Guard founder had realized that he had a nose for all things technical. 'Anything related to technology, I could digest or understand. Be it an iron, fan, motor . . . I could fix them all from the time I was thirteen,' he says. That compensated for his weakness in languages and his lack of interest in sports. His passion was technology. While in college in Irinjalakuda, Kochouseph nursed a dream to become a scientist and get a job in the Indian Space Research Organisation. But as he had scored poorly in the non-science subjects, he could not pursue this ambition.

His first job was in Telics, a company in Thiruvananthapuram that manufactured stabilizers and emergency lamps. Kochouseph joined as a supervisor and immediately made a mark. 'I started off in 1973 with a stipend of Rs 150. Within three years I was working in the R&D division and making some critical changes in the design of circuit boards. By the end of the third year, I was earning Rs 850, equivalent to what my more accomplished classmates from college were earning.'

But the company wasn't doing well. Given his expertise in stabilizers and given Kerala's dismal power condition—voltage fluctuation was the norm—Kochouseph decided to start out on his own and shifted base to Kochi. 'My thinking was that I was earning Rs 850. And I had to earn more. I felt that if I could earn Rs 1000–1500 or Rs 2000, I would be happy.'

His enterprise started off in 1977, in a small shed in Kochi's Kuttoor neighbourhood. Kochouseph hired two SSLC-pass (SSLC, the Secondary School Leaving Certificate, was equivalent to the tenth grade) employees and trained them to help him in assembling stabilizers. V Guard's stabilizers looked better and had more features than the ones available in the market and produced by the big names of that time—Keltron and Neloc, a Tata company. Even though the distributors were a little taken aback when the young Kochouseph priced his product Rs 5 higher than the competition, V Guard's stabilizer quickly found a loyal clientele, because it looked more attractive and had more features.

'Big people, including economists, ask me which year I broke even. I tell them, V Guard was profitable in its first month itself!' says Kochouseph. The V in V Guard stood for voltage.

From ten to fifteen units in the first month, sales shot up incredibly fast. By the time his now trusted lieutenant K. Vijayan joined the company in the early 1980s, V Guard was clocking Rs 20 lakh in annual sales and employed about thirty people. An air force veteran, Vijayan found Kochouseph's transparency and openness a fresh change from the hierarchical system he had come from. 'Though he was four years younger than me, he was like a mentor. He would trust his people and easily delegate work. Within six months of my joining, he went on a trip to the US, leaving me in charge of the operations,' says Vijayan, who is now executive director, administration.

A catalytic moment came in 1986, a moment that is Mithun's earliest memory linked to his father and V Guard.

Inevitably—this was Kerala—labour trouble erupted at V Guard, and protesting workers gheraoed the company premises and even their home. Mithun and his brother were not allowed to go to school for two weeks. Not one to give in easily, Kochouseph went to a priest who had earlier approached the entrepreneur for contracts to develop the company's products. Now, with labour trouble at his factory, Kochouseph realized what opportunity lay in the priest's offer. He could outsource V Guard's operations, including the assembling of stabilizer units, to units run by the priest.

It was a success. Units, each employing up to fifty women, mushroomed across Kerala and other south Indian towns and cities, and in no time there were sixty of them. Each unit was trained and supervised by V Guard executives. But each unit was an independent entity, with its own balance sheet. Simultaneously, the manufacturing presence of V Guard thinned, and its labour force became extremely lean. Almost all the manufacturing was outsourced to these units.

'In hindsight, I could have tackled the labour strife differently. But it was a blessing in disguise. While we had 2,000 people on our rolls, over time, this outsourcing resulted in more than 5,000 being employed indirectly. And, sitting in Kerala, I gave an indirect lesson to our politicians. V Guard has never suffered industrial unrest since,' says Kochouseph. Kerala, home to the world's first democratically elected communist government, had earned a dubious reputation for its industrial strikes that had rendered many companies sick.

Another memory etched in Mithun's mind from his growing-up years is of their father being recognized as India's highest taxpayer in 1993. 'It came in the papers and was a huge recognition. Everyone was now aware of my surname . . . and it was a great boost to his public profile,' says Mithun.

By 2005, when Mithun joined V Guard, the company had complete control over the stabilizers market in Kerala and was fairly well known in the rest of southern India. It was recognized as a fair employer; loyalty was prized and rewarded, and the whole company was like a big family that got along exceedingly well—and also a profitable one, growing by 10–15 per cent annually. After the success of its stabilizers, V Guard's R&D department had developed other products, such as wires and motor pumps over the years.

That is why the IPO came as a shock for everyone, including Mithun. Though V Guard was the undisputed leader in its market and its product, it was almost a nonentity outside Kerala.

However, the IPO gave Mithun the ticket to set about reforming and restructuring the company. By then he was already calling the shots in the sales, marketing and finance departments—Kochouseph had asked everyone in these verticals to report to Mithun after he joined the company. The impending IPO had given Mithun free rein to question the existing practices across departments.

The biggest change was brought about in the sales and marketing function. Until then, this function was divided among the branches. Each branch had a manager, under whom there were about ten executives covering thirty districts. Each of the executives was responsible for selling three to four products in two to three districts. Overall, the sales team comprised about seventy executives located across the southern market. The organization was thinly staffed, which helped in keeping the costs down. But output suffered.

That was primarily because everyone was focused on just selling stabilizers—which were fast moving—to meet their monthly targets. The stabilizers and the company brand were immensely popular in Kerala. This popularity helped the company sell other products under the brand name. But outside Kerala, this proved to be a tough task. Except for stabilizers, none of the other products was making money. The wire business was running losses and the water heater business was making less than Rs 10 crore a year.

The picture changed dramatically in the four years after Mithun took over. Now each branch manager had a category specialist at his branch. So if Bengaluru was a branch, it would have separate specialists heading stabilizers, wires, water heaters and pumps. Each product was handled by ten guys at each branch. While earlier the executive in north Bengaluru was responsible for all the products, now he specialized in just one. For the rest of the products, new hires were made. The team got more focused. So, from about ten persons in the IT capital, the sales force increased to fifty.

At present, the sales and marketing department is headed by a vice president. Under him, there is a head for each product, who is responsible for the all-India sales and profit and loss (P&L). These heads travel all over the country and recruit people for sales and marketing.

As V Guard looked to expand its market beyond south India, it sought to replicate its existing structure everywhere. The team in the National Capital Region (NCR), where there had been just a one-man office since 2003, had expanded in 2008 and now consisted of fifty members. Next, the branches in Kolkata and Thane (in the Mumbai metropolitan region) were expanded in 2010. Mithun decided against entering Mumbai city because stabilizers weren't sold in most parts of the city, which had high-quality electricity supply. In hindsight, it was a good move to be in Thane, where operating costs were much lower than in Mumbai. Also, the timing helped, as V Guard had a presence in the city when Thane's real estate grew exponentially. 'Thane became a hot-bed of activity. So it was a good move,' says Mithun. For the Delhi region too, the first office was set up in Gurugram to reduce costs. And the construction boom in the NCR helped increase numbers for V Guard.

In the south, barring Andhra Pradesh, the company had a fairly good network already. A team was added in AP.

Mithun also pushed for the introduction of more products. The company had only four. Over the years, more were introduced, including switchgears, fans, inverters and even kitchen appliances, such as mixer grinders and induction cookers.

'Starting with fans in 2006, we now have eight to nine large categories,' says Mithun. 'To develop the new products, we groomed internal talent, and then did a bit of lateral hiring. In the case of inverters, we had a good knowledge of electronics. Now we also have solar-based inverters.

'Dad was a technical guy. The R&D team was well developed. There was always this culture of experimentation and finding new things to do. Though the new products weren't profitable, there was enthusiasm to learn and grow, even if you risked losing money. The culture was one of learning. We also had a design team.'

But when it came to distribution, Mithun initiated a major tweak. His father was a great believer in the distributor system, which meant that all the products first went to distributors, who then supplied them to the retailers. Such a system, Mithun believed, was fine so long as it was for a product like a stabilizer, for which margins were high enough to be shared by the company, the distributors and the retailers. But it did not work for other products. Huge retail chains demanded that the company sell its products directly to them and not through the distributors. Kochouseph had refused to do this, and V Guard missed out on expanding its reach. This was one of the reasons why the company had a negligible presence in Chennai, where large retail stores were coming up.

Mithun thought it was time to change this system.

'We had lost many opportunities. Hardware stores like Ratna Fan House in Chennai or the large ones on Govinda Nayakan street were used to buying directly. They will not deal with distributors, especially in something like wires where there is little margin. So I said, for large orders we should supply directly. That opened gates for us.'

From thirty to forty distributors earlier, V Guard today has 300 distributors and 2,000 channel partners all over the country. 'That network of 2,000 partners wasn't there before. V Guard was under-marketed. I told my dad that if a distributor supplies our products and loses Rs 20–30 lakh, he will ask us to compensate him. So I was of the view that we must sell products directly to the retailers. And once we were large enough, we could sell through distributors.'

These measures were helping V Guard up its sales. By 2010, its revenues rose to Rs 454 crore, from Rs 222 crore in 2007, more than doubling. Net profit, at Rs 26 crore, almost doubled too. The improved financial performance reflected in the company's scrip, which zoomed past the Rs 150 mark by the end of 2010.

* * *

In 2010, an important top management change happened for V Guard.

Until then, Kochouseph was dividing his time between V Guard and Wonderla. He would spend the first half of the day at the V Guard office, and after lunch head to the premises of Wonderla. Arun was handling Wonderla operations from Bengaluru, where he had set up the second theme park after the first one in Kerala. Kochouseph kept close track of the operations from Kochi. At V Guard, Mithun was increasingly taking the calls, in consultation with his father.

A lot was happening in Kochouseph's personal life at the same time. He was inspired by the impact organ transplantation had made on Arun's mother-in-law's life. A kidney transplant had helped her regain control of her life and lead a normal lifestyle. Until then, life had been a constant struggle for her. An inspired Kochouseph now decided to donate one of his kidneys. 'He told us seven months before the operation. We were concerned. My dad is a person who, once he decides on something, will do it. We were supportive; Mom wasn't but didn't have a choice,' says Mithun.

While the family worried about complications that may arise from the surgery, Kochouseph went through the process with gusto. He underwent tests for four months and was declared fit. 'Luckily, he has been very healthy,' says Mithun.

Kochouseph donated his kidney to a truck driver, setting off a chain of organ donations. In this chain, one of the family members of the recipient has to donate an organ. Kochouseph became the first donor at the Kidney Federation of India, and is now deeply involved in the initiative.

This step won the entrepreneur countless admirers in the state, in the country and even internationally. As his social engagements increased and he immersed himself in more initiatives, including the controversial stray dog-free movement in the more recent years, Kochouseph found himself spending even less time at V Guard and Wonderla. Stray dogs had become an emotive issue in the state in 2016, after an old woman was mauled by a pack of dogs. In three months—from June to August—the state had recorded more than 31,000 dog bite incidents. Kochouseph firmly believed that the menace should be controlled by limiting the population of stray dogs.

He formalized his social work by setting up KCF (K. Chittilappilly Foundation) in 2012, helping those from the marginalized sections to access healthcare. 'I don't engage myself with V Guard or Wonderla any more. At the same time, I wanted to be gainfully engaged, so I started a real estate venture,' says Kochouseph.

Veegaland Developers, the real estate venture, is now three years old. It has completed two projects; two more are being planned. There is also an 'ultra-luxury' project, where one apartment consists of the entire floor and consists of over 8,000 square feet. This project, targeting high-net worth individuals, will be sold by invitation only.

The V Guard group also includes V Star, founded by Kochouseph's wife, Sheela Kochouseph, in 1995. It started producing nightwear for women, and diversification into innerwear in 2002 has helped turned around the operations. 'It is a profitable venture now, with revenues of almost Rs 100 crore,' says Mithun.

Though the four companies—V Guard, Wonderla, V Star and Veegaland Developers—now come under the V Guard Group umbrella, each functions independently of the other. Kochouseph is the chairman of V Guard and a non-executive director at Wonderla. Mithun, who would take over as the managing director of V Guard in 2012, doesn't sit on the board of Wonderla; and Arun, who is the managing director of Wonderla, doesn't sit on the board of V Guard.

Kochouseph is the single largest shareholder in both companies. Mithun and Arun are the second largest shareholders in the companies they head; at the same time, Mithun holds a minority stake in Wonderla, and Arun has a stake in V Guard.

Mithun and his wife, Joshna Johnson Thomas, also sit on the board of V Star, where Sheela is the managing director.

With Kochouseph focusing on KCF and the real estate company, Mithun was firmly on the saddle at V Guard. But he was not alone at the top. In 2009, a new position of joint managing director was created, and Kochouseph roped in N. Sreekumar, a professional with more than thirty years of experience and who was most recently with Apollo Tyres for eighteen years, in that position. But Sreekumar's stint in V Guard was a short one of just eight months. Mithun declines to explain his early departure, but it was clear that there were differences of opinion between them.

Within five months of Sreekumar's leaving, Kochouseph got Dr George Sleeba as the new joint managing director. Dr Sleeba was a respected industry veteran who had been at the helm of some of the top public sector undertakings in the state, including Travancore Cements and the Fertilizers and Chemicals Travancore Ltd (FACT). Dr Sleeba proved particularly good at handling operations and industrial relations. 'He was a great team leader, and V Guard immensely benefited from his experience,' says Mithun.

By 2012, the company's revenues had crossed the Rs 1,000 crore mark. It now needed someone who could take it pan-India; preferably an experienced hand from the FMCG sector. 'I was heading sales and marketing till then. When I started with the company, the goal was to double the revenues. Not only did we double the revenues, but we quadrupled them. I then felt that to take the company to the next level we needed a seasoned hand, as I was finding myself out of depth.'

The long-term vision was for the company to achieve a top line of one billion dollars. But it was not just about growth, it was also about managing it. 'I always believe that you should bring in as many professionals as possible. V Guard needed to move from being people-dependent to process-dependent. So we needed someone who could create processes and systems.'

This time though, Mithun did the hiring. Even as Dr Sleeba continued as the joint managing director, Mithun got V. Ramachandran as director, marketing and strategy. After joining Hindustan Lever as a management trainee and spending eighteen years there, Ramachandran had joined LG Electronics India as director, sales and marketing. Ramachandran was director and chief strategy officer for the south-west Asia region at LG when he moved to V Guard.

With the experience of having worked in two multinational companies that were among the best in their sectors, Ramachandran brought in deep changes at V Guard. 'He knew the best practices in the FMCG companies. Plus, he knew our industry very well,' says Mithun.

Among Ramachandran's first tasks was to build the company's competitive advantage, and this started with the removal of one pain point that V Guard had had for some time—its after-sales service. What prevented V Guard from expanding its distribution channel was its legacy—the after-sales service was operated by its distributors. Problems cropped up when V Guard's distributors refused to provide after-sales service for products that were directly sold by the company to the retailers. 'Distributors asked why they should spend money on products sold by retailers. We had tied ourselves in a knot,' says Mithun.

In the home state, it was easy for V Guard to monitor its after-sales service. There were almost 500 people on the rolls doing the servicing directly. But in new markets like Delhi, the service was pathetic. Data on product and customers were collected manually, and the information would take up to four months to reach the headquarters in Kochi. It had become common to have customers calling in to complain about the company's poor service. 'It was not that we were intentionally giving poor service, but it was managed badly. We worked on the after-sales service side. And on the supply chain side,' says Mithun.

Now, with Ramachandran by his side, Mithun got Deloitte to implement Oracle Siebel, a customer relationship management software, and appointed 130 authorized service centres, based on the franchisee model. A system was created to monitor them, and a centralized call centre was set up in Noida. This helped the company in two ways. 'It helped us to broaden distribution,' says Mithun. 'Second, the company's after-sales service improved dramatically outside Kerala. There was a unified system to track data on product complaints. Gradually, the complaints dried up.'

Though Ramachandran came in as the sales and marketing head, Mithun also gave him the function of strategy. 'We needed to drive process excellence in each function. So I said, whatever best practices we could bring in, we should.' While Deloitte helped in setting up the after-sales service, Accenture came in for the supply chain, which has hugely improved V Guard's margins.

'This was one of the reasons why we have been able to throw up some good numbers. We slashed our working capital. From having a debt of about Rs 300 crore, today we have a cash balance of Rs 150 crore. We have hugely improved the efficiency of the company. After four years, we thought we should elevate Ramachandran, and that is how he was promoted,' says Mithun.

Ramachandran is now the chief operating officer and also a member of the board at V Guard. The former Hindustan Lever and LG veteran continues to oversee transformational projects at V Guard. It is almost like a joint operation between Mithun and Ramachandran. 'And in some cases, like in corporate communications, I have given him more space. He also works on improvement projects,' says Mithun. Dr George Sleeba, who was dividing his time between V Guard and KCF till 2016, now works full time at the Foundation.

Post-2012, V Guard also changed its HR structure, a transformation that was led by Ramachandran. 'Our structure was very different from that of other companies. We were finding it difficult to hire people to fit into specific roles,' says Mithun. So, new jobs were identified. As lateral hiring increased, salary disparities too rose. To manage that, a compensation study was conducted.

'Ramachandran is involved in almost all aspects of the company. Between us, he goes deeper. I work on broad strategy and on the road map of where the company should go. I manage investor relations and engage with the board,' says Mithun. On the other hand, Ramachandran continues to monitor transformational projects at V Guard.

'It's been five years since he joined, and we have doubled revenues and probably tripled profits. We did Rs 50 crore in profit after tax in 2012. Last year we crossed Rs 100 crore,' Mithun said in late February 2017. The company had a net profit of Rs 151 crore in the 2017 financial year.

Ramachandran is based in Delhi, but ever since he joined V Guard, he spends at least two days of the week in Kochi. The rest of the time, he is either at the Delhi office or is travelling, visiting branches across the country.

* * *

Ramachandran's hiring was a break from the norm at V Guard. Kochouseph's hiring philosophy was influenced by a first-generation entrepreneur's need of the hour, which was to keep employee costs low. His first two hires were what were called 'SSLC-pass'. 'Even if I had hired a graduate, I would have had to train him. So SSLC guys were enough, and even they wouldn't stick around,' says Kochouseph. Later, this belief strengthened when he hired IIM graduates, none of whom stuck on. Kochouseph also looked for loyalty. This meant that he avoided the cream of the talent pool and instead looked for people who could be trained and retained in the company.

Mithun thought differently. 'We are from two different generations. Our outlook is different,' he says. The times had also changed when Mithun joined. And new needs became even more imperative when, post the IPO, the company sought to build new capabilities and improve its financial performance.

While there was pressure to continue with the philosophy that was time-tested, Mithun preferred to look beyond the traditional talent pool. 'I said, if you want to take the company ahead, then we have to hire laterally. We had good guys. But it was not possible for a company of our size to have functional knowledge about each segment of the business. So, be it human resources, corporate communications, IT or finance, I always pushed to get better guys.'

A senior official at V Guard sums up the difference in the philosophies of the two generations: 'Kochouseph tried to extract extraordinary work from ordinary guys. He believed in internal and home-grown talent.' From Mithun's perspective, while he accepted that they did have internal talent, he did not believe it was sufficient for every business function, especially if you were expanding. 'I felt that it worked okay up to a certain point. But once the company reached a higher level, we needed to look further. My philosophy was that if you hired good people from good companies with good practices, then we would be fine.'

With V Guard's new ambitions expanding beyond its home market, the search for talent now meant throwing out a wider net. To attract the best talent, compensation structures were tweaked and a conducive infrastructure set up, including a world-class video conferencing system that connected almost all the offices and plants of V Guard with the head office.

In 2016, another change was brought about. To attract talent in metros like Delhi and Mumbai, offices in V Guard adopted a five-day working week. Before that, only the second Saturday of the month had been a holiday.

Most from the team at V Guard responded positively to this change. But there were some who were out of sync with these new trends. They were given time to adjust to the new systems, but when they could not, they were given 'generous ESOPs and asked to leave'. Then there were some old-timers who no longer fit the seat they were occupying. This included the head of a large branch (state); there was a major lapse of judgement on his part when it came to keeping accounts, and he was asked to leave.

Apart from the HR department, the marketing department too saw changes. This was the result of Mithun's MBA stint in Australia. As part of the course, Mithun had done a case study on Amazon as a challenger brand (this was in 2003). The management course in Melbourne had opened Mithun's eyes to managing and growing a brand with an understanding of the science behind brands.

He brought the learning to V Guard, which continued to focus on the traditional medium of marketing—print—even as the broadcast and later, the digital, mediums were changing the way companies built perception around their brands. In 2006, V Guard was spending about 70 per cent of its total ad budget—amounting to about Rs 10–12 crore—on print advertisements. 'I got the feeling that we were not leveraging the budget properly,' says Mithun.

He knew that advertisements needed to create a perception around the company's brand. But that was not possible by doing only print. 'In print you can only do offers. If you want to run a consumer deal or retail a product like a sari, then print works. But we are not a retail company,' Mithun told his men. 'For us it is about creating perception, a lifestyle perception. You need to create the imagery, that is not possible in print.'

A staple V Guard ad in a newspaper would include a complete list of dealers in the region. But, over time, the advertisements were more about providing the contact details of dealers than sending a message about the product. While the phone numbers and addresses of dealers were needed in a new market that V Guard had entered, this practice was otherwise a waste of money. Also, as its list of dealers grew, it started eating into the advertisement itself.

Cutting down on print ads was not easy. Over the years, the company had built relationships with newspapers, and a cut in budget would also not go down well with his own men. But

Mithun didn't relent. 'One April [at the start of a new financial year], I cut [the budget]. I said we would sign new deals entailing less commitment. In other states, we started giving ads in the local languages.'

The cut led to some displeasure among the veterans, especially when the budget was slashed for the Kerala market. Mithun assured them of more funds if the business suffered because of the budget cuts. It didn't, as sales in Kerala continued to grow by more than 20 per cent annually.

'We changed agencies and got a media buying agency. Gradually we started spending more on electronic media, first in the other states and then in Kerala also. So, for some of these changes I faced resistance. But the good thing was that everyone was willing to experiment,' says Mithun.

Now V Guard's print spend is less than 20 per cent of its total advertisement budget, from the earlier 70 per cent. 'We changed the way we spend money. That was a big change, and it helped,' says the managing director.

Mithun also changed the agency that had created V Guard's commercials. This was tricky, as the older agency had been with V Guard since the 1980s. Another sticky point was that the agency's head was close to Kochouseph.

But now, as V Guard wanted to woo customers outside Kerala, Mithun wanted campaigns that would find appeal among non-Malayalee customers too, something the earlier agency, being based in Kerala, could not have done.

To match its ambition, V Guard hired national agencies— first TBWA for a few years and then Publicis, which continues to work with the company. 'You could make out the difference in the ads. This helped us to change the image,' said Mithun.

He was open to having a brand ambassador for the company, especially if it was possible to have someone who would take the brand to the next level. Mithun wanted a film star from among the A-listers. But then, such a star would want to endorse all the products in the stable and demand Rs 1–1.5 crore for each. That would be unviable. And Mithun wasn't interested in the second-rung stars. 'I will not degrade the brand, especially when you are trying to create a perception,' said Mithun.

He was, however, open to using a second-rung actor in a TV commercial in which the script was king so that the actor didn't come across as the brand ambassador. The company had followed this principle earlier, before Mithun had joined, roping in Anand Mahadevan, a well-known face on TV, for its commercial.

While some of the older V Guard commercials had jingles, the more recent ones depend on scripts that use humour and have a storyline.

* * *

One of the more daring marketing campaigns by V Guard was its associate sponsorship of Kochi Tuskers, the IPL team that lasted for just one season before the team owner's franchise was terminated by the Board of Control for Cricket in India (BCCI). Though the deal lasted just a year, the sponsorship had a lasting impact on consumers.

The V Guard logo was displayed on the sleeve of the Kochi Tuskers' official jersey. But there were difficulties in accommodating the kangaroo along with the company logo on the T-shirt sleeve. Though the mascot finally did find a place on the T-shirt, the difficulty of fitting it on the sleeve set off a debate between Kochouseph, Mithun and Ramachandran: was it time to do away with the kangaroo?

The question led to an exercise to change the logo, which always appeared with the image of the kangaroo. But Mithun would allow this only on one condition: 'The logo change can't be just about the logo. Many companies have changed their logos, but that hasn't changed the way they work. I believed that a logo change should happen along with a change in the philosophy and direction of the company.'

Meetings and discussions followed, and a call was taken to involve the entire organization in the exercise. Workshops were held across offices. Distributors and other partners were informed.

'We hit upon this philosophy that we should build products that are thoughtfully engineered for the customers. That should be the core focus going forward. That would mean we would be consumer driven and get out of the industrial business,' says Mithun.

The project, now in its third year, has seen V Guard exiting from its industrial business such as industrial UPS and industrial cables. 'We are now entering many new categories. So we should get out of any other category that is small and insignificant,' says Mithun.

Mithun wants the exercise to reflect in the culture of the organization, to bring in a kind of intuitiveness that will also rub off on the products they make. When the new product line-up was discussed, questions such as 'why are pumps always kept outside the house?' or, 'why are inverters placed under the staircase?' were discussed. 'We wanted our customers to interact with our products. We wanted the products to be more intelligent.'

The first product line to deliver on this promise will be new-generation water heaters from the company. It has the 'Internet of Things' built into it. A user can control it from anywhere in the world through an app on his phone that is synced with the water heater. The heater is self-diagnostic and can tell what's wrong with itself and, with a click of a button, can register with V Guard's customer relationship management for service.

There are similar plans for next-generation solar inverters and for ceiling fans with in-built lights that can be customized to light up a room in different colours. By Diwali in 2017, V Guard plans to offer four new product categories that will embody this new-found philosophy.

'We are going to see more interaction, and products will be more intelligent. We are changing the packaging and look of our products and have revamped our product line-up. We just communicated this to our distributors and retailers . . . they have been positive,' says Mithun.

And now the rejuvenated company will get a new logo. Mithun got in touch with Landor Associates, the brand-consulting firm based in San Francisco, to design a new identity for the company. Landor, which counts BMW, Nike and the Taj Group as its clients, has come up with a new logo for V Guard. And for those wondering if the kangaroo remains in the new look—it surely does. It is just that it is no longer sedentary, but now has a leaping posture—an image of action. The new logo is sleeker and has a stamp of the premium.

V Guard was all set to unveil its logo and new products during Diwali in 2016, but the demonetization drive delayed the launch. Fresh plans have lined up for the launch of the new line of products and the redesigned logo during the 2017 festival season.

* * *

Kochouseph's Facebook page has nearly seven lakh likes. His posts, mostly in Malayalam, are widely liked and commented on. He is constantly in the news. He always has firm opinions on public issues. Last year, he was in the thick of action when he was one of the leading voices in the stray dog-free movement in Kerala.

Being socially conscious comes naturally to Kochouseph. Growing up, his father made sure his children were aware of their surroundings. In his book—*The Gift*—Kochouseph narrates an incident in which his father asked him not to go for the school excursion as a few children in the neighbourhood weren't going because they could not afford to. It was his father's way to make sure that Kochouseph never felt superior and was inclusive in his outlook.

The V Guard founder has made sure that his own children, who grew up in relative luxury compared with his childhood, also value money. Mithun used to cycle to school, and in college, he and Arun had to make do with a monthly allowance which was fixed. He also taught them to value time, ensuring that the family was always two hours early at the airport, or ready right in time for a movie, otherwise which they would not be taken along.

After Mithun graduated from St Joseph's College in Bengaluru, Kochouseph asked his son to get some work experience. 'There was no pressure to join the family business immediately,' says Mithun, who spent nearly two years at Deloitte and then at HP. These stints opened his eyes to the corporate world. 'At Deloitte, I worked on audit and due diligence, and got an understanding of how companies functioned,' says Mithun, who got to work closely with companies such as Apollo Tyres and Taj Hotels. At HP's backend operations in Bengaluru, Mithun closely observed how a company quickly scaled up operations on the back of processes.

When an attempt at learning chartered accountancy didn't work out, Mithun went to Melbourne to do an MBA. Studying and working with classmates from different countries and varied temperaments, Mithun picked up important people skills. 'One [classmate] was from a finance background, and another from marketing . ¿. there you learn to understand and accept differences. People are not like you. There is a perception that Americans were very loud, and they were. But you realize it is part of their culture.'

This early exposure meant that he came into the family business with a perspective very different from what he obtained at home. The near debacle of the IPO was a sobering experience, helping him to appreciate the immensity of the challenge ahead. The success that came thereafter was not a solo effort, and he agrees. 'It was not like I came in and told them [the team in V Guard] we have to be a Rs 2,000-crore company. It was never my own initiative. The initiative came from them. Somehow we had to bring the share back up to Rs 82 and save face,' says Mithun, crediting his team for V Guard's showing over the last decade.

These challenges also fortified his belief that V Guard has to make the transition from being people-dependent to becoming process-oriented. While, till at least 2010, V Guard was associated with its founder (and Kochouseph continues to be a brand in himself), the coming years will see the promoters distancing themselves from the public image of the company. 'The intention is to build an institution, an institution that will last a couple of centuries,' says Mithun.

This, in a way, also suits Mithun. A private person—in complete contrast to his father—Mithun is rarely seen making public appearances. While Ramachandran takes care of most of the media interactions, Mithun comes in when it is necessary to engage investors, making appearances on business channels during the earnings season. He makes sure to attend company meetings and address employees, but stays away from industry meets, realizing that if he agrees to attend one, more invites will follow.

At the same time, he makes sure that the organization is represented in all these meets, including those organized by the Copper Council of India, where V Guard is one of the programme partners. 'I know it is important to learn what's happening around the world. But in today's Internet world, it is much easier now to get information without having to go out. Also, even if I don't attend events, my colleagues represent us, and they debrief us once they are back.

'I just like the privacy. Personally, I would like not to get the kind of attention we usually do. My dad's and V Guard's publicity were intertwined. But I have made it is clear it should be separate in my case.'

Little wonder then that one of his idols is Amancio Ortega, the elusive founder of Inditex, which owns brands such as Zara. 'My greatest role model, when it comes to making your work talk, is the founder of Zara. He is the world's second or third richest person. But you won't find any interviews of his. He is worth about $70 billion, and he runs the biggest fashion empire in the world. I read a book about him, and he is an inspiration.'

The book—*The Man from Zara*—is a bestselling story of how Ortega built his empire. The legend is that Ortega has given interviews to just three journalists in his long and successful entrepreneurial career. Mithun hasn't been that reclusive, but has limited his interactions with the media and cherry picks whom he will talk to.

'So it's possible to have privacy and still build a successful business. He is my role model. You don't have to be very public,' he says.

Mithun maintains privacy in his personal life too. At least, he tries to. But he could not on his wedding day. While the second-generation entrepreneur wanted the wedding to be a small, private affair, where he could offer his friends an experience, the ceremony eventually turned out to be one of the biggest social dos in the state. Almost 8000 people were in attendance. Kochouseph, making sure that his son's wedding was celebrated in as big a way as possible, had ensured the grand attendance.

'He is close to very few people,' says Mithun's wife Joshna of her husband. 'He has a close group of friends with whom he likes to spend time.' Joshna's father, a businessman in Dubai, used to help Kochouseph sell V Guard products in the early days of the company.

When with friends, Mithun, who stores about 30 GB of EDM and rock music in his phone, likes to hit the dance floor. 'He loves dancing, and enjoys the *thappan kuthu* kind too,' says Adarsh Varghese, a close friend who is managing director of the Kochi-based Imperial Group.

Mithun's only exception to this insistence on privacy is his involvement in Round Table India and the Young Presidents' Organization (YPO). Round Table is a social networking and charitable organization consisting of men in their twenties, thirties and early forties. It was founded in the UK in 1927, and in India is involved in several projects that give children from poor families access to education.

Mithun is a founding member for YPO's Kerala chapter. This organization is a global network of young executives, and has about 24,000 members in 130 countries. It has 600 members in India, including thirty-five in Kerala. 'Am occupying the education chair this year. So I have been busy organizing ten to eleven education events this year,' says Mithun.

This is the kind of forum that is ideal for someone like Mithun. Membership in YPO is only by reference, and only those who handle business worth at least Rs 100 crore are eligible. Moreover, a family can be represented by just one member. There is an emphasis on members who have a 'legitimate business and don't have overt political connections'.

'They have great educational programmes and have had great sessions with senior industry leaders and people from other walks of life,' says Mithun.

Apart from Ortega, Sam Walton, the founder of retail giant Wal-Mart is also one of Mithun's idols. 'It is fascinating that he grew the business fastest after he had hit the sixties. He talks about hiring people . . . one of the reasons Wal-Mart has become so big is that it hired the right people at the right time,' says Mithun.

And he often talks about the concept of core competency, a term introduced by C.K. Prahalad. 'I'm a believer in core competence. We should do what we do best. You can build a multi-billion dollar business on a single product. So why should one look outside?' he says, when asked about diversification.

'People might call V Guard a conglomerate now. But we are a set of different companies.

'I would like to diversify within the company. But we shouldn't get into anything unrelated. It can be distracting. If I want to do something, that will be under a different company. But I don't have the time for that. This is enough,' he says.

To ensure the organization's focus, V Guard has stopped buying land for the last seven years. Kochouseph had made it a practice to buy land whenever the company expanded and needed more space. 'But now we prefer to take space on lease. Things have changed, and the way business is run has changed,' says Mithun.

* * *

Things have surely changed at V Guard. Every morning, even as Mithun is on his way to office, he gets an inventory report of the company. The sales report also comes in at 10 a.m., and is updated at 2 p.m. and 6 p.m. The frequency of the sales report doubles when it is close to the month end, when the managing director needs a closer look at the numbers.

The reports are generated automatically by the company's system, using SAP analytics. The system gives inventory information division-wise, and data for the day, month and the last quarter. The sales report contains tables specific to products, states and branches. Mithun also gets product-wise operating margins and ROCE on a quarterly basis.

The system has been in operation for three years now. Before it was set up, the data used to be manually entered. The review process was also less exhaustive. For instance, only the overall sales used to be reviewed, and not the sales of each product division.

Mithun also uses the review system to keep abreast of what is happening and to monitor operations. The management structure at V Guard has the board at the top, chaired by Kochouseph. It includes C.J. George and Ullas Kamath of Jyothy Laboratories as independent directors. Ramachandran, who is also on the board, has the vice presidents of marketing, manufacturing, product development, R&D, legal and corporate communication under him. Each vice president has a reporting structure under him.

The senior management does a monthly review of all the divisions and the twelve product categories. At present, review is also done of the 'transformation' work of rehauling the supply chain. It is a project headed by the COO, Ramachandran.

Once a quarter, Mithun reviews the twenty-seven branches. 'It's done through VCs. Once a year, they come down, and it's almost like a sales conference. Initially, we used to bring them down every quarter. Then we started having VCs every month. Now, during the annual conference, we have team-building activities and entertainment, and share plans for the next year.'

The managing director typically spends the first two weeks of the month in reviews. The next two weeks, he gets involved in the special projects, or travels. 'Next month, I am visiting Sikkim and will be later visiting all the new manufacturing units,' Mithun said in February, 2017.

While he regularly visits the branches, the company's aggressive expansion has meant that there are branch sites

Mithun still hasn't visited. 'I have not been to central India yet, to places such as Raipur. It will take a while to cover them all . . . Ram [Ramachandran] visits two-three branches every month,' he says.

Mithun also chairs a meeting every day at V Guard's headquarters at 12.30 p.m. The management committee meeting includes the COO, Vijayan, Anthony Sebastian, who handles the supply chain, the CFO and the two vice presidents of marketing. 'It is held when we don't have the monthly meetings. This meeting is important to take ad hoc decisions and to bring any issue to the table as may be necessary.'

With these processes and systems in place, Mithun is building a V Guard that is independent of a central figure. 'The first part of V Guard's life was about growing and consolidating it. Then, in the last ten years, it was driven by individuals like the COO and me. But now we are in the process of institutionalizing these systems so that we can bring out better products faster. The company will be beyond any individual,' Mithun says.

And he is also thinking of scale. Though he didn't give a direct answer to questions on his revenue target, Mithun does slip in mention of a 'billion dollar company' a couple of times in his conversation. He wants to hit that mark from his India operations before stepping out overseas. Mithun doesn't want to repeat the mistake of his bigger peer, Havells, a company that he otherwise greatly admires.

Havells, the Delhi-based company, had acquired a European company, Sylvania, in 2007, spending nearly Rs 1,000 crore on it over the next seven years. But Havells struggled to make good of the buy, and in 2015 divested 80 per cent of its stake in it for Rs 1,340 crore. It has used this money as a war chest to consolidate its India business. In February 2017, the company acquired Lloyd's consumer durable business for Rs 1,600 crore.

Mithun has been following the development closely. Even as he is putting in place a system in V Guard that will quicken the pace of organic growth—coming out with new products and getting into new geographies—the thirty-six-year-old is also scouting for acquisitions. 'We haven't made an acquisition till now. We are scouting for one. I can say that by the end of this year, we will be able to announce something.'

The acquisition, according to the plan, should either cement V Guard's position in the market or help it diversify into a related segment. These segments would include kitchen appliances and switchgears.

'India is growing, and few countries are growing at the same pace. It is easy to grow when the economy is growing,' says Mithun. The industry, he says, is bouncing back after the demonetization move, which did have an impact on the numbers in the third quarter. V Guard's top line grew by 10 per cent, against 15–17 per cent in the first two quarters. But the company's profit still grew by 30 per cent in the third quarter. Mithun sees better days once GST is implemented. The Goods and Services Tax would make operations difficult for the unorganized sector, which now makes up for almost 40 per cent of the market.

Mithun would eventually want to make V Guard a multinational company. His mother's company, V Star, already sells in the Middle East. He is waiting for V Guard to gain an ideal scale—a billion dollars in revenue—before stepping out of the country.

* * *

My Learnings

+ Take risks.

If you guys don't want to take the risk, then you will not get the returns [told to one of the erstwhile investors who exited the V Guard stock early, only to rue his decision later].

+ Change is the word.

The IPO changed me. It changed V Guard.

+ Surround yourself with people smarter than you.

I was heading sales and marketing till then. When I started with the company, the goal was to double the revenues. Not only did we double the revenues, but we quadrupled them. I then felt that to take the company to the next level we needed a seasoned hand, as I was finding myself out of depth.

+ Keep looking for talent.

I said, if you want to take the company ahead, then we have to hire laterally. We had good guys. But it was not possible for a company of our size to have functional knowledge about each segment of the business. So, be it HR, corporate communications, IT or finance, I always pushed to get better guys.

+ Get the marketing strategy right.

In print you can only do offers. If you want to run a consumer deal or retail a product like a sari, then print works. But we are not a retail company . . . For us it is about creating perception, a lifestyle perception. You need to create the imagery, that is not possible in print.

* Avoid cosmetic changes.

The logo change can't be just about the logo. Many companies have changed their logos, but that hasn't changed the way they work. I believed that a logo change should happen along with a change in the philosophy and direction of the company.

* Think long term.

The intention is to build an institution, an institution that will last a couple of centuries.

* Never align promoter interest with that of the company's.

I just like the privacy. Personally, I would like not to get the kind of attention we usually do. My dad's and V Guard's publicity were intertwined. But I have made it is clear it should be separate in my case.

* Focus on core competency.

I'm a believer in core competence. We should do what we do best. You can build a multi-billion dollar business on a single product. So why should one look outside?

4

T.S. Kalyanaraman

It is difficult to miss the dominance of gold jewellery shops in Thrissur's High Road. As one drives down the road from National Highway 544 and towards Swaraj Round in Kerala's cultural capital—home to the famous Vadakkunnathan temple—one notices countless stretches of gold jewellery shops, their sequence broken sometimes by a textile outlet or a fruit juice shop. This isn't surprising. Thrissur—with a population of three lakh—has 700 outlets selling gold jewellery, one of the many reasons it is called the gold capital of India.

Its gold legacy can be traced back to 1 AD when Roman and Arab traders bringing gold with them would stop at the now lost port of Muziris in Kodungallur in Thrissur. The next push for gold in Thrissur came centuries later under the reign of Shakthan Thampuran. During the 1800s, the ruler invited about fifty Syrian Christian families from other parts of what were then the Malabar and Travancore regions to set up businesses in Thrissur. One of the businesses was the manufacture and retail of gold.

Today, almost three-fourths of the 1000 kg of gold sold every day in Kerala, itself the largest market for the metal in the country, is made in Thrissur. There are 2500 units or cottage factories within a twenty-kilometre radius of the city, where 45,000 craftsmen work round the clock to produce jewellery that is transported across the country and also exported. Quite a few of these goldsmiths can be found toiling away in small rooms on top of the jewellery shops on High Road, bent over their tools.

Given the city's tradition and history of gold, it was hardly surprising when T.S. Kalyanaraman decided to set up a jewellery shop in 1993. He was just one more jeweller among the hundreds in Thrissur.

Kalyanaraman had been running a textile shop in Thrissur that his father, T.K. Seetharaman Iyer had bequeathed to him. Iyer, who ran five textile shops, had handed down one each to his five sons. A generation later, Kalyanaraman had a similar plan. 'I wanted to set up two jewellery shops, one each for my two sons,' he says.

The idea for a jewellery shop had come from the customers at his textile shop. Many of his clientele would come to Kalyan Textiles for their wedding shopping. They would suggest that Kalyanaraman open a jewellery shop too. That would make things easier for them, as clothes and jewellery are the two most important purchases for a wedding, they would tell him.

His wife, Rama, who had grown up in Chennai and had witnessed the great popularity that the city's well-known utensils shop Rathna Stores enjoyed, suggested diversification into stainless steel kitchenware. Rathna Stores' iconic four-storey outlet is situated in Chennai's shopping hub of T. Nagar, and stocks almost everything stainless steel. But after hearing out his customers, Kalyanaraman was sure that jewellery was the best bet for diversification.

Diversification was the clear way forward because Kalyanaraman didn't want to expand further in textiles. His brothers were in the same trade and Kalyanaraman didn't want to compete with them by expanding his business. What would happen if his big textiles shop drew away customers from his brothers' shops in Thrissur? A jewellery shop resolved this sticky issue.

But Kalyanaraman's ambition was not limited to just two shops, as was his initial intention.

If the opening of his jewellery shop in 1993 was any sign, it was just the start of an astounding entrepreneurial journey. At 4000 square feet, Kalyanaraman's outlet was the biggest in Thrissur at the time, and among the biggest in Kerala.

Unlike the other jewellery stores in the city, Kalyanaraman's outlet was heavily stocked. 'Till then, the local jewellers used to display only a few select pieces in their shops. The idea was that the customer could choose one from the display, order the piece . . . and it would be delivered within a few days. If the order was for a wedding, then it could even be weeks before the jewellery was handed over to the customer,' says Ramesh Kalyanaraman, the younger son of the company founder.

But Kalyanaraman's mind was that of a textile shop owner. 'In textile shops, you buy and take home something like a sari or a shirt immediately. So I thought we should do the same in the jewellery shop and keep a big variety of pieces and let customers buy on the spot. Yes, it would require a big place, but by God's grace we got a big space,' he says.

Kalyanaraman travelled to Kochi, Kottayam, Thiruvananthapuram and even Chennai, studying jewellery stores in those cities. Most of the shops he came across were small—300–500 square feet. 'So I thought, why not start a big shop that will impress the customers and where I can keep a wider variety of items.'

Many of his competitors, friends and relatives advised him against opening a big showroom. 'They said it would be a big failure, that the shop would run maximum for a year, and that sales tax people would disturb me. But my mind was tuned to the textile business. By God's grace and our customers' blessings, we got fantastic business from the start.'

Kalyan Jewellers' first showroom broke many a convention. Built where earlier a popular hotel stood, the new showroom was air-conditioned, with dedicated car parking—a complete novelty in Thrissur. Customers were greeted by an artificial waterfall, and once inside the large expanse of the store, they were well attended to at the counters by a large staff. The people of Thrissur had never seen so many gold ornaments under one roof before this.

The other crowd-puller for the store was its inauguration itself, which was done by two of the leading cine stars of the Malayalam film industry of the time, Murali and Geetha. The two were still enjoying the success of their 1990 film, *Lal Salaam*, and crowds thronged the new store to see them.

It will be unfair to give all the credit to Kalyanaraman for this marketing coup. His father Seetharaman Iyer, in 1972, had successfully employed the same marketing tactic when he got popular playback singer Yesudas to open the textile shop that Kalyanaraman later inherited.

But few would have had the guts to pay cine stars to cut the ribbon at a jewellery store back in 1993. But Kalyanaraman did, and this created a great impact. The opening of the store was well reported and created the hype that generated footfalls. The entrepreneur needed all the attention he could get. He had borrowed money from banks and from his father, and had also put a large part of his savings into the new venture. The total investment was Rs 75 lakh, and Kalyanaraman had to make sure it didn't turn out to be a damp squib.

He needn't have worried. In the first year, Kalyan Jewellers' first shop in Thrissur clocked Rs 60 crore in revenues. It was a success that took the businessman himself by surprise, but it emboldened him to do much more.

* * *

Kalyanaraman's older son, Rajesh Kalyanaraman, had joined the business with the opening of this first outlet. He had just completed his MBA from Bharathiar University in Coimbatore. Two years later, when Kalyanaraman's younger son, Ramesh, completed his education, Kalyanaraman opened his second jewellery outlet, this time in Palakkad. He was among the first jewellers to expand and step out of Thrissur.

This was just the beginning. Over the next twenty-two years, Kalyan Jewellers expanded to thirteen states in India. In 2013, Kalyanaraman set up shop in the Middle East, and now has a presence in Kuwait, the UAE and Qatar. In 2016, the jewellery retailer's network crossed the 100-store mark and its revenues touched the Rs 13,000 crore mark. Kalyanaraman plans to add seventeen more in 2017. The year could see him enter new international markets, including Sri Lanka and Singapore.

In 2014, Kalyanaraman's business got validation by one of the marquee private equity firms, Warburg Pincus. The

American firm invested nearly $200 million in Kalyan Jewellers for a 24 per cent stake. 'Warburg Pincus's investment in Kalyan Jewellers is the largest private equity investment in the jewellery industry in India, and is an acknowledgement of the company's highly talented team, its pioneering role within the industry, and its commitment to the highest levels of customer service,' said Vishal Mahadevia, managing director and co-head, India, Warburg Pincus.

More validation was in store for Kalyanaraman. A year later, he entered the Forbes Rich List, the hallowed group of super successful entrepreneurs. He is now ranked among the richest in the world, with a net worth of $1.4 billion (as on 26 March 2017).

'I can still see Ramani [as he is called by his cousins and brothers] standing there at the textile shop, serving his customers, cutting cloth and packing it. While he has remained as simple as he was then, today he is talked about all over the world,' says Kalyanaraman's cousin, T.S. Anantharaman.

A chartered accountant by training, Anantharaman founded and sold a successful financial company; he is now chairman of the Catholic Syrian Bank and also sits on the board of several firms. 'If thirty years ago you had told me that Ramani would become one of the largest jewellery retailers in India and would be featured in the Forbes list, it would have been news to me,' adds Anantharaman.

How did the soft-spoken Swami (as he is known by the locals in Thrissur), who is mostly seen in a crisp, white shirt, dhoti and sandals, and is most comfortable eating curd rice and idli, climb to the top of the corporate ladder? The man himself doesn't see his rise as rocket science. 'I have followed the basic principles of business that my father and my grandfather had instilled in me,' he says.

'Sell at low prices, try to sell more and get a reasonable profit. From that profit, give a small amount to family, god, and to the poor for charity.'

While this philosophy is central to Kalyan Jewellers' business model that focuses on high volumes and low margins, Kalyanaraman also implemented at his company the important shop skills and discipline that his grandfather, and later his father, inculcated in him.

* * *

In almost every conversation about his success, Kalyanaraman goes back to the lessons he got early in life, both from his father and grandfather, T.S. Kalyanaraman Iyer. He converted those lessons into the pillars on which his business is built. Take, for instance, the discipline that the jeweller inculcated early in his gold business.

When Kalyanaraman opened the company's second outlet, in Palakkad, he was following the script that he had initially planned—an outlet each for his two sons. But when the Palakkad outlet also proved to be a winner, he knew there was scope to do more.

Palakkad, the rice bowl of Kerala, is close to the Tamil Nadu border and a drive of just about an hour and a half from Coimbatore. Coimbatore is known for its industries, and is a hub for small and medium enterprises. In no time, the Palakkad outlet started getting customers from Coimbatore. 'We soon realized that with so many customers coming from Coimbatore, it would make sense to open an outlet in that city,' said Ramesh. After opening a store in Coimbatore, the same rationale that brought them there took them to their next city, Erode, which is a two-hour drive from Coimbatore.

The initial expansion of this retail network was gradual. By 2012, almost twenty years since opening its first outlet, Kalyan Jewellers had about thirty showrooms—all of them in south India. The largest number was in Tamil Nadu, then in Kerala, Karnataka and Andhra Pradesh in that order. There was one in Puducherry too.

In these twenty years as they expanded, Kalyanaraman and his two sons had perfected the art of jewellery retailing. For instance, running the second outlet in Palakkad, they understood the importance of having a sound infrastructure to control the business.

Though Ramesh was handling the Palakkad outlet, he was based in Thrissur. His mother, Rama, was adamant that her younger son should be home every day; later, she relented a bit, insisting only that he should spend at least a few days of the week at home. This meant that even as Ramesh was travelling about seventy kilometres back home after closing the Palakkad shop at 7 p.m., someone in Thrissur had to take stock of the day's accounts.

To facilitate that, Kalyanaraman bought a leased line network, which enabled communication between the two branches, including exchange of important data. 'We had the line in 1998. So sitting in Thrissur, we could see the accounts of Palakkad,' says Rajesh. So if a stock, say two kg of gold, was taken from Thrissur, did it show in the system in Palakkad? 'We could check the stock. And also do rudimentary accounting . . . we observed and learnt. It was important because we needed that data to plan our purchases too,' says Rajesh.

As the company gradually expanded its footprint, this infrastructure was replicated at all its branches. And the headquarters in Thrissur had a clear view of the daily operations in each of its branches. 'Our software is strong. Right now we are working on building our own advanced platform with a third party. It is a central server billing system,' says Rajesh. The headquarters is connected by leased line with all the showrooms in India and overseas, just the way it is in the case of banks. Be it a branch in Tamil Nadu, Kerala or in Punjab, the billing is done and recorded in Thrissur.

The discipline of keeping stock and auditing accounts was drilled in early in the Kalyan family. Kalyanaraman's father was a master in accounts. Those were the days when tax rates were high, and with seven textile showrooms to be managed, the cash books were looked into diligently. 'After every week he would count the cash and record it. He was that disciplined. He was strict,' says Rajesh, of his grandfather.

A commerce graduate, Seetharaman Iyer would keep records of every shop's accounts going back to more than ten years. His room had a huge cupboard containing the records of all his shops. The books were stacked under the shop's name. Seetharaman Iyer was so respected for his financial acumen that many in the city, including Thrissur's chief commissioner, would come to him to resolve their complicated tax issues.

That 'religious accounting' was inherited by Kalyanaraman. 'Father was extremely strict in keeping accounts, as perfect as possible. Earlier, we had a local auditor who could come and audit every month. The books would be ready by the fifteenth of every month. Now the auditors are Deloitte,' says Rajesh. 'We have been paying tax very systematically and that's how we have been always. We often joke that if not for the taxes, we could have grown faster!'

* * *

Early on, Kalyanaraman also realized the importance of having a loyal and sincere workforce—a must when it comes to a business dealing with gold. Moreover, his people at the counter were the face of the company. It was important that even as the retail footprint expanded, the quality of customer service didn't fall. Every new outlet needed to have the same standard of service as exemplified by the first one in Thrissur.

For starters, his recruitment philosophy was simple. While an employee's basic education was important, the biggest emphasis was on his or her commitment and sincerity. Efficiency was a close second. 'Even if you are not 100 per cent efficient but are committed fully, then it is okay. It is the way a teacher talks about a student, that "his marks might be a little low, but he works hard". That works for us. A little low in marks is okay, as long as you are a good student,' says Ramesh.

Initially, the family rallied around, built and managed the new outlets. Kalyanaraman and his two sons would travel extensively to plan the initial phase of expansion. Over time, as more people were hired, a core team of staff was built. Most of the business heads have been drawn from this team, which has been with the company for fifteen to twenty years now. In short, the emphasis has been on grooming internal talent.

Every time a new branch is opened, some of the experienced employees are posted at the outlet. It would be their responsibility to train the new recruits for that outlet. The aim is to make sure that the new hires understood the Kalyan culture. The system—where the old train the new—is repeated at each new outlet.

'This is the chain. And that's how we expanded,' says Ramesh. 'It is otherwise very tough to open ten stores every year. For ten stores, you would need a staff of about 1000. How do we train these people, especially when we don't have any formal training programme? For instance, my father would say that he doesn't want a sales executive in the conventional style, but someone who can sell in accordance with our brand philosophy.' The company now has a staff strength of 8000, and leverages this asset to aggressively expand its retail network.

'Don't sell by telling lies, we tell our staff,' says Kalyanaraman. 'It often happens that a customer sees about ten products and, say, likes one which she wants to use for daily wear. But the salesman knows that that product is not for daily use. If he tells her that, the customer might walk away, but that is okay with us.'

The company abounds with examples of executives who started at the bottom of the organization but now occupy senior positions. One such employee, who has not studied beyond the tenth standard in school, started work at Kalyan as an office boy and slowly started attending to customers. Satisfied with his service, clients would come back and ask for him. The seniors recognized that and put him on a sales job. Over the years, he progressed from being the head of a counter, then head of a department and later a branch head, to become an area manager. Today, he is one of the most promising business heads in the company.

Others have seen a dramatic rise in their salaries. For example, Ramesh's secretary, who started with a monthly salary of about Rs 1000, now earns in six figures every month.

'When we assess a staff member, more than his education we check his handling of a situation. How does he move with people,' says Rajesh. 'Our attrition rate is low, even though we don't give over-the-moon remuneration. It's respectful. And we have a wonderful work environment. We are open and don't impose, and prefer to take decisions after discussion,' he adds.

* * *

Kalyanaraman's father had started taking him to his textile shop by the time he turned twelve. Initially it was the promise of a masala dosa at the end of the day that prompted the young boy to join his father at the shop, but over the years he started to enjoy working at the outlet. He would tend to customers at the counter, selling them lungis and saris. It was important to understand the mind of a customer. They may not provide a clear answer to questions like, 'What kind of sari would you like to buy?' But by observing their body language, one had to understand what their likes and dislikes were.

Kalyanaraman also picked up some of the tricks of the trade: 'Not every customer is comfortable talking about his price preference. Few customers are comfortable when asked direct questions like, "What is the price range you are looking at?" Some of them do not like to divulge this in front of their wives. In many families, the man may not be the decision-maker. Sometimes it is the wife, the sister or the daughter. So you have to pamper them to be able to sell to them and ensure that they return.'

Ramesh and Rajesh picked up these secrets too. In jewellery, for instance, a sales executive has to follow the eye movement of the customer to understand what he or she really likes.

'We were in the eighth and tenth standards, and during Onam or summer vacations we would be at the shop. People would ask if we were "Swami's sons". They liked it that they were interacting with the owner's sons,' says Ramesh.

* * *

In 2012, Kalyanaraman readied a war chest of Rs 90 crore to launch a marketing campaign that would take the company beyond the southern markets. It was not an easy decision. His cousin Anantharaman recounts his conversation with Kalyanaraman about this.

'We were in Kenya for my nephew's wedding. The whole family, including Kalyanaraman and his two sons, were there. One day, while the others were out on a safari, Ramani and I got talking. That's when he told me, "I have signed on Amitabh Bachchan and am spending so much money." I asked him how he had the strength and the guts to do what he had. He looked this way and that, and said, "I think it is the blessings from above."'

It was a big bet. All of Kalyan's thirty-five outlets until that time were in the southern region, and now with the marketing campaign featuring the Big B, Kalyan was set to make a splash in the western and northern markets. The superstar, among the A-listers in Bollywood, commanded a fee that exceeded the value of stock at the Kalyan outlet in Ahmedabad, the first outside south India.

'. . . for a national player who has a strong message to communicate to prospective gold buyers, what better ambassador could be there than brand Bachchan? We expect the association to give us instant brand identification and recall, and clear differentiation from day one,' the entrepreneur told a news publication.

Kalyanaraman knew that a lot of money was involved. 'But he was not bothered about the monetary aspects. He wouldn't even ask when you could break even. There was a long-term goal. If you are confident, let's do it, he would say,' recalls Ramesh.

The marketing campaign helped Kalyan Jewellers get noticed. The pitch—My Gold, My Right—was that customers were currently being cheated by jewellers, as there was no guarantee that the gold they sold was standardized and unadulterated. Kalyan Jewellers, on the other hand, was selling jewellery with the stamp of BIS (Bureau of Indian Standards), which certifies product quality.

A superstar vouching for the purity of gold, one of the biggest assets held by middle and lower-middle class homes, had the desired effect. Today Kalyan continues to have Amitabh Bachchan as its brand ambassador. In fact, Bachchan is not the only endorser of the brand. There is a long list of endorsers, including his daughter-in-law, Aishwarya Rai Bachchan.

For each of the southern states, Kalyan has a different brand ambassador—Manju Warrier in Kerala, Prabhu in Tamil Nadu, Shivarajkumar in Karnataka and Nagarjuna in Andhra

Pradesh. Kalyan's was one of the most detailed, expensive and comprehensive marketing campaigns for any jewellery brand, and perhaps for any brand in the country.

'Jewellery is a different kind of product. An item like bread, or even a piece of clothing, is standardized, and the same thing is available in markets everywhere. Sure, in a place like Punjab, a clothes retailer might stock more of the bigger sizes than his peer in Kerala, but the product is largely the same. But not in jewellery,' says Ramesh, who heads marketing at Kalyan.

A jeweller faces a unique challenge. He sells traditional products. Jewellery designs in India keep varying according to the tradition of a state or a region. 'Designs that move in Tamil Nadu may not move in Kerala. In fact, even the designs that move in Thrissur may not sell in Palakkad,' says Ramesh. Kalyan is one of the few jewellery stores to recognize this, and aspired to be both a regional brand in each state, and also a national brand of appeal in the Hindi belt.

In fact, Kalyanaraman learnt this early. When he opened his second outlet in Palakkad, he realized his mistake in stocking almost the same kind of designs that were displayed in his first store in Thrissur. 'Now we know that every market is different and that we can't stock the same item everywhere. So now, before entering a market, we find out what moves, what stock size, budget and other components are required in the region where we are opening a showroom,' says Ramesh.

While the marketing campaign of educating customers had begun in Kerala, it was soon taken to other states. 'It was education. And we needed a superstar who could convince people. Or someone whom people could believe. All the campaigns were about purity.'

The message had to be same in every market—Tamil Nadu, Karnataka, Andhra Pradesh and north India. 'For each market, we wanted someone who was a legend and had the backing of tradition. Prabhu was Sivaji Ganesan's son, and he was endorsing a product for the first time. It was the same with Shivarajkumar, who was the son of Kannada movie legend Rajkumar. Then we went to AP. There we got Nagarjuna, Akkineni's son.' Nationally, Sushmita Sen endorsed the brand in 2011. And in 2013, Bachchan.

Signing up Amitabh Bachchan was a coup of sorts, and Kalyan's association with him continues.

With these stars as endorsers, the launch of a new Kalyan outlet turns out to be grand affair. Be it the inaugural outlet in Chennai that was opened in April 2015, or the launch of stores in Dubai in 2013, Kalyan now makes sure to fly down all its stars for an opening. The presence of these stars ensures huge media coverage, resulting in hype that stokes people's curiosity to visit the outlets.

In recent years, the social media has been abuzz with photographs of Kalyan Jewellers' events. After the Chennai opening, there was much sharing of photos of Kalyanaraman, his sons, Bachchan and others dining at Prabhu's house in the city. Last year, during Diwali, Kalyanaraman hosted a party at his house in Thrissur. Apart from the star endorsers, other celebrities such as Sachin Tendulkar and big names from the local film industry were present. Photographs from this do again made the rounds of the social media showing Kalyanaraman busy attending to his guests. The stars from outside Kerala were flown down in Kalyanaraman's private jets. It is also said that Bachchan and his wife Jaya Bachchan stayed back for a night at the Kalyan home.

While the setting was far less glamorous, the launch of the Kalyan Textiles shop in Thrissur forty-five years ago was as big a talking point.

The year 1972 was a big milestone for Kalyanaraman. He got married that year. And his father opened the textile showroom for him the same year. The shop—Kalyan Textiles—continues to run. It is located close to the Thrissur bus stand, and opposite the municipal office. Inside, the moments from that 1972 opening have been framed on the walls. One photograph has an almost unrecognizable young Kalyanaraman busy at the preparations for the opening. Another shows Yesudas, the iconic singer, cutting the ribbon.

'At that time Yesudas was very famous. We were insistent that a famous person should inaugurate the shop as people will then get to know its location, and the brand will get exposure. I had a thing for that,' says Kalyanaraman.

He says that the company was among the first textile shops to advertise in the local theatres. Decades later, in the 1990s and early 2000s, as the company gradually expanded, it would get Malayalam film stars to open its new stores.

Later, the company appointed superstars Mammootty, and still later, Mohanlal, as its brand ambassadors.

* * *

People in Thrissur—those from the gold industry and even Kalyanaraman's relatives—had often wondered if Kalyanaraman would step out of Thrissur and shift base to a metro like Mumbai or Delhi. After all, Kalyan Jewellers' meteoric rise in the last ten years has been ambitious . . . and would a small city like Thrissur match those ambitions?

'I don't think they will ever do that,' says Anantharaman, the cousin. 'They are rooted to the village and the temple. At heart, they are the very same, simple Thrissurians; not the sophisticated dollar billionaires of the world . . . I have closely known some of the other billionaires from Kerala and outside. But I haven't come across any like Ramani,' he adds.

The family's history gives us a glimpse of what makes for Kalyanaraman's staunch belief in tradition.

The family traces its roots to Kumbakonam in Tamil Nadu's Thanjavur district. The Brahmin family was known for its priests, and many of its members were advisors to kings. In the early part of the twentieth century, the family migrated to Thrissur, basing themselves in Thrikkur, a nondescript village about fifteen kilometres from Thrissur town.

One of the family elders was a dewan to the Maharajah of Kochi. The king called upon the dewan and others in the community to create enterprises and generate jobs. Giving heed to the call, the dewan, who was Kalyanaraman's grand-uncle T.R. Ramachandra Iyer, sowed the family's first seeds of business by setting up Seetharam Mills in the 1940s. It was the state's first spinning mill, and Iyer was conferred the title of Rao Bahadur by the king.

Iyer invited many from his family and those known to him to work in the mill. All the Brahmins who came over settled down in an area known as Pushpagiri Agraharam, which was home to Kalyanaraman till 2015. The Agraharam's life centre was the Sitarama Swamy temple that was built by Iyer.

Though the mill was later taken over, post-Independence, by the communist government, the family continued doing business in textiles. 'Ramani's part of the family is made up of businessmen,' says Anantharaman, who became a chartered accountant at the age of nineteen. 'We have plantations, and most of the people down the generations have been professionals,' says Anantharaman, of his part of the family.

Kalyanaraman, who was born in 1951, says some of his earliest memories revolve around the strict and disciplined life that his grandfather, T.S. Kalyanaraman Iyer, led—a regimen that his father later passed on to the joint family. The day would start with the reading of newspapers, followed by breakfast together and then proceeding to the shops. When the family got a car, all the men would travel together to the shops. The same car would then drop the children, with their bags packed in the boot, to their schools.

The men would come back home together for lunch, and in the evenings, everyone would head home together again after pulling down the shutters at the shops. The shops would be closed by 8–8.30 p.m., even if the competitors kept their doors open till much later.

Iyer, says Kalyanaraman of his father, was the first municipal chairman of Thrissur. He was a follower of Gandhi. Just like the Father of the Nation, Iyer would meditate on Sundays and keep a vow of silence. And again, like Gandhi, Iyer would wear just a dhoti.

'Father, like Grandfather, was a disciplinarian. After lunch, he would check if we had gone to the shop or were still sleeping. At the same time, overworking was not allowed. Father would say business should be a pleasure, not a pressure. Treat it as a hobby. With pressure, he would say, you will feel the heat, lose your cool and scold the staff. They should be treated like family. If they are happy, they will treat your customers well and business will be good,' recounts Kalyanaraman.

Seetharaman Iyer encouraged his sons to spend time at the shop and to engage with the customers and understand their needs. Kalyanaraman, as mentioned earlier, was a man about the shop since age twelve. A few years later he was asked to manage the counter and handle the cash, learning the importance of financial management. Even today, the staff at Kalyan Textiles talk about Swami's strictness in maintaining the account books and tallying transactions at the end of the day.

It was only after the shops were handed over to Kalyanaraman and his brothers that each family moved into individual houses. But all of them stayed within the Agraharam. The temple was a meeting point for them during the morning pujas. They would also get together during the Ramnavami festival.

The larger family continue the tradition of running a community kitchen at the temple for the duration of the Ramnavami festival. All the members lend a hand in the preparations and serving, and Kalyanaraman too, joins in when it is time to serve the food. In the night, Kalyanaraman joins his sons and other relatives in the procession in which a golden chariot is brought out of the temple and taken around it. Kalyanaraman had donated the Rs 5-crore chariot in 2013.

Kalyanaraman's childhood friends, many of whom live in the Agraharam, talk in wonder about how Swami hasn't changed a bit even after becoming a billionaire. One of them is D. Ananthanarayanan, a constant presence at the Kalyanaraman family functions and Kalyan outlet openings. 'In all these years, and despite his wealth, Swami hasn't changed,' he says. In 2013, when Kalyanaraman opened his outlets in Dubai, he flew down Ananthanarayanan and his other close friends for the inauguration. It was a momentous occasion for the friends, as this was the first time Kalyan Jewellers was opening an outlet outside India.

Traditional but Unconventional

Steeped in tradition though he was, Kalyanaraman had the uncanny ability to gauge a situation and take decisions that were completely unconventional. Take, for instance, his decision to take his family out of the Agraharam.

He had built three houses in Sobha City, a modern township on the Thrissur–Guruvayur highway. One for himself and one each for his two sons. Each house, more like a massive villa, has been built for Rs 75 crore. One more is being built for his daughter, Radhika. 'Our families are becoming bigger. So we need bigger houses,' he told me in 2015. Ramesh moved into the new house in 2015, followed by Rajesh and finally Kalyanaraman himself. All the villas sit in a common compound. A private helipad, the first in the state, is close by.

Kalyanaraman bought his first jet in 2012. It was a seven-seater Embraer Phenom, carrying a price tag of Rs 30 crore. A year later, he added to the fleet with a Canadian Bell 427 helicopter for Rs 48 crore. Many in the state and outside were surprised at this 'splurging'. But Kalyanaraman had his rationale for acquiring the planes. Ramesh explains:

'Earlier, to reach any of our outlets, we used to travel by road. But as we expanded beyond Kerala, and then in the northern and eastern regions of the country, we needed a faster commute. This is important because driving to the Nedumbassery airport [on the outskirts of Kochi] takes about an hour and a half. Add to that the time for the security check. Then the return journey takes an equal amount of time.

'We calculated that we spend at least six hours a week just going to the airport and coming back. That is equal to a full working day. We wanted to travel fast, cover as many places as possible and get back home. The investment [in jets] has proved to be very fruitful for us,' says Ramesh.

'Swami is known to make quick decisions. With the jets, he also quickened the pace of his expansion,' says P.V. Jose, chief patron, Jewellery Manufacturers' Association—the industry body in Kerala—and a long-time associate of Kalyanaraman's. 'By travelling in their own jets, they sometimes cover retail outlets in two or three places.'

The company had two jets and a helicopter till recently. But the first aircraft was damaged in the 2015 floods in Chennai. Kalyan Jewellers' chief operating officer, Sanjay Raghuraman, had flown to the city for a meeting. Parked in a hangar, the flood waters damaged the aircraft beyond repair. Now the family is getting a new aircraft.

To ensure the safety of the company's legacy, the three—Kalyanaraman and his two sons—often travel separately, even if they are headed to the same destination. If they are staying in the same hotel, the three take rooms on three different floors.

'It is not about us, but about the company and the employees. Now, more than 20,000 families are dependent on Kalyan Jewellers. Father often says, "Me, you or Rajesh, if something happens to any one of us, our families will suffer a loss, but they will be secure financially. But it will impact 20,000 other families. For that you have to take care of yourselves."' That is why, even when they are travelling by road, the three take separate cars. For the Chennai opening, the three drove to the metro separately in their Rolls-Royces.

* * *

Opening the second outlet in Palakkad was a daring move that shocked the local jewellers in Thrissur. But that was just the start. Years later, the whole country took notice when Kalyanaraman led the opening of Kalyan Jewellers' outlets in the UAE—not one, but six on the same day. The six outlets included those in Dubai, Abu Dhabi and Sharjah, each of which has a sizeable population of Indian expatriates. 'He has done quite a few things that have been a first for the industry. This was one of them. To inaugurate two, three or six outlets in a day was unthinkable earlier. Not just in India, but the world over. One outlet needs marketing. For each additional outlet, it takes a little more marketing and a little more investment,' says Jose, Kalyanaraman's industry peer.

It was also a risky venture, given the economic conditions in the Emirates after the 2008 subprime crisis and global slowdown. The real estate sector in Dubai was taking a hit, and the overall sentiment was not very encouraging. But again, Kalyanaraman wasn't looking at short-term gains.

'We felt there was huge scope in terms of the market, availability of products and customer base,' Kalyanaraman told a news website.[1] And that is why he followed almost the same model, which he was perfecting in India, in the new market too. All the six new outlets

---

[1] 'Kalyan Jewellers to Rewrite Jewellery Retailing in UAE', Indiantelevision.com, 28 December 2013, http://www.indiantelevision. com/release/y2k13/dec/decrel103.php.

were huge, each of an average floor space of 5000 square feet spread over two floors. The showrooms also had a separate floor just for diamond jewellery, claimed to be a first in the Emirates.

The company invested Rs 250 crore in the new market, which was said to be the single biggest venture by an Indian company in the local jewellery sector in the Middle East. The openings, with all the Kalyan brand ambassadors in attendance, made a big splash in the media.

Kalyan would go on to expand its presence in the Middle East by adding outlets in Kuwait and Oman. In 2016, it did a repeat of the Dubai opening in Qatar, launching six outlets there. The company was growing its business in the region in the 'healthy double-digits' and wanted to increase the share of its business from the Gulf Cooperation Council (GCC) countries to 40 per cent of its turnover. Kalyanaraman said that was his 'medium-term target'. The latest investment has taken Kalyan's network in the region to twenty-one outlets, with a manufacturing unit in Sharjah too.

In India too, Kalyanaraman has taken the unconventional route. In Chennai, Kalyan Jewellers was among the last entrants among the major jewellers in a highly lucrative gold market. 'It was important to get the proposition right,' Ramesh told me during a press conference in Chennai to announce the unveiling of the brand in that city. The outlet opened in 2015, and was claimed to be the largest in the country; on display were 600 kg of gold in an area of 40,000 square feet. It was also an emotional moment for the family as Ramadevi, Kalyanaraman's wife, grew up in Chennai; her father's house was just a walking distance away from the Kalyan outlet in T. Nagar.

T. Nagar in Chennai is often dubbed as India's biggest jewellery retail hub. Most of Kalyan Jewellers' competitors were already present in the neighbourhood. This included Malabar Gold, the local favourite, GRT Jewellers, and Joyalukkas, claimed to have the largest outlet in India (though it was said[2] that its size hadn't helped it, and that the brand was struggling to make its presence felt in the city).

But Kalyanaraman and his sons were confident of their plans. 'We have customized our offering keeping in mind the local taste and culture. Chennai is becoming a cosmopolitan city. Take half of our staff, between them they speak ten languages,' Rajesh told me. The company had invested Rs 200 crore in the outlet, its biggest investment in a single store in the country.

The strategy has worked. In less than two years after opening its first showroom, Kalyan Jewellers has added four more in the city. The last two—in Anna Nagar and Velacherry—were added in late 2016. The three-storeyed outlets are of over 7,500 square feet each. At the time of their opening, Kalyanaraman said the city now contributed to almost 10 per cent of the company's top line. He has invested nearly Rs 900 crore in Tamil Nadu state, which has more than twenty of his outlets today.

At the same time, the Kalyan Jewellers' founder has been careful not to venture into geographies where it might not be easy to operate, given the political conditions. For example, Saudi Arabia is a big market for jewellers. Despite the recent challenges due to the dip in oil prices, the kingdom has a flourishing economy. It also has a sizeable Indian population, especially from Kerala. It is no brainer for Kalyan to open an outlet there; and it makes sense given its strategy for the GCC

---

[2] Prince Mathews Thomas, 'Golden Big Daddy', *The Hindu Business Line*, 24 April 2015, http://www.thehindubusinessline.com/blink/work/golden-bigdaddy/article7137383.ece.

market and push for more revenues from there. It appointed a team of advisors, including legal experts, and found that local regulations required many conditions to be fulfilled before an outlet could be opened. Though the Kalyan promoters didn't reveal what these conditions were, Kalyanaraman dropped the plan for Saudi Arabia.

'If it's too complex, let's do it later,' he told his sons. The message is to steer clear of anything that would put undue pressure on the management. 'The business shouldn't govern you, we should enjoy it. It shouldn't feel like pressure. So don't do it,' Kalyanaraman advised Ramesh and Rajesh.

* * *

Sometimes the best-laid plans go awry. And sometimes one's strategy can be tweaked for something more promising. That is what Kalyanaraman did with My Kalyan, a sub-brand that he floated in 2010 as a chain of service centres. The idea was to create outlets that were smaller, nimbler and more accessible to customers who wanted to book in advance their wedding purchases, or were interested in schemes like gold insurance, advance purchase and vouchers.

According to Kalyanaraman, My Kalyan would educate customers about gold standards, and help them make the right decisions. 'Buying jewellery is an emotional decision; however, with the spiralling cost of gold, it is also a huge investment,' he says.

These stores were much smaller than the jewellery outlets, and were of 250–600 square feet. Most of these stores— numbering almost 600—were opened in the smaller towns and even in semi-rural regions. My Kalyan was part of a strategy, the smaller centres drawing customers, functioning as spokes to the hub, which was the larger jewellery showroom.

Within a year, Kalyanaraman altered the offerings at these centres. While My Kalyan continued to give investment advice to prospective customers, they also started stocking diamond jewellery. And given that the focus of these stores was beyond the metros and tier-1 cities, these diamonds were in the affordable range, costing between Rs 8000 and Rs 25,000. This change came about in 2015.

'We expect our affordable diamond portfolio to contribute Rs 100 crore in the new financial year,' Kalyanaraman was reported as saying in early 2016. The strategy would make Kalyan Jewellers among the largest sellers of diamonds in the country, bring it in head-to-head competition with Tanishq, the Tata concern which too has a line of affordable diamond jewellery. Kalyan Jewellers plans to expand this network to 1000 stores, taking the company deeper into the market.

By getting into the affordable diamond jewellery segment, Kalyanaraman is extending his basic business model for the gold vertical—a focus on volumes by offering affordable rates and no insistence on high margins.

While the model has reaped benefits for Kalyanaraman, not everyone is a fan. This includes Anthony Thottan from the Thottan family, among the first to set up a jewellery shop in Thrissur. His great-grandfather Thottan Kunjipalu had founded the company—Thottan Kunjipalu Rappai and Brothers—in 1894. Over the decades, this company has created a reputation for hand-crafted jewellery. But despite its rich legacy, the company is yet to venture out of Thrissur, where it has two outlets. In 1998, it started an exports division.

'The jewellery industry is fast separating into two groups,' Thottan told me in 2015. 'On the one side are companies that are looking for quantity, and on the other are those that are focusing on quality. We sometimes take fifteen days to make a jewellery set. Others do it in a single day,' says Thottan, in what appeared to be a not-so subtle hint at the business model of Kalyan Jewellers.

Others, like P.V. Jose, a wholesaler and exporter of gold jewellery, are unabashed admirers of Kalyanaraman. 'The retail business is difficult. Apart from the investment that one needs, the business is also about gaining the trust of the customers. Many people have tried, but no one has made it as big as Swami,' Jose says.

According to Jose, it is Kalyanaraman who best understands the mindset of the Indian customer. 'Swami focussed on the B and C segments of customers, for whom gold is like an investment and an asset. They use it for emergencies and prefer buying gold to opening a bank account,' says Jose. On the other hand, customers from the A segment already have gold traditionally, and are less frequent buyers.

Kalyanaraman focused on the B and C segments. And his marketing, which focused on the purity and standardization of gold, struck a chord with the customers who wanted to ensure that their gold was genuine and would get them the prevailing market rate if they sold it in the future. 'Swami has told his people in the shops to ensure the best service to anyone who has come to return/sell back gold. He knows the pulse of the common man. This ensures positive publicity through word of mouth,' says Jose.

Kalyanaraman has also taken the lead in representing the industry. While he flies in his private jets to Chennai, Bengaluru or Delhi to meet industry peers or to make presentations to policy makers, the Kalyan Jewellers' founder is equally at home addressing the goldsmiths. 'He attends their meetings and talks to them, suggesting ways to improve their work. He also motivates them, assuring them that they can match the skills of international artisans,' says Jose.

That Kalyanaraman could think out of the box was evident in the Warburg Pincus deal. The PE giant had earlier made an investment in the Indian jewellery industry, only to burn its fingers. Over a period of time, it had picked up a majority stake in Vaibhav Gems—an exporter—for Rs 247 crore in 2006. But it was downhill for the company since then, and Warburg exited Vaibhav Gems in 2011 for less than Rs 20 crore, making one of its biggest losses in the country.

In Kalyan Jewellers, the investor was again betting on the industry, but was hoping it had picked the right company. Its investment in Kalyan Jewellers was the biggest of its kind in the industry.

For Kalyanaraman, who was being pursued by other investors too, the Pincus investment opened up avenues like never before. Now he had a war chest of Rs 1,200 crore to aggressively expand his company's footprint in India and overseas. In the ensuing three years, the company intensified its marketing efforts, doubling its retail network and crossing the Rs 10,000-crore mark in revenues.

Were these vigorous efforts, though fuelled by the PE money, also pushed by the PE investor? There are quite a few instances in India Inc of companies who have lost their way trying to expand quickly after getting money from investors.

'Yes, their blood is different,' says Ramesh, talking about PE investors. 'They want fast growth and high returns, but we can't promise them everything they want. We didn't seek them out. We were comfortable, and it was the investors seeking us out with high valuations. We have been telling [the investor] that you can't be in the driver's seat.

'Yes, people think we are aggressive. This is not about aggressiveness. This is about confidence. We open six or seven outlets in a single day. The Chennai outlet is the world's largest. But this is confidence, and we are well prepared.'

The Two Pillars

'His sons are like his two arms. While Swami's is the final word, the two brothers do their research very well before doing anything. Who else has grown so fast in India?' says Jose.

There is no denying the role Rajesh and Ramesh have had in the staggering growth of Kalyan Jewellers. And to Kalyanaraman's credit, he has allowed his sons to expand their wings. While in the earlier generation, the patriarch was a forceful figure, both at home and office (shop), Kalyanaraman has maintained a subtle balance.

'We continue with the patriarchal system. But Father is friendly; my brother, father and I are like friends. While Father makes sure we are disciplined, he is not overly strict. Our grandfather was not like that. He wanted everyone around him to follow in his footsteps,' says Ramesh.

Their early years seem to have mirrored those of their father's. Growing up in a joint family, the cousins were more like friends, and all would head out to the shops during the vacations. Their early lessons in business, just as they were in Kalyanaraman's time, came from the hours they spent at the counter interacting with customers.

By the time the two sons completed their studies and joined the business, Kalyanaraman had recognized their interests and given them compatible responsibilities. Rajesh, who had done his BCom and MBA, always had a penchant for numbers. He was asked to manage the company's finances. Ramesh, the most outgoing of the three, looked like a natural choice to head marketing. 'Father knew that Rajesh was more mature and conservative, good traits for a finance guy. While Rajesh was an income, I'm an expense,' laughs Ramesh.

The two have separate teams, and there is a clear communication line that prevents employees from getting confused as to whom to report to. 'Only when we need to take a joint decision do our paths meet. Then we go our separate ways again,' says Ramesh.

Over the years, Kalyanaraman has let them take decisions, allowing them to make mistakes too. At the second outlet, in Palakkad, they got the product mix wrong, not realizing that customer preferences here were different from what they were in Thrissur. That learning now helps them to plan their retail expansion. Similarly, the controversy generated by the 'racist' advertisement showing actor Aishwarya with a dark-skinned boy holding an umbrella over her head, was quickly doused.

'Though I head marketing, Father has made sure that our proposition is correct. He asks us to avoid gimmicks to increase sales. He wants us to do things that will be remembered and respected. He talks little. And when he does talk, one does listen.'

Apart from mentoring them, Kalyanaraman also got them to seek counsel from the best minds around, including his cousin Anantharaman. While Rajesh and Ramesh were deeply involved in creating the white paper on Kalyan's expansion beyond Thrissur, Kalyanaraman asked them to confer with Anantharaman and take his advice as to whether their plan would work. 'Their numbers were good. I asked them if they were confident. They said, "yes, *dhairyam unddu* [yes, we have the courage]",' recounts Anantharaman. Since then, the nephews would often call out their uncle for advice.

As the company expanded, Kalyanaraman not only groomed managers within the company, but also hired laterally. 'I have seen family businesses going up and then going wrong. Professionalism is very important,' says Anantharaman. He gives the example of his father-in-law's thriving business that went bust for want of the right people.

Kalyanaraman heeded his cousin's advice. Sanjay Raghuraman, who was earlier with HDFC, was appointed as chief operating officer in 2012. 'Coming from a private company, I was pleasantly surprised at Kalyan's execution capability,' says Sanjay.

'It is when you are not able to do something as well as you want to that you put another person on it,' says Ramesh, about hiring professionals. 'We hire laterally only when we see a gap. Not because we want to create a post.'

The infusion of professionals into the management helped the father and sons to strengthen the organization by creating systems and processes. At present, Kalyanaraman chairs the company board. Rajesh looks after purchase and finance, and Ramesh is responsible for marketing and HR. Both the sons are executive directors. The CEO reports to the directors. Sanjay, who handles operations, has a business head for every state. Each business head oversees a team of regional managers. My Kalyan has one business head but a different set of regional managers for different zones. Each regional manager is responsible for a set number of stores. And each store has a manager and a sales team.

Every Saturday, the top team sits for a day-long meeting. The directors, the COO and the CFO too attend this meeting.

Despite the company's pace of the retail expansion, Kalyanaraman and his sons make sure to visit each outlet at least once a year. 'We get a feel of the place when we go to the branches. We might be there for just thirty minutes. But sometimes that is enough to learn what is happening on the ground and for an idea to emerge,' says Ramesh.

The three also talk to the employees when they visit the branches. 'The staff then know they are being taken care of and that there is someone whom they can approach. Otherwise, they would be only seeing us in videos or photos. Often, people don't leave a job because they are unhappy with their salary or the owners but because they are unhappy with their boss. We keep track of how many people leave their job under one manager. So we do have a system,' says Ramesh.

One of the most integral components of that system consists of the sourcing centres. Kalyan Jewellers has twelve sourcing centres that manufacture jewellery. Each sourcing centre specializes in a specific design or style. 'People from different states have different tastes. In Kerala, lightweight jewellery is preferred; in Tamil Nadu, the temple style is popular. As a brand we have to ensure that we offer the variety,' says Rajesh.

A typical Kalyan showroom will have products from multiple sourcing centres. 'We can't get the Mumbai-made black beads in any other place. So when the authentic product is available, then the customer is happy,' says Rajesh.

Each of these sourcing centres has 100–400 people. All the centres are connected to the head office through a software that helps manage the inventory and check quality.

'Software has played a very important part in our success. Without it, it would not be possible to control the organization. For instance, we have enabled customers to subscribe to our loyalty programme though a software. Another software helps our backend, and also helps data to be updated every day,' says Rajesh.

Payments done on the Kalyan system are synchronized through an SBI platform, which enables payments to suppliers, customers and even governments. 'We are already doing cashless transactions. The industry is heavily regulated, and it is very difficult for the human mind to manage it efficiently. It is all software driven. That's why we can sit here in Thrissur.'

Kalyanaraman, who continues to personally call up to ten customers every day to get their feedback, has institutionalized the practice. A 24/7 call centre now dials every customer for his or her feedback after a purchase is done. Did the sales representative give the customer the proper information? Did he explain the pricing method, or the making charges? . . . These are the kind of questions asked. 'We don't ask the customers if they will come back to Kalyan. Our main focus is that they shouldn't feel cheated,' says Rajesh.

Thanks to these systems and processes, the three directors have almost paperless desks. 'I come to office like a professional.

I arrive at a particular time and leave at a particular time,' says Ramesh, as he sips lemon extract (it's good for burning fat, he says).

This is another lesson that Kalyanaraman has ensured his sons learn—to balance work with family life. 'Father would tell us that you can't finish all the work in a day. You can complete it the next day. But be with your family. Your family doesn't need your money after some time, but they need you and your time.'

Rajesh is given to stretch his office hours. But unfailingly, he will get a call from his father enquiring if he has left office. 'It is okay for you not to leave. But your team has a family and they are also waiting,' he would tell him.

Sundays are sacrosanct for Kalyanaraman. He likes to catch up with his brothers, and the whole family meets up.

Should the need arise, he or one of his sons also host meetings at home. Though informal, these meetings keep the father–sons team a step ahead of the industry—like the Sunday meeting Rajesh hosted for friends and peers soon after the demonetization move of the central government to discuss and understand the impact of this step on their business.

In many ways, the sons take after their father, including in their food habits—they are teetotallers and vegetarians. 'They don't think about anything else but their business. Other billionaires might indulge in activities like clubbing, or perhaps dabble in politics. But I haven't heard Swami and his sons talking about anything else. The gold business is their profession, passion and hobby,' says Jose.

It is tempting to speculate on the future of Kalyan Jewellers. Yes, there is expansion. Within the company corridors there are talks about hitting the 200 store-mark. The earlier talks about an initial public offering of shares have resurfaced. Perhaps Warburg Pincus, which invested in 2014, might soon look to exit, and an IPO could be the best route for Kalyanaraman to not just bid goodbye to an investor, but to also raise money for the next round of expansion.

If his address to his top management during the Diwali festivities is any indication, he would want the company to take stock of and consolidate its current scale of business before pressing for more expansion. 'We have 104 outlets now. It is okay if we don't make it to 200. But we need to maintain the trust, name and reputation that we have earned till now,' he told the gathering, which included his sons and the top officials of the company.

It is not that Kalyanaraman is not looking beyond jewellery at all. There is the real estate business that he started separately under the banner of Kalyan Developers. The company, which has expanded outside Thrissur, is co-owned with his son-in-law R. Karthik, who is heading the operations. The billionaire also wishes to venture into the education industry. He almost froze plans for it in 2014, but wasn't satisfied with the location. 'We want to build an international-standard school here in Thrissur,' says Ramesh. As is now the norm, Thrissur will be their starting point for all businesses, before they venture out. 'Everything started from here, and I have a belief that whatever we do from here will succeed. That belief is what matters,' says Kalyanaraman.

But there is another, bigger item on his agenda that he will have to take up sooner or later. Like his grandfather, and his father, Kalyanaraman will also have to take a call on the legacy he leaves behind. Will Kalyanaraman follow in the footsteps of Kalyanaraman Iyer and Seetharaman Iyer who divided the family assets among their sons? The number of shops in the Kalyan fold has multiplied by many times. 'They [the sons] know their strength lies in their unity. Still, if they want to separate in a way that doesn't hurt the business, they can,' the gold magnate had told me.

As he does before every decision he takes, for this one too, Kalyanaraman would be seeking divine blessings at the temple in Pushpagiri Agraharam. Every day, when he and his family members step out of their homes, a trip to the temple is mandatory before they head to their offices, shops or schools. Even when their private jet takes off, it flies over the temple. 'It is for the blessings of Sri Ramaswamy,' says Kalyanaraman.

* * *

My Learnings

+ On the future generation, his two sons.

   They know their strength lies in their unity. Still, if they want to separate in a way that doesn't hurt the business, they can.

+ Thinking out of the box.

   In textile shops, you buy and take home something like a sari or a shirt immediately. So I thought we should do the same in the jewellery shop and keep a big variety of pieces and let customers buy on the spot. Yes, it would require a big place, but by God's grace we got a big space.

+ Old is often gold.

  I have followed the basic principles of business that my father and my grandfather had instilled in me.

+ Being open to new ideas. On branching out as nuclear families.

  Our families are becoming bigger. So we need bigger houses.

+ The customer is king. Don't cheat him/her.

  Don't sell by telling lies. It often happens that a customer sees about ten products and, say, likes one which she wants to use for daily wear. But the salesman knows that that product is not for daily use. If he tells her that, the customer might walk away, but that is okay with us.

+ Think about the employees. Don't overwork them.

  It is okay for you not to leave. But your team has a family and they are also waiting.

5

Rituraj Sinha

A meeting was on; Rituraj Sinha was sitting in the back of the room with other freshers who had recently joined the London office of Halifax, the British bank. In front of them, and closer to the meeting table, sat the seniors. And at the head of the table was the boss. Rituraj was listening attentively, jotting down notes. He and a few of his colleagues were responsible for recording the minutes of the meeting.

Rituraj had joined Halifax with stars in his eyes. It was while studying business management at Leeds University Business School that he first began to take an interest in banking. The world of sharply dressed young executives, deals and big numbers was alluring to the young graduate.

It was all far away, geographically and otherwise too, from the security business that his father R.K. Sinha had founded in Patna. The company, Security and Intelligence Services (SIS), provided guards to companies for their offices and industrial facilities. Though Rituraj had grown up wanting to join the family business and take it forward, the course in Leeds had given him much to think about. He now wanted to cut his teeth in banking and see if he was up to it.

He had graduated from Leeds University Business School in 2001 and joined Halifax. But after a few months there, the twenty-one-year-old was feeling a little disillusioned. While he was expecting to straightaway get into the thick of action and experience that high of concluding deals, there he was now, jotting down notes.

Sitting in the back of the room taking down notes from the meeting that day, a realization dawned on him. The banking sector was a massive machine and he was a very small cog in it. 'I thought to myself, I don't know how much time it will take me to get to the chair in front of me and then to the head of the table. It could take me forever. I realized that it was neither an easy nor quick process,' he says. As his disillusionment increased, the youngster's mind often went back to India, and to the family business.

Then, on 11 September that year, associates of Osama Bin Laden crashed planes into the twin towers of the World Trade Centre in New York. Two other planes crashed into the Pentagon and into a field near Pennsylvania. In the following weeks, as the American government made plans to invade Afghanistan in search of Bin Laden and the rest of the Al-Qaeda terrorists, countries all over the world beefed up their security networks. From airports to factories, companies too took steps to increase surveillance and ensure the safety of their people. Security had suddenly become a top priority the world over.

Rituraj didn't fail to notice this change in the security industry's profile. The dreams that he had had for SIS, and the many things that he wanted to do at the company now looked seemed definite possibilities. Even his project at Leeds University was on diversification of the security business in India through an introduction of the cash logistics segment in the domestic market through a foreign partner.

A security business in India was now beginning to slowly look more exciting than his mundane life here in London. The question hung in front of him—should he take the flight back home or hang in here for some more time?

The final pull towards home came when his father, called RK by friends and peers, made Rituraj an offer he couldn't refuse. 'I told Rituraj he could come back and take over the company. I would take a mentor's role. I realized that both of us had different perspectives; I had studied in a municipal school, he is an alumnus of Doon. I don't have an MBA like him. So it was best that father and son did not have a direct reporting relationship,' says RK, recounting his conversation with his son to me at our meeting in 2012 for a story I was doing for *Forbes India* magazine.

RK, who had founded SIS in 1974, had shifted to Delhi with his family in the early 1990s. He was asking his son to join the business because he now wanted to fully immerse himself in matters social and political, which had been his passion since his growing-up years in Patna.

The two factors—increasing opportunities in the security industry and his father's offer—convinced Rituraj to come back home in 2002, after about three years in the UK.

In SIS, the scion had inherited a mixed bag. At that time, it was a Rs 23-crore company. Though its founder had moved to the capital, most of its operations were still concentrated in the eastern part of the country. It had an office in Bengaluru—its sole presence in the south—and was absent in west India.

As was the norm then with security firms, SIS was filled with retired police and army officials—right from the senior leadership to the bottom of the organization. Decision-making was slow; the company didn't have any systems or processes, and was yet to start saving data about its clients and businesses. Growth had stagnated in the recent years, increasing by only about a crore of rupees a year.

While it was still a profitable business, SIS's cash flow was in a mess, a problem that besets many security companies. This business doesn't need high capital as there are no factories to be built or retail networks to be set up. That means security companies don't collapse because they fail to grow or because they run into losses. They get into trouble when they take on bad contracts where money gets stuck, payments get delayed and employee motivation plummets.

'There is a downward spiral that sucks you down, and you go from one problem into another. You spend your time firefighting rather than building a business,' says Rituraj. The situation at SIS was exactly this when he joined the business.

At the same time, Rituraj says: 'What I inherited was a fantastic business. Not for its revenues or its scale, but for the intangibles. Three or four fundamental ideas that my father ingrained in the business early on are still the pillars of SIS's development.' RK had the foresight to start a training academy for his employees. Later, he also began a graduate training programme that helped attract young talent. Both the initiatives would prove to be path-breaking in the industry, not just in India, but the world over.

At the same time, RK had managed to lure into his company one of the best talents he could get—his son. Ever since he joined, Rituraj has been the catalyst that has taken SIS right to the top of India's security business.

SIS has grown exponentially in the fifteen years since Rituraj joined the business, from a Rs 25-crore company to a diversified security company that is clocking Rs 5,000 crore currently. Its staff strength has increased from about 9000 in 2002, to about 1,50,000 in 2016. It is the biggest Indian company in the security business, second only to the multinational giant G4S in the domestic market. And SIS is among the top five in every other business that it has entered—cash logistics, pest control and facilities management.

So how did Rituraj pull it off?

* * *

Partner at Work

After three years of living in the UK, Rituraj had got used to standardized systems and processes. The dissertation for his course had opened his eyes to other companies in the security industry, like Securitas and G4S, and how they function.

The world was completely different at SIS. Even after nearly thirty years of its inception, the company was functioning like a start-up. Each and every decision needed the nod from R.K. Sinha, who was either constantly travelling or was busy with his political and social life. Decision-making took a toll. It didn't help that the senior leadership consisted of retired army and police officers who were used to a bureaucratic set-up. 'They always worked around a safe decision,' says Uday Singh, RK's childhood friend, who came on board as the group CEO of SIS in 2002.

There was a very clear danger that SIS could miss the opportunity to capitalize on India's growth story. Fuelled by the boom in sectors such as telecom and retail, the demand for security was increasing, and SIS needed to be nimble on its feet to make the most of it.

No one knew this better than R.K. Sinha himself. While he had ensured that there would be a renewed energy and aggressiveness in the company by getting Rituraj in at the helm, he also needed someone who had the professional experience to bring about that change in SIS.

He found that man in Uday Singh.

Both he and Singh were from Patna, and their families knew each other. While Sinha took the entrepreneurial route, Singh had opted for the professional world. After graduating from the Birla Institute of Technology and Science (BITS), Pilani, he had stints at companies such as the Steel Authority of India Ltd (SAIL), JSW Steel and Praxair. Sinha would often invite his friend to address employees at SIS. Singh's persistent emphasis on systems and processes and the need to scale up the business had made an impression on Sinha.

When he invited Singh to join SIS as the group CEO, the professional was not sure at first. Having spent years with leading national and multinational companies, Singh had some doubts about joining an industry that was largely unorganized. But the challenge of building a company and scaling it up made him eventually accept his friend's offer.

'I told RK that we had a great friendship. But SIS was his baby and it could be possible that we will have conflicts,' Singh says. His friend then made him a promise. 'I know you and you know me. You can be sure that once you take over, you have control of the company. I have other ambitions.' Sinha kept his word. 'I can keep my hand on the heart and say that he kept his word. He never ever interfered,' says Singh.

The arrangement could have become complicated when, six months after Singh joined, Rituraj took over at SIS. Though Sinha asked Singh to mentor the youngster, it was unclear how the two would work together.

On paper, the two were the ideal combination of a young man's restlessness and an older veteran's professional experience and stability. It was just the medicine that SIS was looking for. But could a professional group CEO work independently when the promoter's son had joined the business and would eventually take over the company? Would their age difference also lead to conflict?

That both are still around after fifteen years, Singh as the group CEO and Rituraj as the group COO, is testimony to the sound values SIS is built on.

There are a few things that each did to make theirs a successful combination. First, let's look at what Uday Singh did right.

From the very first day, Singh had noticed a real zeal and energy in Rituraj. SIS, familiar to the young man since he was a toddler, was already a part of his DNA. 'He knew the meaning of, and what it takes, to be a guard, without even working in the company,' says Singh.

Also, as a new-generation entrepreneur, Rituraj came with a lot of new ideas for SIS. Singh gave each of them serious thought, sharing with the young man his honest opinions. But always, he left the final decision to Rituraj. For instance, the Chubb deal in Australia (SIS acquired the Australian company in 2007) was a call that was entirely Rituraj's. As a promoter, it was the younger man who had to decide whether his company would put money in the deal. But when it came to operations at the acquired unit and its integration with the parent company,

Singh stepped in, making the most of his experience. He had earlier worked in multinationals and was well versed with their systems and process-oriented functioning.

Uday Singh has been extremely conscious of the fact staring him in the face. 'I was conscious that he was the promoter of the company. And I would fade out,' says Singh. 'I tell him, "I have a choice in that, I can retire. You don't. You are tied to the company for perpetuity."

'I also believe my joining this company was an act of god. There is no rational or logical reason why I should have joined SIS. And I didn't expect Rituraj to be so good in his value system and strategy.'

On his part, Rituraj was equally aware that he was a *bachcha* surrounded by executives who were his father's peers. 'I was in my early twenties then. Nobody said it to my face, but it was like, *bachcha hai, seekhega phir karega* types,' says Rituraj, as he looks back at the initial years. He was surrounded by Colonel sahibs and Brigadier sahibs for whom hierarchy and seniority were sacrosanct.

Not surprisingly, his ideas, including suggestions to introduce systems and processes, met with resistance. He could have bulldozed the senior guard into agreeing to his view. After all, he was the owner's son, the future big boss. 'Then I realized that you can't be their boss if you want to get anything done. You cannot think that you are the owner's son and can start giving directives . . .' For instance, he couldn't tell P.K. Sharma, a former Border Security Force (BSF) commandant, and now executive director, operations, at SIS, that his strategy for recruitment had to change. 'His first reaction would have been—"man, I have done this whole my life and you are telling me that I'm wrong?"'

Rituraj decided to reach out to these seniors, spend time with them and listen to their views; he would then present his own views and try to make them see reason. He did this and shared his experiences from his time in the UK, where he saw other companies following varied strategies. 'You have to make them understand your view point and then win them over. One by one. And over a period of time.'

There were a lot of debates and questions, and Rituraj welcomed them. 'Change is a process. The seniors' initial resistance helped me shape my communication, people and conflict resolution skills. All that came in very early. So it was a good experience.'

His inexperience, in hindsight, was a blessing in disguise. 'You are young, and sometimes ignorance is bliss. You don't know how hard it will be to accomplish something. You are pushy. You are highly ideas-oriented. And sometimes, that conviction is also because of lack of understanding, of how painful the execution of those ideas can be.'

He also knew that this was a battle that he needed to win. This was a battle within the company and he had to be inward-focused. 'Unless you win the confidence and support of the team within, you can't go out and start making a difference on the other side, which is the market. The first battle had to be fought inside.'

While he questioned almost every practice at the company, it was also already understood that many processes would have to go through a rethink and re-engineering. The sales team, for instance, sometimes consisted of just one person. The company had no brochure to present to potential clients. There was no strategy on how and to whom to sell. And worse, there was no pricing template. The situation was similar in departments such as customer service and quality control.

Over time, processes were created and standardized. People were pushed to follow the processes. Decision-making was decentralized, as there was no reason why each and every decision should be made at the corporate office in Delhi. A guy in Bengaluru didn't have to write to the Patna or Delhi office to get clearance for everything.

The initial murmurs of resistance and disapproval faded, and over time turned to appreciation. Things started changing, and slowly, even the seniors began to acknowledge Rituraj's contribution. It helped that the youngster called everyone 'Sir', and didn't mind being addressed by his name, even by younger colleagues.

Once, the team was taking a break after an intense meeting on how to bring about operational changes at the company. Rituraj was sipping tea. He was joined by P.K. Sharma, the former BSF commandant, and now executive director, operations, at SIS, who said, 'Rituraj, in Bihar, when the TV signal is weak and does not pick from the antenna—we use a booster. You know, you are SIS's booster.'

Rituraj's strategy and steps to implement them were aided by SIS's growth, driven by Uday Singh's changes in the processes and systems. Within five years of Singh's and Rituraj's joining the company, SIS's revenues grew five-fold to Rs 150 crore. That brought in a degree of recognition to both Singh and Rituraj. It made things easier for them to drive the change. People, both within the company and outside in the industry, started talking about the company's growth. 'Success actually enables you to bring about larger reforms as you are more acceptable. In 2006–07, I started thinking about diversifying in two directions—multi-services and going overseas,' says Rituraj. A year later, he would start the cash management business in partnership with Securicor.

Ritraj is effusive in his praise of Uday Singh. 'While I have given him the respect due to a mentor, he has done the heavy lifting of moulding himself around the circumstances. He has been a great help. I give him a great deal of credit. He is twice my age. In the initial years, we had a different equation, he was way senior to me. He was chief exec and I had evolved from the college boy into somebody learning the ropes, and then had stepped into an industry-level leadership role in my company and the larger industry. He had the tough part of continuing to work with me and allowing me my space.'

From the start the two had forged a relationship that allowed them to agree to disagree. Each would give the other the chance to make his point. 'He has allowed me the opportunity to prevail, to have the last word . . . he has been here over a period of time because he is the right guy for the job. That gives you the conviction to communicate clearly with him . . . and not every conversation between us is positive or pleasant,' says Rituraj.

Rituraj was careful to strike a balance in the power equation between himself and the senior management. Be it with Uday or other senior officials, he didn't want to be seen as having the last word just because he was his father's son. 'That is a very bad way to manage people. And a good way to get abuse outside the room. I have always believed that you have to earn your stripes. And once you do that, if you have the conviction that something has to be done a particular way, you are no longer concerned that people behind you might say, *"Yeh toh owner ka son hain, isliye iski baat sunni par rahee hain"*.'

Rituraj has developed a working relationship with the rest of the senior management too, along the lines he did with Uday. 'He has given space. I give him the inputs and make sure that I don't hide anything. Here I am able to voice my opinions fully, and it is not like you have to follow whatever the promoter says,' says Dhiraj Singh, president, SIS, who is responsible for the new businesses.

It helped that Uday Singh was based in Bengaluru. So he took charge of the security business's operations in the south and the west, while Rituraj handled the north and the east. Rituraj had a natural penchant for marketing, public relations and banking relationships, and managed these responsibilities. Singh took care of the capex-related matters. When it came to HR, even if Rituraj found someone to take care of it, he would take Singh's counsel. Singh coordinated with the labour officers and managed the force, an important function in the security business.

The chemistry between the two had to be good to send clear communication to men down the line. A sign of even the slightest friction between the two was enough to set the rumour mills working overnight to create confusion among the rank and file. Also, the troublemakers needed to know that no one could play around with the two top men and attempt to plant the seed of doubt or mistrust between them.

'If you have a good relationship and trust the other, and they (the employees) know about it, then nobody plays around with you. Trust is the most critical factor at the top management level. If only one person is running the company, then it's okay.

If there are two, you don't want to be taken advantage of,' says Uday Singh.

The intensity of the partnership between the senior colleague and the upcoming young promoter was evident to all during the recent road show for the company's IPO. Most of the time, the two would travel together to meet potential investors. They did 130 roadshows abroad. It was clear that both had to be there to keep the company's best foot forward—a professional, veteran CEO and a dynamic, young second-generation entrepreneur. If there were ten meetings lined up for a day, the two would attend a few together and split the rest between them.

A frequent question the two were asked at the roadshows was about Singh's future. With the group CEO soon to hit the seventies, it was predictable that investors would be keen to know about the company's future plans. What will happen once Singh retires? Did Rituraj plan to take over the operations entirely? Or, were there other transition plans? Would someone else take over from Singh?

The answers to these questions also provided a clue as to what Rituraj was thinking about his own role in the coming years at SIS.

But before we get to the answers, let's visit another big part of Rituraj's strategy to expand SIS—acquisitions.

* * *

A Shopping Spree

Rituraj made a calculated decision to leave the banking industry, but he made deal-making the centrepiece of SIS's growth. 'SIS's revenues have grown ninety-three times over the last ten years. During this period, we have incubated five businesses from scratch, done three joint ventures and four acquisitions. Add to that, we had two rounds of PE, and I am now doing the IPO roadshows,' said Rituraj, during the run-up to the company's going public.

But the start of this deal making was marked by a series of failures.

Within a year of his joining SIS, Rituraj began executing his college project at Leeds. The project was about bringing the cash logistics business to India. This business involves the transportation of bank notes, replenishment of cash at ATMs and safekeeping of cash and bullion.

The project envisaged a joint venture between SIS and Securicor. Rituraj had presented the project to a panel of three professors in Leeds University. One of them wrote this on the project sheet: 'This is so good that you should actually consider doing it.'

To bring the concept to India, Rituraj's project had zeroed in on Securicor, which had an extensive cash management business internationally. 'It had a big cash logistics business, and I felt there was a great opportunity in India, especially with the growth of the Indian banking sector. Moreover, cash management is a little more evolved compared with the guard business, and gives higher margins,' says Rituraj.

Like a good student following his professor's advice, that was the first deal Rituraj pursued. He had approached the management of Securicor Asia, which saw the potential the proposal held for them. A management agreement was made for ratification by Securicor's board of directors. Rituraj was eager that it happen quickly; he wanted to start rolling out the business in India. But then he got a call. 'Have you seen the news?' the caller asked him. Confused, Rituraj surfed the television channels. And there it was—G4 and Securicor, both companies listed on the London Stock Exchange, had agreed to a merger in July 2004. G4 was already present in the cash logistics industry in India. So it didn't make any sense for the merged entity to go ahead with the deal with SIS.

One of Rituraj's dreams had just fallen off the cliff. He didn't take it lightly. 'Those were the early days, and he was out there to prove himself. He would put in days and nights on what he was doing. He wouldn't sleep,' says Pallavi Sinha, Rituraj's wife. Rituraj spent two days shut up in his room after he first heard the news.

'This one was my first transactions. And I thought it was going to be my big break . . . after all, it was an extension of my dissertation at college, and I had had this idea for many years. I was too emotionally invested and it didn't work out. It was a good lesson to get early in life,' says Rituraj.

But then, the second transaction also failed. Rituraj realized there was something that he had to get used to—rising up after a failure.

The second one was a joint venture (JV) with Securitas, the global giant in the security business. Rituraj and Uday Singh had met that company's top officials, Thomas Berglund and Hakan Winberg, in Poland. Conversations led to the two sides signing a term sheet for a proposed JV in India in 2007. But just before the deal could be sealed, the top management at Securitas changed and the new CEO decided not to go ahead with the JV.

Disappointed, but again not defeated, Rituraj next approached George Chin, president, Chubb Asia, the

Singapore-based unit of the Australian security company. Chin heard out the young man. He didn't agree to a deal. Instead, he made Rituraj an offer—'Will you work for me? I'm looking for someone to head the India business of Chubb.' Rituraj was flattered, but politely turned down the offer.

When Rituraj was not travelling overseas pursuing these deals, he was camping in Mumbai reaching out to private equity (PE) firms for money. But there was no success. 'I probably created a record for the number of bad PE meetings one can have in a calendar year. I used to be camped in Mumbai trying to raise PE money,' says Rituraj. 'But we were a small company of close to Rs 100 crore [in 2007]. And there was no appetite among the PE guys [to invest in a security company]. We had gone in too early.'

By 2017, Rituraj had three failures to show for every successful deal he had cracked.

But almost each of the failures came with a silver lining.

Regarding the first deal, Rituraj thanked his stars that it didn't happen as fast as he had wanted it to. 'If I had signed a JV with Securicor and done some work, and then they had done the deal with G4S, we couldn't have stopped them. And we would have had to live with the consequences.'

The second deal with Securitas might have failed, but Thomas and Hakan invested in SIS, a huge vote of confidence for the company and its top team. 'Its people made me invest in SIS,' said Hakan. 'People are the most important aspect in a security company. You need a culture and need to stand for something. RK had made sure that the culture of being a family was central to SIS.'

In Uday Singh, the two investors saw a sound professional. 'He was like a mentor, and focused on processes,' said Hakan. 'And Rituraj had all this experience of growing up around a security business. He had respect for guards and, like his father, focused on the culture. And at the same time, he was entrepreneurial and visionary . . . these three things—culture, professional CEO, and a visionary second-generation entrepreneur with strong roots in the business—was a good combination.'

The Securitas deal also put Rituraj in touch with Randhir Kochchar, who was one of the advisors to the deal. He knew SIS's numbers and Rituraj's proposals. So when he joined D.E. Shaw—the global investment management firm—he readily agreed to put money in SIS. The deal was done in seven days, and DE Shaw took a 14 per cent stake in SIS in late 2007.

Six years later, when Randhir was looking for an exit from SIS, he brought in his friend Ajay Relan and Jayanta Basu, founders of CX Partners. 'The deal with Relan got done over a casual conversation in his house,' says Rituraj. For DE Shaw, it was a great deal as they got a return of seven times on their investment in SIS.

'Failed deals have given me a lot of confidence. I understand that it's okay for not every deal to be successful. And I think you never lose, even in a lost deal. Every failed transaction gave me something. The Securitas deal got me Thomas and Hakan. And a failed conversation with Chubb Asia got me George Chin who helped me do the deal with UTC, the American multinational,' says Rituraj.

The UTC deal remains Rituraj's biggest ever, giving him his career's biggest high. It was the Tata Steel–Corus deal equivalent for the Indian security firm.

* * *

It was mid-2007, and Rituraj was busy scaling up operations at SIS and adding businesses. SIS's security firm had expanded to forty branches with 30,000 employees.

Despite his initial failures in securing deals, Rituraj was able to execute some important JVs. He might have failed to get Securicor for the cash management business, but he managed to rope in Prosegur—the world's second largest cash management company—to set up a JV with them in 2006.

It was in August 2007 that Rituraj heard about an opportunity in Australia. UTC, the $56-billion American multinational, was selling its Australian security arm Chubb. UTC had acquired Chubb in 2003 to enter the fire and security business, but within five years it was in exit mode.

Australia was foreign territory for Rituraj. He hadn't even travelled to the country, to say nothing of having an idea of the local industry there. To get a better picture, the first person he called was George Chin who, since offering Rituraj a job, had retired from Chubb Asia.

The deal made sense. A developed security market like Australia added to SIS's top line and bottom line, and also brought with it more advanced practices and processes. A mature market would also balance a dynamic, fast-growing business in India.

There was a problem, though. Chubb was more than seven times SIS's size, which by 2007 had touched Rs 150 crore in revenues. Senior officials at SIS asked Rituraj where they would get the money for buying Chubb. And how would they manage such a big company from here in India? It was a risk, Rituraj admits—one that could have broken SIS.

But the twenty-seven-year-old was confident, even quite emboldened by the events around him. He had read *Cold Steel*, which had chronicled Lakshmi Mittal's acquisition of Arcelor in a thriller-like account. Closer home, Tata Steel had completed the acquisition of Corus in a $12 billion deal. As in the case of SIS and Chubb, both Mittal Steel and Tata Steel were smaller than the companies they had acquired.

But the banks weren't very confident about Rituraj as a potential buyer. Citigroup, which was managing the sale of Chubb on behalf of the latter's parent company, the US giant UTC, refused to give Rituraj access to company information for due diligence. 'First show that you have the money to buy it,' he was told.

The Rs 300 crore that DE Shaw had paid for a 14 per cent stake in SIS now came in handy. With the backing of a well-known PE firm, the young entrepreneur was able to convince SBI and ICICI to lend to him. He convinced them that there were enough opportunities to turn around Chubb's business that had an EBITDA (earnings before interest, tax, depreciation and amortization) of less than 2 per cent.

Finally, a year later, in August 2008, SIS acquired Chubb for an undisclosed sum. 'He was really happy with the Chubb deal,' says Pallavi of Rituraj. 'It was an exciting deal and he had taken a huge risk, and not everyone was convinced it would go through. He made it happen.'

By the time I met Rituraj for the first time in 2011, Chubb (rechristened MSS Security) had been turned around. Though its revenues were stagnant at $350 million, the EBITDA now stood at 8 per cent. Rituraj had initiated a slew of measures to cut costs. These included the sale of loss-making businesses and the shifting of offices into less expensive spaces.

The deal had turned SIS into a Rs 2,100-crore company, the largest Indian security firm. Rituraj was thirty-one years old.

Since the Chubb deal, Rituraj has added two more international companies—ServiceMaster and Terminix—as his business partners and formed JVs with them. Later, in December 2014, SIS Prosegur, the cash management JV, acquired the India business of ISS, a Danish major. The deal made SIS Prosegur the second largest cash management company in the country.

In August 2016, SIS bought a majority stake in Dusters Total Solutions Pvt. Ltd, a leading facilities management company, for an enterprise value of Rs 175 crore. Through Dusters, SIS added 25,000 employees and clients in the southern and western parts of the country. The deal also made SIS one of the top three players in the facilities management industry in India.

Rituraj is not done, and is hungry for more deals. Many might term his attitude as one of haste. But the group COO of SIS is following an international trend among security companies. He explains it this way:

'Every security company that has managed to hit $500 million in revenues has gone to $2 billion in less than seven years. So there is something about this $500-million mark. It might take you many years to reach here. But after that, because you grow by mergers and acquisitions [M&A], you scale quite rapidly.'

He is taking this insight seriously; and has found a way to access the central factor in deal making—money.

Capital and fund raising is difficult in India, especially when it comes to financing acquisitions. Indian banks have regulatory restrictions when it comes to funding M&As. Even if a bank is convinced about a deal, it needs collateral to lend against. But the security business is asset-light. 'If I have huge assets, I will never have a 30 per cent return on capital,' quips Rituraj.

So when it comes to India's security industry, few companies have managed to raise money for M&A. 'Whoever cracks the code to get large sums of money for M&A is going to take this market,' prophesies Rituraj. And he is making sure he is going to prove this.

Though Rituraj has the choice to dilute more equity in his own company to raise money, he has seen too many entrepreneurs taking this route and ceding control of their companies to investors. 'I would never want to do that. With investors determining strategy, you will lose the culture and philosophy that lie at the centre of your security business . . . If you are too focused on getting results quarter to quarter, you will never reap long-term benefits.'

So he, assisted by the SIS finance team, has found a unique way to raise debt. As soon as the Australian arm repaid the loan that was raised to finance the 2008 acquisition, Rituraj sent his finance team to National Australia Bank (NAB) to raise A$80 million in revolving finance at a 5 per cent interest rate. The revolving credit line meant that Rituraj didn't have to identify his acquisition targets before raising the money. NAB has sanctioned the money to SIS, enabling Rituraj to go out shopping for deals.

And the sweet part of this arrangement is that this loan of A$80 million has been raised against the Australian business's annual profits of $20–22 million. This helps SIS save on tax and use the profits to repay the loan and interest. 'I have converted the Australian business into a cash cow to fund our growth here in India,' says Rituraj.

He used part of that A$80 million to buy Dusters, and still has more than half of that money left to pursue more deals in the domestic and overseas markets.

Rituraj continues to push for more JVs. In February this year, he signed a second JV with Prosegur, with whom he already does the cash management business. Now the two partners have entered the business to consumer (B2C) segment, a first for SIS, to offer alarm-monitoring and response solutions for homes and small businesses.

With the IPO money expected to add to SIS's reserves, Rituraj is eyeing more deals and JVs to take SIS to the target of Rs 10,000 crore in revenues that he has set for it as part of the Vision 2020 plan. Though he is yet to announce this publicly, his team at SIS knows that their boss is relentlessly pursuing this goal.

Five years ago, while talking about his plans for the company, Rituraj had admitted that 'overheating' SIS is a risk, given the momentum of organic growth of the business. That risk continues. SIS is already growing at nearly twice the industry rate—its security business grew by 30 per cent last year, and the cash management business expanded by nearly 40 per cent. Now Vision 2020 entails a consolidated growth rate of 20 per cent year-on-year, and a return on capital of 30 per cent for the company.

This is a tough target. But those who have known Rituraj are not surprised.

'Even back then [when both were in school], he would talk about the family business and share what he wanted to do at SIS. After all these years he has been able to pull it off,' says Pallavi. She met Rituraj at an economics tuition class in Dehradun, when both were preparing for their class twelve board exams. Pallavi was studying at the Welham Girls School, and Rituraj at the Doon School.

'From the first day I met him, when he joined Doon, he looked like a focused guy. He knew what he needed to do and would be very systematic and organized in the way he went about achieving that,' says Shekhar Nagar, who was Rituraj's classmate at Doon. 'For the first time I saw someone making plans, using stick-ons and all. And this was more than twenty-five years ago,' adds Nagar, who runs Toyota franchisees in the Delhi NCR.

This discipline helped Rituraj accomplish something that very few in the history of the Doon School had achieved.

* * *

The Doon School, founded in 1935, is often ranked as the best residential school in India. It attracts the cream of society, and some of the country's best known bureaucrats, businessmen and ministers—including a former prime minister—are its alumni.

R.K. Sinha had always valued good education. His family has been one of professionals—among his older brothers were a lawyer and a bureaucrat, and his younger brother was a professor. He was the first in the family to become an entrepreneur, actually an accidental entrepreneur. His is an interesting story.

R.K. started out as a journalist. He had made a name for himself as a reporter in *Searchlight*, a paper owned by K.K. Birla. He had covered the 1971 Bangladesh liberation war. But his hard-hitting stories weren't received well by everyone. Very soon he got a call from the owner himself.

RK met K.K. Birla in a hotel in Patna and treated the young reporter to a hearty lunch. Later he said, 'You write very well. But *bahut theekha likhte hon* (you write very harshly). And if you continue this, then any fine morning—you know Indira Gandhi is a very whimsical lady—within no time my sugar mills in Bihar and UP will be closed. And thousands of workers will be unemployed.'

The message was clear. By the time RK returned to his office, the general manager was ready with his termination notice.

In the evening RK went to meet Jayaprakash Narayan, the political activist and social reformer. 'So, the Marwari has fired you?' JP asked him. 'It is time that you did something for the public,' the leader, who would in the next few years lead the opposition against Prime Minister Indira Gandhi, told RK. JP advised the young man to help ex-army personnel get jobs.

RK started off helping ex-servicemen to get jobs in factories owned by businessmen whom he knew. Very soon he was inundated with requests for more retired army personnel. 'For about ten years, it was like doing a special service without expectations of any gain. But gradually it became a full-fledged profession.'

Rituraj's earliest memories are of his father building the security business. On Sundays, it was a ritual for his father to conduct his recruitment of new employees on the lawns of their home in Patna. Every Sunday, scores of men, mostly retired police and army officials, would turn up to see his father.

Drives to Ranchi, his mother's maternal home, were never straight. His father would often take detours, calling on new and old clients, or visiting sites where his employees were at work. 'Not that he wanted to take us along on his work rounds. But he was an entrepreneur at work and wanted to make the most of time and opportunity. I remember driving by and stopping at Nawada and Hazaribagh, en route to Ranchi,' says Rituraj.

It was said that by the mid-1980s, SIS had more than 500 employees, and RK, who recruited each of them, knew them all by their names. Many a times RK would invite retired army officers home, and over lunch or dinner, their jobs would be secured. For young Rituraj, it felt as if there was no boundary between family and business, and as he grew up he realized that the family culture was central to the business that his father was building.

Rituraj also remembers going to the training academy, which his father had set up in 1984, during the holidays. While his father was at work holding sessions for his new recruits, Rituraj would hover around, too young to understand what exactly was going on but beginning to get a hang of what his father, an entrepreneur, was building, and accepting SIS as an important part of his life.

The training academy was path-breaking for the security industry, both in India and overseas. 'None of the international players at the time—Group 4, Securitas, Pinkerton or anyone else—had taken this step. The reason was two-fold: the industry was growing at such a pace that the number of ex-servicemen available couldn't fill the vacancies on offer; and the customers' requirements were changing as well,' writes Hakan Winberg, the former Securitas senior executive, in the chapter on SIS in his book, *Approximately Right 3 Journeys*.

He adds: 'The second point is very significant. The customers were realizing that ex-servicemen were very good at a particular style of guarding. They were always well turned out, good at saluting and responding "yes, sir" or "no, sir", but when it came to performing the actual duties of a guard they tended to behave as if they were dealing with an enemy rather a visitor or customer.'

RK's residential training academy, where each batch gets trained over ninety days, continues to be one of the cornerstones of SIS's rapid expansion. 'In retrospect, it's apparent that if you want to build a service business, a manpower-intensive service business, there is nothing more fundamental than training. My father did that; he was ahead of his times,' says Rituraj.

In 1986, RK added a graduate training programme at the academy to attract young graduates and train them. Both the initiatives attracted attention, and within a year, Group 4 (which later became G4) requested to visit the academy and see what RK was doing.

Rituraj also remembers the first computer his father bought in the late 1980s. 'I would sit at it and play Pacman-kind of games. The computer was a pretty novel thing.' For RK, it was an important decision to standardize payrolls as his employee strength was growing. He was among the first in the country to own a mobile phone, and as technology evolved, SIS men were seen with pagers, wireless walkie-talkies, mobile phones and computers.

By the early 1990s, RK was thinking about shifting to Delhi, from where most of his new clients were coming. It was a natural transition for a growing company. And he decided to send his son to the Doon School, which accepted students from the seventh grade. Rituraj joined the seventh grade at the institution.

* * *

'A large part of who I am today is because of Doon. For one, it offers a fantastic environment. For all-round development of a youngster, Doon is one of the best boarding schools. I made the most of what was available,' says Rituraj.

As a student, Rituraj was competent but not brilliant. He was usually among the top ten in his class. He was also a decent sportsman, but no Usain Bolt. Rituraj could run 400 metres in fifty-six or fifty-seven seconds and was a handy opening bowler in the school's cricket team. He was also in the school's hockey team.

'He was not a naturally gifted sportsman. Or an extremely bright student. But it was the sheer doggedness with which he went after a goal that set him apart,' says Praneet Mungali, another one of Rituraj's friends from Doon.

The Doon School has a merit system that awards students for excelling in sports, studies and extracurricular activities. Students who excel and get a set threshold of points in each of these three streams are awarded 'colours', which consisted of blazers—the Games Blazer, the Duke's Blazer and the Scholar's Blazer. Early on, Rituraj, though not a natural sportsman or a scholarly genius, set his sights on these awards.

He took part in debates and enthusiastically participated in outdoor activities. While in the eleventh grade, he scaled Imja Tse, also known as the Island Peak, in eastern Nepal. The twenty-day expedition saw Rituraj and the rest of the group from the school flying to Nepal and landing at the Lukla airport, the highest in the world. From there they proceeded to the Mount Everest base camp.

'Each of us was given Rs 1000 for the trip. We gave the money to Rituraj, who planned and managed the trip for us. He would list our requirements and then budget money for everything—from food to accommodation. We would just relax!' says Nagar. During the trek, if any of his schoolmates was lagging behind because of the tough terrain and rough weather, Rituraj would be at his side, goading him to go on. Four of the boys, including Rituraj, scaled the summit.

Outdoor activities like the expedition, or the cycling trip he did to Chandigarh from Dehradun, were meant to teach students punctuality, leadership, organization skills and budget management. As his friends say, Rituraj was seeped in these qualities.

The script was the same, even for the weekly outings the students made. Each student could withdraw Rs 50 by cheque from a nearby bank where their parents had deposited money for them. Rituraj and his friends would get together, and it was Rituraj who would chalk out the expenses and decide if they could afford the balcony ticket for the movies or would have to do with sitting in the front row; how many naans each could have, whether they could afford butter chicken; and whether they could have an iced drink each or would have to share. 'I learned a lot of life skills. You will never learn these skills if you are staying with family,' says Rituraj. Many of these skills would come into play later in his life.

Rituraj was one of the few students who represented the school and the country at the Round Square Conference, at the chapter held at San Jose in the US. He was the school prefect as well as the house captain. At the prefect council, he would have a say in matters ranging from mess food to the punishment policy.

When his school days drew to a close, it was no surprise that Rituraj was among the very few who got not one, but two blazers—for studies and extracurricular activities—missing out on the rarer third one, for sports, by just half a point.

'He was very sure about himself. It was not arrogance or even confidence on his part. He knew himself very well, and was very clear,' says Mundali.

Perhaps that was what attracted Pallavi to Rituraj when they first met at their economics tuition class. Or maybe it was his organizing skills. 'Very organized for a boy,' says Pallavi, with a laugh. Both were in the last year of school. She was initially reluctant to get into a relationship with him. It was awkward for her, having studied in an all-girls school, and she was unsure as to how her conservative Punjabi family would react to their relationship. 'But what is meant to be, will be,' she says.

It surely helped that Rituraj was effortlessly well turned out. 'My friends were very jealous. They would say, "You have a boyfriend who is so prim and proper," and I would say, "Ya, I don't understand that myself!"'

After school, the two kept in touch though they were so far away from each other now—Rituraj in Leeds and Pallavi doing her BCom at Delhi University. When Rituraj came back from the UK in 2002, Pallavi had shifted to Pune to do her Masters. With her parents pushing her to marry, it was time for Rituraj to meet them. Differences between the two families— one a Punjabi from Rishikesh and the other a Bihari settled in Delhi—had to be sorted out.

Pallavi didn't have to worry much. After her father met Rituraj for the first time, he told his wife, 'You know, Varsha, even if we search for a match, we won't find a boy like this one for our daughter.' On her part, Pallavi met Rituraj's mother, who took at an instant liking to the young woman and took it on herself to convince the rest of the family that the marriage should happen. Rituraj and Pallavi got married in 2004.

The two now have three children—two daughters and a son. While Rituraj is an indulgent dad—he picks up cakes for his daughters from the coffee shop of a hotel—he seems to be working hard on perfecting this role too.

His secretary, Natalie Hansda, has to call Pallavi before chalking out Rituraj's schedule for the month. The schedule is prepared around events at school and home, as Rituraj insists on being present for the parent–teacher meetings and for his daughters' school annual days. When his elder daughter complained that her friend's father cooked for her and her own dad did not, Rituraj turned to YouTube, and within weeks perfected some Thai dishes. Every Sunday, he either takes the family out to lunch, or asks the staff to move out of the kitchen so he can cook a mean meal. His Thai chicken crepe, says Pallavi, is the best. 'He just picked it up. He has a knack for everything,' she adds.

While at home he has played the role of a father and a son— getting the best doctors overnight to help RK get back to his feet after complications set in owing to diabetes—to perfection, at SIS he now has to ensure smooth operations.

* * *

One of the qualities working for Rituraj is his ability to seamlessly wear two hats. 'Rituraj has the optimum mix of the professional and promoter mindsets. He can wear both hats comfortably and can change them at will,' says Dhiraj Singh.

At the same time, Rituraj realizes the importance of balancing the two aspects too. 'When we were a small company and setting up new businesses, it was perfectly okay to have an entrepreneur mindset. But if you have built a Rs 500-crore cash business, the second largest in the industry . . . you need a more process-oriented and systems-oriented administration. Entrepreneurship is important. But I think it there is great sense in the argument in defence of professionals driving larger organizations.

'I had my very hands-on management going for fifteen years. I want to continue that, but I also understand that I need to concede more space to professional managers. CEOs have to function like CEOs and not like my assistants. They can't look to me for directions.'

Following this philosophy, a new organizational structure has been created in SIS over the last three years. Under this new business umbrella, each brand has a head, who in turn reports to Dhiraj Singh. For the past year and a half, Rituraj has been doing monthly reviews with the brand heads and Dhiraj. The review session is recorded, updated and sent to Rituraj for his thoughts. It is Dhiraj who then takes it forward. 'If I get behind them every day—why did you do this, why did you open this branch, don't do this . . . I will be intruding into their space,' says Rituraj. For some businesses, like the recently acquired Dusters, Rituraj does a quarterly review.

With Dhiraj, Rituraj has coffee sessions over which they discuss critical issues. They do not discuss how to increase revenues by so many percentage points, but more fundamental matters. For instance, this year the two might agree on the need to build stronger regional management, or a stronger IT system. 'We agree on a broad plan and I let the management run it.'

Apart from these formal, recorded meetings, the two WhatsApp each other too. If a decision has to be made on a matter, Rituraj does it instantly, or the two chat over the phone, which happens once a day.

This arrangement helps Rituraj counter one of the biggest criticisms of his business model—that it would be better off specializing in one area, like the guard business, rather than diversifying into several. While competitors like Rahul Nanda of Tops Security have aired this view in the past, closer home, investors such as Hakan say that cash management is a difficult business, and in the coming years Rituraj might have to take a call on which business to specialize in.

'It is rather simplistic to say that diversification will come at the cost of specialization. Not necessarily. If you can balance diversification and specialization, that is special. Similarly, people say you can't grow and improve quality at the same time. But, why not?' asks Rituraj.

'I have diversified and also specialized. My facilities management business . . . you can call it a diversification. But by itself it is the fourth largest and fastest growing in India. My facilities management guys are not talking about security. They are not talking about cash. They are specializing in that business. I have diversified and specialized, and that is the way forward, I think.'

Adds Dhiraj Singh, 'Our approach is that each business is independent. We bring the right leaders. Within all these businesses we have presidents, who function like CEOs. We believe that by providing these businesses opportunity and support from our side, we will be able to grow them independently.'

At the same time, each business makes the most of the corporate brand, uses the SIS backend, including payroll systems, and depends on the senior leadership for funding and for establishing government relationships. The pan-India infrastructure of the group also helps it incubate new businesses.

The security business has a president, and the cash management vertical has a country manager. The Australian and international businesses are handled separately.

The system has helped Rituraj focus on three important requirements—hunting for the best talent, identifying new businesses and new partners, and fund raising. To help him in these three areas, Rituraj is aided by teams.

With this new structure now taking off, Rituraj has an answer to the questions raised by potential investors during roadshows on professional management at his company. And when they ask him about Uday Singh, he shares with them what has been in the planning for three years now. A strong second rung of leadership, below Rituraj and Uday Singh, has been built. Each of these leaders comes with a sound professional track record and, as in the case of Dhiraj Singh, who is an IIT-Mumbai alumnus, each is of a strong pedigree.

With time, some of these leaders will be assimilated into the top rung, which will take the form of a group management committee. This will ensure that SIS, even after the exit of Uday Singh, is led by professionals backed by the promoter.

Remarkably, neither Rituraj nor RK is on the board of SIS. Rituraj's mother, Rita Kishore Sinha, represents the family's interests on the board, which is headed by Uday Singh.

RK, who is now a BJP member of Parliament in the Rajya Sabha, says, 'Rituraj is doing pretty well. I have no hesitation in saying that he is doing better than me.'

Rituraj himself is non-committal about his interest in politics. He evades the question and says, 'I have an interest in politics, for sure. I have deep interest in making an impact in social services. I think what we ultimately crave is recognition. That is the most satisfying thing.

'I am creating 1000-plus jobs every month. What India needs most today is jobs. And not for engineers and doctors. But for the underprivileged from rural India and for people from the backward sections who do not have proper qualifications.'

These are no empty words. As part of the Central Advisory on Labour and Unemployment set up by the central government, Rituraj lobbied for the recategorization of security workers, from the unskilled category under minimum wage to the skilled category. When he first proposed the idea, the minister for labour, Bandaru Dattatreya, smiled and looked at the secretary, who was sitting close by, and said, 'We will do this. Because until today I have never seen a businessman talking about increasing the wages of labourers.'

Rituraj, who has made his mobile number available to his employees, asking them to call in case of need, gets at least twenty-five calls from them daily. He knows his industry peers won't be amused, but he firmly believes it is a step in the right direction. In fact, he sounds bewildered that a step such as this is even questioned. 'We have the opportunity and also the responsibility to do something. Especially if you can make an impact, then it's not an option (not to do it). I find it difficult to believe why someone successful doesn't hear the inner call to make impactful changes in society.'

With 150,000 employees at 9000 sites across 600 districts of India, Rituraj has already made an impact.

* * *

My Learnings

+ · Listen to your colleagues, don't impose on them.

 Then I realized that you can't be their boss if you want to get anything done. You cannot think that you are the owner's son and can start giving directives . . . . You have to make them understand your view and then win them over. One by one. And over a period of time.

+ Earn the respect of the team. Respect, unlike the business, can't be inherited.

 Unless you win the confidence and support of the team within, you can't go out and start making a difference on the other side, which is the market. The first battle has to be fought inside.

 That is a very bad way to manage people. And a good way to get abuse outside the room. I have always believed that you have to earn your stripes. And once you do that, if you have the conviction that something has to be done a particular way, you are no longer concerned that people behind you might say, 'Yeh toh owner ka son hain, isliye iski baat sunni par rahee hain'.

- As you rebuild, ensure that the company enters a growth trajectory. Nothing succeeds like success.

Success actually enables you to bring about larger reforms as you are more acceptable. In 2006–07, I started thinking about diversifying in two directions—multi-services and going overseas.

- Failures will disappoint. But don't get bogged down by them. The learning from them is invaluable.

Failed deals have given me a lot of confidence. I understand that it's okay for not every deal to be successful. And I think you never lose, even in a lost deal. Every failed transaction gave me something.

- Entrepreneurship is good. But to build scale, you need systems and processes.

When we were a small company and setting up new businesses, it was perfectly okay to have an entrepreneur mindset. But if you have built a Rs 500-crore cash business, the second largest in the industry . . . you need a more process-oriented and systems-oriented administration. Entrepreneurship is important. But I think there is great sense in the argument in defence of professionals driving larger organizations.

- You might be the owner. But your colleagues, especially the good ones, can easily get jobs in other companies. So respect them, and their space.

I had my very hands-on management going for fifteen years. I want to continue that, but I also understand that I need to concede more space to professional managers. CEOs have to function like CEOs and not like my assistants. They can't look to me for directions.

+ Diversification is good, but be careful. Build the capability to ensure that each diversification also becomes a specialization.

It is rather simplistic to say that diversification will come at the cost of specialization. Not necessarily. If you can balance diversification and specialization, that is special. Similarly, people say you can't grow and improve quality at the same time. But, why not?

6

Vikas Oberoi

It was just another day at his office in Andheri, Mumbai, for Vikas Oberoi, the second-generation promoter of Oberoi Realty. It was late 2001, and the young real estate developer was going through some documents when his secretary called. A broker had come to meet him. Vikas was not amused. The man didn't have an appointment. But since he had taken the effort to come all the way to the office, Vikas decided to meet him.

The moment the broker entered the room, Vikas got straight to the point, 'What is it?' The broker had come with a piece of information. There was a land parcel along Mumbai's Western Express Highway that was on sale. 'Mr Oberoi might perhaps be interested in it,' said the broker.

Vikas was. Ever since he was a teenager, there were few things that excited him more than the prospect of buying land and building a property on it. Of all the aspects of getting a structure up, it was the design of the building and the rooms that excited Vikas most.

When the broker asked Vikas to have a look at the land, the entrepreneur first took out a pencil and paper to draw a map.

He drew the Eastern Express Highway and the road that turned from there to Film City. 'I don't see any land here. Isn't that the Aarey Milk Colony?' he asked the broker. 'No no. There is a company called Novartis and it has land here that it wants to sell,' said the broker, pointing at Vikas's hand-drawn map.

Vikas had always thought the land mentioned by the broker was an extension of the Milk Colony. 'There were a lot of trees . . . one could easily miss it,' he said. He was now intrigued and immediately called for his car. With the broker settled in the passenger seat, he drove to the site.

When they arrived at the site, Vikas could scarcely believe what lay in front of him. 'My god,' he muttered to himself. The land parcel was of sixty acres, beautifully vegetated and superbly located. Vikas later came to know that the land actually belonged to Ciba-Geigy, which had merged with Sandoz in 1996 to form Novartis, the global pharmaceuticals company.

Land was critical for developers like Vikas. And any land wouldn't do. A developer needs to know the scope of developing the land—would an apartment or a mall here attract buyers and customers? Would the flats command a good price? That is why the best of developers have the knack to identify a land's scope better than the rest.

Vikas immediately understood that this land in Goregaon was a gold mine. He needed to meet the owners. But the broker didn't know them. 'Then how do you know it's up for sale?' Vikas asked him. 'Somebody told me that Knight Frank, a property consultant, has been appointed to sell this land parcel,' answered the broker.

Vikas was not convinced. He decided to check with Knight Frank. Though a real estate developer, Vikas still hadn't worked with the international property consultant. He called their Mumbai office to inquire. 'You are right sir,' said an executive at Knight Frank, 'Novartis is selling that land parcel. The process has started. Too bad, we are already on round one of bids and we can't entertain new ones.' The line was disconnected.

Vikas didn't want to let go of the opportunity without trying a little more. He called up the managing director of Novartis India, Dr E. Schillinger. Vikas introduced himself and told the Novartis MD that he was interested in buying the land, even though Knight Frank had informed him that the process had already started and fresh entries were not being entertained. Vikas requested Dr Schillinger for help. The Swiss German was more than willing. 'Nothing much has been done. I will give you the data sheet and you can give your bid,' Dr Schillinger told Vikas.

Excited, Vikas and his team studied the numbers and in no time sent in their bid. While the bids were being examined by Frank Knight, Vikas decided to befriend Dr Schillinger. Though Oberoi Realty had by then built a reputation for timeliness and its projects fetched a good response from buyers, the company perhaps wasn't big enough, at least in the eyes of others, to be seen as a serious contender for the Novartis land parcel. Vikas wanted his bid to be taken seriously.

He called Dr Schillinger and asked for an appointment to meet him. But the Novartis MD was only ready for a telephone conversation. A few days later, when Vikas tried again for an appointment, this time saying he needed a piece of information, Dr Schillinger asked him to depute someone to collect the document that contained what he wanted.

Finally, Vikas came up with another idea. He called up Dr Schillinger and said he was on the way to 'town' (south Mumbai, in local parlance) and wondered if he could drop by for five minutes. Vikas knew no one would turn down a request for a five-minute meeting. Dr Schillinger agreed.

Vikas had no plans to go to 'town', but now drove from his Andheri office to the Novartis office in Worli to spend five minutes with Dr Schillinger. Over the next few days, these visits became the norm. Vikas would drop by at the Novartis office for five minutes, sometimes make coffee for himself and Dr Schillinger, and the two would chat.

For each question that the Swiss German would ask about the property, Vikas would give an honest answer. If the others were telling Dr Schillinger that the land parcel 'had problems', then Vikas told him that it was like a 'piece of gold and beautiful'. The Novartis MD was pleasantly surprised by Vikas's frankness and appreciated it.

Apart from Oberoi Realty, at least five other real estate developers had put in their bids for the land. Vikas had bid top dollar, and when the bids were opened, his bid emerged as the highest. But there was a problem. 'I can't give it to you because internally we have a number in mind, and unless we get that we won't make a deal,' Dr Schillinger told Vikas. The board of Novartis India had now asked Dr Schillinger to individually sit with each bidder and negotiate. He had started the process with Vikas, who was the highest bidder.

Vikas readily agreed to match the number the board was looking for. He didn't want Dr Schillinger to engage with the other bidders. There was a risk that he might be overpaying, especially if none of the other players raised their bids; but it was a risk he was willing to take. He requested Dr Schillinger to prepare the papers for the agreement.

In February 2002, Oberoi Realty announced the acquisition of Novartis's sixty-acre land parcel for Rs 100 crore. It was one of the biggest land deals in the country, bringing in a lot of attention to both Vikas and the company.

While the attention was good, being in the limelight also upped the stakes for Vikas. It was now up to Vikas to make the most of the land. If planned well, this opportunity could take his company to great heights.

To develop a land parcel as big as this, Vikas used common sense, as well as thought out of the box. Goregaon in 2002 wasn't a place that Mumbaikars thought of when it came to buying a house, or even when it came to entertainment. 'If you ask a customer to write a big cheque for a house that we think he should buy, it may not happen,' says Vikas. So instead of building just a residential complex, Vikas opted to build a 'city within a city', which had the infrastructure that would attract its future residents. He named it Oberoi Garden City.

Vikas started with a mall. 'There was no mall here. It would become a natural attraction for people to drive to this location. Even if this area was in the middle of nowhere earlier, now suddenly there would be things happening around the mall,' says Vikas.

Named Oberoi Mall, the shopping centre was the first of its kind in the area and drew in the crowd from residential neighbourhoods such as Malad (East) and Kandivali (East). Over 300 popular brands had their outlets in the mall. Retail chain Central's first outlet and Home Centre's largest outlet in

Mumbai were here. The crowds also came in to watch movies at PVR's six-screen multiplex that could seat 1,900. The mall had parking place for 1000 cars, one of the biggest in the city; and it was the first mall in the country to get a LEEDS certification, a global benchmark for design, construction and operation of green buildings. Within 100 days of its opening in 2008, Oberoi Mall had registered two million footfalls.

Having made a mark with the mall, Vikas also opened the Oberoi International School the same year. Classes started with thirty-eight students. The pupil strength would grow to 1,630 by 2016. Managed by his sister, Bindu Oberoi, the school was designed by architects from Singapore and includes a 400-seat auditorium.

The last part of the infrastructure came in the form of a five-star hotel. 'A wise man once told me that a city revolves around a five-star hotel. So we said there is no five-star hotel in this entire belt and we should build one,' says Vikas.

But the five-star hotel was envisioned in a way not seen before. On a visit to New York, Vikas stayed at the Mandarin Oriental hotel, which stretches from the thirty-fifth to fifty-fourth floor of the Time Warner Centre. Apart from the hotel, the centre also includes TV studios, offices of big corporate names and condominiums. It was the largest such structure in New York.

After staying at the hotel and having understood the novelty of the mixed use concept, Vikas knew he wanted to do the same in Goregaon. While he had initially intended to build a commercial building that would house corporate offices, now Vikas told his team that the building would also have a five-star hotel. When the building, named Commerz, finally opened in 2010, its thirty-two floors included the Westin five-star hotel from the eighteenth to the thirty-second floor. The building itself was the result of an international collaboration. Architects and design consultants came from the US, Singapore, Canada and Japan, and the civil contractor was India's infrastructure biggie, Larsen & Toubro.

The Westin's opening, in January 2010, was at an opportune time. The financial markets and business newspapers had begun talking about Oberoi Realty's planned initial public offering, or IPO, and the hotel was a good way to build curiosity among prospective investors.

This was not the first time that Vikas was raising money. In 2004, he had formed I-Ven Realty Ltd along with ICICI Venture to purchase a four-acre plot in a prime location in Worli from another pharma company, Glaxo SmithKline. Later, in 2007, Morgan Stanley's Special Situation Real Estate Fund had invested $152 million in Oberoi Realty for a roughly 10 per cent stake.[1] Anand Madduri, executive director of Morgan Stanley's Asia-Pacific property portfolio, claimed the deal was the single largest foreign direct investment (FDI) in India's real estate sector.

To get the stake, Morgan Stanley had to fend off serious competition from similar high-profile investors, including Warburg Pincus and Citibank's Citi Venture Capital International. It was not difficult to see why these big names were interested in investing with Vikas.

A news report[2] said: 'The Morgan Stanley realty investment of $152mn for a 10.75% stake implies that Oberoi Constructions

---

[1] Gurbir Singh, 'Morgan Fund Invests $152 Million in Oberoi Realty Firm', *Hindustan Times*, 17 January 2007, http://www.hindustantimes. com/india/morgan-fund-invests-152min-oberoi-realty-firm/story-Oabivdu5Gui7LNkgY7rXkO.html.

[2] Ibid.

has derived a valuation of a little over $1.4 billion. Since Oberoi Constructions has a turnover of a little over Rs 600 crore per year, the high valuation by international investors is largely a derivative of the high asset value given to the land banks built up by the company.'

The land bank had grown since the Novartis land deal, after which Vikas was on a shopping spree. He bought the Worli land in 2004, and a year later, signed two more land deals. He purchased 24.47 acres in Andheri (East) for Rs 106 crore, and twenty-three acres in Mulund for Rs 221 crore. There was a pause in the buying as the market went on an upward swing during the 2007–08 period, before the global financial crisis spoiled the party. Vikas was prudent enough not to buy assets at the peak of their valuation. A year into the crisis, he made his move and acquired just a little over three acres in Worli for Rs 300 crore.

After the success of the mall, school and hotel at Oberoi Garden City, Vikas also started to build the first residential project, named Oberoi Exquisite. It was a premium project, with each flat priced upwards of Rs 4.55 crore. There was also Commerz 2, the second commercial project in Oberoi Garden City. The company was also building another residential project, this time on its Andheri (East) land. Vikas also was looking out for more land deals. All this meant he needed money, and it was time for a larger play. That's where the IPO came in.

A listing would not just bring in the money, but would also raise the company's profile. Up to that time, many were confusing Oberoi Realty with Oberoi Hotels, the premier hospitality chain whose promoters have the same family name. Many news and analyst reports, while introducing Oberoi Realty, would explain, 'unrelated to the Oberoi hospitality group'. Vikas himself had been a low-profile entrepreneur, preferring to stay away from the limelight. There was one exception, though. In 2005, he created a flutter in the press and in Bollywood after marrying Gayatri Joshi, a well-known model who had just a year earlier debuted in her first and only feature film, *Swades*, co-starring Shah Rukh Khan.

Days after Oberoi Realty filed its DRHP (Draft Red Herring Prospectus) in January 2010, business journalists and brokerage analysts began to write about how the company was different from its peers. A DRHP is a legal document mandated by the Securities and Exchange Board of India, which provides details of a company's IPO. It contains information about the company, its promoters, its business model, and provides information on what the money is being raised for.

Rating agency CRISIL Research said,[3] 'In the past 28 years, the promoter, promoter group and the company has developed 30 projects under the brand name "Oberoi", totalling 3.9 million square feet. ORL (Oberoi Realty Ltd) enjoys a very strong brand name in the market due to its track record for good quality construction and hence commands a price premium for most of its projects.' CRISIL rated the IPO 4 out of 5. Many analysts gave it 5/5, 'indicating strong fundamentals'.

The prospectus elaborated on how the company intended to spend the Rs 1,200 crore that it hoped to raise through the IPO. Of the total amount, Rs 777 crore would be spent on

---

[3] CRISIL Research, 22 March 2010, https://www.crisil.com/Ratings/Brochureware/News/CRISILResearch_ipo-grading-rat_OberoiRealty.pdf.

construction of ongoing and planned projects, and the rest on acquiring land. 'This is somewhat unusual, since most of the real estate public offerings have been made with an objective of paying off debt,' *VCCircle*'s Manish Tulsian wrote in his news report.

Most unusually, unlike other real estate companies, Oberoi Realty had minimal debt—just Rs 11 crore that Vikas has lent the company in his personal capacity. The company had a cash reserve of Rs 312 crore. The previous year, it had revenues of Rs 455 crore, with a net profit of Rs 252 crore. This set Oberoi Realty apart from other companies, including DLF.

The biggest real estate company in the country, DLF, had a debt of over Rs 20,000 crore[4] in 2010. Its founder, K.P. Singh, had seen his fortune slide, from over $30 billion in 2008, to less than $10 billion in 2010. The story was not very different for many of the other high-profile real estate companies and their promoters.

'In the case of Vikas, every banker and lender felt he had the strongest balance sheet,' says Deepak Parekh, chairman of the Housing Development Finance Corporation, or HDFC, the country's leading housing finance company. 'He had cash and was never in financial trouble in all the years I have known him. Vikas is the least leveraged developer that I was aware of. Even today I can say that. He is the least leveraged developer.' Deepak Parekh has known Vikas for over twenty-five years.

Oberoi Realty was not very big. It had over the years developed about four million square feet of real estate, and at

---

[4] 'DLF's Debt Rises by 800 Crore', Rediff.com, 01 February 2011, http://www.rediff.com/business/report/dlf-debt-up-by-800-crore/20110201.htm.

the time of going for the IPO was developing about two million square feet. In comparison, DLF had over fifty million square feet of real estate under construction. But investors were no longer big fans of DLF. The company's scrip was down to Rs 250 per share in mid-2010, from a high of nearly Rs 1,250 just two years earlier. In Oberoi Realty, investors now saw a real estate company 'with strong fundamentals'.

Even with all these accolades, Vikas had to make sure that the listing was successful. 'One day we got a call from JP Morgan India [one of the lead managers[5] of the IPO]. They told us there is a small window before the mega IPO of Coal India and asked if we would be interested in doing the listing then,' recounts Saumil Daru, chief financial officer at Oberoi Realty. 'VO [Vikas Oberoi] was interested, and asked when we should start the process. The JP Morgan people said we would have to start the next day, and VO said okay.'

Vikas and Saumil embarked on a whirlwind tour, meeting investors in India and abroad. 'We left on a Saturday night. On Monday we were in Singapore, on Tuesday in Hong Kong and a day later we were meeting investors in London,' says Saumil.

On that same day, the two proceeded to Paris for a meeting and then flew to New York. 'That day, breakfast was in London, lunch in Paris and dinner in New York, thanks to gaining time as we moved westwards,' says Saumil. To save time, the two would shower and change at airports, not bothering with hotels. 'We took a Friday night flight out of Boston to Mumbai. The following Monday we met investors in Mumbai, the next day in Ahmedabad and landed in Chennai on Wednesday,' says Saumil.

---

[5] Lead Managers and Book Running Lead Managers (BRLM) are involved with the complete process of an IPO.

Though the travel was hectic, the two had a bigger task of convincing investors to invest in Oberoi Realty. The focus was mainly on Vikas, the promoter. 'They wanted to understand who this person was,' says Saumil. In one of the meetings, when the topic came to the company's top line, business model and the focus on the premium segment, Vikas said, 'Buildings have an ability to change people's moods. As you drive past an area, if you see a good building, it uplifts you. Your job as a developer is not just to build buildings but to contribute to the city's skyline. If you want to make good buildings, money will be a by-product. But if the intention is to make lots of money, then good buildings need not be a by-product. So our focus is clear. People want to have Oberoi homes. And Mumbai is a city where people are aspirational and are willing to pay the premium.'

The investors bought into Vikas's vision. 'I believe if any other developer had that land in Goregaon, he would have built forty buildings of six to seven storeys each. The place would have been just another nagar, with several lanes snaking around, and that's it,' says Saumil. 'What we are doing instead is to build nine buildings of forty storeys each . . . so Vikas has completely changed the landscape.'

The investors also bought into the company's business model, especially that of Oberoi Garden City. The Oberoi Mall, for instance, had emerged as a good annuity business. 'Today it gives me 100 per cent return on the cost that I incurred,' says Vikas. 'Even if I spent Rs 125 crore building it, every year my rental revenue from the mall is Rs 125 crore.'

By the time the listing was done, Oberoi Realty had managed to rope in nine foreign and domestic anchor investors. These included big names, such as Eton Park, AllianceBernstein, Prudential, ICICI Prudential and Birla Mutual Fund. Anchor investors[6] are marquee institutional investors who are invited to subscribe to shares ahead of an IPO to boost the popularity of the issue and provide confidence to potential investors.

Vikas and Saumil struck the gong at the Bombay Stock Exchange on 20 October 2010, marking the listing of Oberoi Realty. The stock opened at Rs 271, touched a high of Rs 299 and then closed at Rs 280.05, above the issue price of Rs 260. Overall, the shares were oversubscribed 12.13 times, and the portion reserved for the qualified institutional buyers was subscribed 22.15 times.[7]

A *Business Standard* report[8] said the subscription for Oberoi Realty's shares broke a three-year record: 'There were three realty IPOs this year so far. DB Realty was oversubscribed 2.63 times, Nitesh Estates 1.13 times and Vascon Engineers 1.16 times. Godrej Properties IPO was oversubscribed by 3.56 times last year. No real estate company came up with an IPO in 2008. Analysts said the appetite shown for Oberoi IPO is likely to encourage some other realty firms to hit the market with their public issues.'

---

[6] Samie Modak, 'Who Is an Anchor Investor', *Business Standard*, 27 October 2015, http://www.business-standard.com/article/markets/who-is-ananchor-investor-115102700806_1.html.

[7] 'Oberoi Realty Gains 8% on Listing', *The Hindu Business Line*, 21 October 2010, http://www.thehindubusinessline.com/todays-paper/tp-markets/oberoi-realty-gains-8-on-listing/article1007153.ece.

[8] PTI, 'Oberoi Realty IPO Oversubscribed 12 Times', *Business Standard*, 08 October 2010, http://www.business-standard.com/article/markets/oberoi-realtyipo-oversubscribed-12-times-110100800195_1.html.

Oberoi Realty got a multi-billion dollar valuation, putting it up there among the real estate biggies like DLF and Unitech. Vikas, though already regularly featuring on Forbes India's Rich List, was now a confirmed billionaire. After the listing, an investor asked Vikas, 'How will this change ORL?' Vikas answered, 'What we have been doing and the way we have been doing it has worked for us, and has made us reach here. It's tried and tested. And you backed me in the IPO for this track record. So I just need to keep doing this, but on a larger scale.'

And if one had asked Vikas who had been the biggest influence in his life, he would have said, 'My father.'

* * *

Vikas had tears in his eyes. His father, Ranvir Oberoi, who was at the steering wheel, couldn't understand why his seventeen-year-old son sitting next to him on the passenger seat had become so emotional.

The two were on their way back home after meeting a landowner, who had a few years ago sold two tracts of land to Ranvir. He was now again selling some land, about three acres. Vikas was very interested in the land and had convinced his father to meet the landowner.

'We will take one acre,' Ranvir told the landowner. Vikas tried to convince his father to take all three. 'No, there is too much stress otherwise too. We can't buy all three acres,' Ranvir replied firmly. Angry and upset, Vikas retorted, 'Okay, then let's not buy anything. Let's go.' Ranvir agreed.

But now in the car, Vikas's eyes had welled up. 'What's the matter?' his father asked. 'This is not how it should be, Dad,' Vikas said. 'We will never grow like this.'

Ranvir melted. He took a U-turn, went back to the landowner and bought all three acres. He was also angry. Vikas had emotionally blackmailed him into buying the land. And, while other teenagers whined for bikes and cars, here was his son crying for land! 'What's wrong with you?' an exasperated Ranvir asked Vikas.

The story wasn't finished yet. Ranvir and Vikas struggled for months to get the land cleared by authorities to start its development in 1988. But they couldn't. Frustrated, the two went back to the landowner to let him know of the problems they were facing. At the landowner's office, Vikas saw a small model of a building. 'I'm getting that done on another small parcel of land. I am starting the construction now,' he said.

'That's unfair,' Vikas told him. 'How can you build and develop land when we are struggling to clear the land that you sold us?' Chastised, the landowner made an offer. 'Do you want the land? Take it, but I need fresh payment and I won't adjust with the last deal,' he said. Vikas jumped at the offer. His father was horrified. But he could only say, 'What's wrong with you?'

Father and son bought the land in Mumbai's Andheri-Lokhandwala neighbourhood. 'That's the land where I really started building,' says Vikas, who took over the project. Though it was a small, seven-storeyed residential building, he wanted to set an example. Vikas went to one of the best building contractors. 'How long will you take?' Vikas asked. 'Seven to eight months,' was the answer.

Vikas started a marketing campaign and promised customers to deliver their flats within twelve months of starting construction. Apart from hiring one of the biggest contractors around, Vikas also hired reputed architects. And he finished the project in eleven months' time. It was a big success. Vikas was just nineteen.

'The building kind of changed the way people looked at us and the company,' says Vikas. But instead of soaking in the compliments that were pouring in, Vikas knew that none of this would have been possible without his father. 'Even though people gave all the credit for the speed (with which the building was commissioned) to me, nobody really understood the fact that I wouldn't have been able to do this, had not my whole family, company, my dad and I not gone through the process. I learnt from those mistakes, that's why I'm here. Had my father, or we, not made those mistakes I would have been never been here,' says Vikas.

The process of learning really began for Vikas when he was just eleven, when his father had begun the real estate company.

Vikas's passion for real estate comes from his father. But real estate was not what the family was initially into. The family was into trading. Ranvir's father, born in the Pakistan of undivided India, had moved to Mumbai even before Partition. Though the division of the country saw the family lose three-fourths of its wealth, the business in Mumbai kept them afloat. While Ranvir continued with the family business, he found his passion in real estate. All the profits from the trading business would be used to buy real estate. Ranvir had decided that there was no investment like real estate, which was sound and gave good, predictable and reliable returns. Even as he would park his surplus money in flats and tracts of land, he advised his friends to do the same.

Soon he had a following of people who would go by his word to invest in real estate.

Following his passion, Ranvir had built a network of contacts with builders and contractors. He loved to travel, and every time he got back from an overseas visit, he would drop in on his developer friends and tell him about the buildings he saw, their design, their colour, and so on. He would show them pictures of water fountains or lobbies, giving his friends new ideas for their next projects.

Ranvir had a small office in Maker Chambers in south Mumbai's business district of Nariman Point. And one of the friends with whom he often shared his ideas was Dr A.S. Maker, the construction magnate who had built many of the buildings in Nariman Point. One day, after one more of their typical chats on buildings and design, Dr Maker asked Ranvir, 'You know so much about real estate, why don't you become a developer?'

It was as though Ranvir had been just waiting for someone to make that suggestion. He took the advice seriously. Soon enough, he sold off his trading business and used all the money to buy two land parcels. 'I am not just an investor any more,' Ranvir announced to his family. 'From now on, I am a developer.'

For young Vikas, this was like music to his ears. From as long as he could remember, he had grown up listening to his father's tales about real estate deals. At the dining table in the family's small flat in Santa Cruz, Vikas would listen wide-eyed to these tales. They whetted his curiosity, and he craved to know more. 'I was very interested and intrigued. And I considered those stories great.'

Vikas was eleven when his father made the transition from investor to developer. His impressionable mind soaked in all the information around him. Architects and builders would come home to discuss the residential apartments that his father was building on the two land parcels. Once an architect was explaining a project to Ranvir and took out a pencil and started drawing on paper. Vikas, sitting close by, was hooked by the beautiful pencil and the designs the architect drew. The amazement on his face was so obvious that the architect gifted that pencil to the wide-eyed boy. It would remain a prized possession with Vikas for years.

Ranvir was delighted to see this interest in his son. He had already told Vikas, 'I'm starting the business for you. I hope you are interested.' His son couldn't be happier. Over the next few years, even as Ranvir went about constructing his first building, he would include his son in his meetings and take him to the sites too. When Vikas joined college, he would be done with his classes by 11.30 a.m. and come to his father's office by noon. He would remain there with his father until 8 p.m., putting in eight hours of work like a professional.

Vikas was like an intern. Ranvir would make him do almost everything. Vikas would attend to phone calls in the office and would be sent by his father to meet important clients. 'But Dad, I am just eighteen and with about two years of experience,' Vikas would say. 'Rubbish, you have thirty-two years of work experience, thirty of mine and two of yours,' Ranvir would say, and send him on his way to the meeting.

Some days Ranvir would hand Vikas a list of customers who had booked apartments and ask him to collect cheques from them. 'So I would sit down and make phone calls and tell them, you have pay us Rs 20,000 or 25,000. Those days flats were selling at Rs 4–5 lakh,' says Vikas. If a customer asked for two days' time to pay, Vikas would make a note of it and then call the customer back after two days. If someone requested him to collect their cheque, Vikas would ensure it was collected and deposited.

There was also a list of people whom Ranvir had to pay. There was pressure to make these payments, so the collection of money from customers also had to be timely. 'We had to ensure that we had enough money to pay the suppliers,' says Vikas. The youngster was fast learning to juggle the two sides of the business.

He was also learning from the challenges his father faced. Ranvir had borrowed money from the banks to develop the two land parcels. But he couldn't sell enough flats on time to make the interest payments. Vikas could see that his father was under stress. Matters came to a head when Ranvir was forced to sell their house in Santa Cruz to repay his debt, and the family moved to a rented apartment.

'That's the time I realized debt is something one should be wary of,' says Vikas.

Also, because the scale of the development was small, one couldn't afford the best of contractors and suppliers. The ones who were hired had limitations when it came to scaling operations or executing on time. 'When you are small, everything around you is of the same scale. These are typical start-up challenges,' says Vikas. These drawbacks delayed their projects. What should have taken four years to develop, eventually took almost eight years to be completed.

But if not for the challenges and failures, Vikas wouldn't have learnt important lessons. 'All my learning came from all the mistakes that were made executing that first project.

My father would teach me about all the things that didn't go right.

'That's why I won't call them failures, but the project had taken a lot from my father and taught him what not to do in the business. And his learning came to me on a platter. That made a huge impression on me,' says Vikas.

Ranvir also allowed his son to make mistakes. 'He was very generous on that aspect. He would allow me to fail. It was very important. I would do things without fear of being reprimanded or of being thought a failure. I had a permanent safety net that my father had created,' says Vikas.

By the time the two projects were over, Vikas had become a part and parcel of the business. No one really noticed when he made the transition from being a curious teenager to someone who started contributing to conversations, advising his father, giving his opinion and eventually taking over the mantle of responsibility at the company.

He was now full-time at work and discontinued his college education. In between, alarmed that his son was not living a 'normal youngster's' life, Ranvir would push Vikas out of the office and ask him to hang out with his friends; or, in the mornings, ask him to play a round of squash before heading to office. 'You won't know and time will slip out of your hands and you will regret not having enjoyed your younger days,' Ranvir would tell his son.

Even in sports, Vikas was ambitious. He started off with table tennis and was trained by a coach. Then his attention went to badminton. He was twelve when a friend took him to see lawn tennis, and he immediately picked up the sport. And the longest he played any sport was cricket. 'I could bowl, bat, keep. I would do everything that my team wanted of me,' says Vikas.

But Vikas was happiest going to work. 'I never missed anything because I was enjoying work so much. My highs in life were different . . . I had friends and would hang out with them, or play squash or cricket. But I was doing less of this than others of my age,' says Vikas, who would sometimes head out to Wellington Club after work to play squash with his friends, and follow it up with dinner at a restaurant.

But Ranvir knew that his son had a zeal for the business. He showed his confidence in his son in several ways. Once, when an associate called saying a cheque was ready for collection and inquired who would sign the agreement, Ranvir said Vikas would do it. 'Are you serious? He is just a kid,' said the associate. But Ranvir knew better, and it was Vikas who signed on the dotted line.

'That was one thing about my father . . . I had 100 per cent power in the business, even when I was just twenty-one. I had as much right in the business as he had. I could sign the entire company off. That was the kind of blind faith and love that he had,' says Vikas.

It came to a point when Ranvir asked his staff to follow Vikas's instructions. They no longer needed to refer to him for decisions. 'It was amazing. And that kind of made me more responsible, conscious and cautious, but without any pressure. That was the beauty,' says Vikas.

But Ranvir couldn't understand his son's appetite for land. After Vikas's first project that was completed by the time he was nineteen years old, the youngster continued with his shopping. When a land parcel, including nine plots, came up for sale in the market, Vikas again went for everything that was available. 'Have you gone mad?' his father asked. But to no avail. Vikas had his way.

With every buy, Vikas scaled the business. When land was available in Kandivali's Thakur Complex, Vikas asked for fifteen lakh square feet. Until now, he had never bought a plot bigger than 1.2 lakh square feet. The landowner agreed. But when the twenty-one-year-old went back home to inform his father, Ranvir freaked out. He told Vikas to make do with three lakh square feet. But the youngster was passionate; he was so eager about the work and so firm in his belief that he could pull it off, telling his father that he needed the scale to do good work and to attract talent in the form of architects, contractors and designers, that Ranvir was convinced and assented to the deal.

It helped that by then the company had earned a reputation in the market for its timely delivery and for the quality of its flats. Vikas had created a sound model. For each project he would do the maths. He would pace the development of a project in such a way that it would complement the pre-sale of flats. He would sell just enough to cover the land costs and some part of the construction. As Oberoi Realty's scale of operations increased, the company was now regularly churning out projects and delivering flats.

It also mattered that Vikas was careful about the brand's sanctity. 'As I speak, I can actually say that I don't have a single project that is a ghost project. I don't have a single project in which I have not given occupation certificates to the customers, or a project which is complete but in which people are unable to stay because of regulatory issues. That was our discipline from the beginning. Customers know that we will only launch a project once we have all the approvals.'

This discipline bore fruit, and Oberoi Realty acquired a loyal following among the investor community. Vikas was now used to meeting and conferring with people twice his age. 'I was able to connect with them. For me, age was just a number. As long as I was doing my part and the person sitting opposite was doing his part, it didn't matter . . . even if I was half his age.'

The increasing pace of development showed in the top line growth of Oberoi Realty. While its annual revenues used to hover around Rs 30 lakh when the first two projects were being developed, the company was later growing by five to ten times every year. While earlier the company employed five people, by the time the company went for the IPO, it was employing 773 people.

By 1998, the twenty-nine-year-old Vikas had already spent over a decade in the business. A year earlier, he had also enrolled for the Owner/President Program at Harvard Business School. Not only was it a step to complete his education, but Vikas also realized it was time to build an organization and prepare the company for the future. The Program, which included three weeks of classes annually over three years, would help him do that. 'Also, I needed to attract good talent, people who were well educated and would be talking a particular language. I needed to understand them,' says Vikas.

The Harvard course coincided with the rechristening of the company. From Oberoi Constructions, it now became Oberoi Realty.

His first project after the renaming was to develop the Kandivali land. 'It was exactly the kind of project I had dreamed of building—there was a swimming pool, gym . . . everything that I wanted in a residential development,' he told *Outlook Business* in an interview.[9]

He was now equally focused on building the organization.

Building the Organization

As Deepak Parekh points out, it benefited Vikas that his was a one-man operation: 'Other developers have large families. With Vikas, his is a one-man show. His decision is final, and he doesn't have to consult anyone. This helps in faster decision-making and also ensures that his organization is full of professionals.'

Vikas created positions as the need for more professionals arose in his growing company. Many of his colleagues, whom he had hired just before or after the turn of the century, including the company's chief architect, continue to be with him. Saumil, the CFO, joined in 2002. Earlier, until 1997, he was working with a chartered accountant who was auditing Oberoi Realty's books. When he left the chartered accountant, Vikas offered him a job at Oberoi Realty. But Saumil, looking for experience, joined Arthur Andersen, the accounting firm that later surrendered its licence in 2002 following the Enron scandal. A few years later, Vikas approached Saumil again as Oberoi Realty was growing fast and he needed a CFO. This time, in 2002, Saumil agreed.

When the company needed a professional for marketing, Vikas hired Reena Kundnani, who was at TechMahindra,

---

[9] Shabana Hussain, 'Towering Ambition', *Outlook Business*, 22 June 2013, https://www.outlookbusiness.com/strategy/feature/toweringambition-336.

handling marketing for India, Africa, the Middle East and Asia-Pacific.

Vikas continues to be involved in recruitment, though in the final stages. Everybody who joins the company meets Vikas before getting the offer letter. He doesn't interview them. That is done by the respective department head and the HR staff. 'I meet them because these are the people who are going to work for my company. And how much am I investing? Just a minute or two. And that fellow is going to be happy too.'

He shares with them the company philosophy and briefs them about their departments and whom they are going to report to. Rarely have these meetings gone beyond five minutes. If he feels unsure about the 'vibe' that he gets from the candidate, he asks HR to dig deeper and find out more about him or her.

While Vikas welcomes these new recruits, he avoids using flowery words like 'we are all family' or 'welcome to the family'. As far as he is concerned, the candidate is being recruited because he is expected to do his job. Everything else, including getting an invite from the boss for dinners, is a by-product of working well. 'I think all this flowery language is a lie. Companies that use such jargon don't blink even once before firing the very same people whom they so "lovingly" welcomed. Employees like to have a fair conversation and like to know where they are going.'

Vikas followed the same principle when it came to formalizing systems and processes in the organization, creating and building them as the need arose. Whenever he thought there was a disconnect between what his people were selling and what customers were expecting, Vikas sought to clear the miscommunication by creating a process.

'I would be very uncomfortable if we were doing a deal and the client said "you misunderstood me". That means either I am lying or backing off. I didn't want this confusion to erode our brand name. If miscommunication is clarified before the deal is done, then it's good,' says Vikas. If there are any sticky clauses, it's better to tell the customer beforehand, not when he comes to deposit the first cheque.

This focus meant that even before Vikas got an IT system to support the processes, the company had a paper-driven system that was well defined.

The first software the company got was Tally, used for customer relationship management. In 2007, Vikas agreed to Saumil's suggestion to get SAP. It didn't matter that under SAP one couldn't 'play with numbers' and the system was now straight-jacketed. 'That's how our business should be run,' said Vikas. He got Deloitte to document all the processes, and SAP implemented them. To adhere to SAP's global standards, processes were tweaked. Oberoi Realty was one of the earliest real estate companies in India to implement SAP.

On compliances too, Vikas was particular that all of them be met. As the scale of the business increased and the company was working with the likes of L&T, Vikas made sure that if something needed to be done, even at additional cost, it was done. 'There has to be a difference between the way we play cricket in our backyard and in Wankhede [the iconic cricket stadium in Mumbai]. So if we are playing at that level, let's then adapt ourselves to that level. I am ready to absorb the costs,' says Vikas.

These systems and processes helped gain the customer's trust. The entrepreneur understood the importance of keeping the brand name intact in a sector where customers were increasingly becoming suspicious of developers and their promises. That was another reason he was averse to debt. He had learnt his lesson watching his father struggling to repay loans. Now, to be debt-free had become a part of company's strategy.

'We feel that if at all you take a debt, you should make sure it is a long-term debt [which has a lower interest rate]. Always have a contingency plan to make the interest payments. If X source has dried up, then make sure there is a Y source to keep paying the interest,' says Vikas.

After his shopping spree post the Goregaon land deal, Vikas's company had a debt of Rs 200 crore. But he repaid it using his sales revenues from projects in Andheri and Goregaon.

A debt repayment default not just ruins a business model, but also breaks a customer's trust. 'When a customer buys a house, he writes the biggest cheque of his life. So for him, trust is everything.'

And trust, says Vikas, comes from the credibility built on your reputation in the market. If you have borrowed money and can't repay, then technically you are bankrupt. 'No customer wants to give his cheque to a bankrupt company . . . when I ask a customer to write a cheque, I am putting my reputation on the line. I can't be defaulting on my loans. I don't want any cash flow mismatch. That's the way I want to run the company,' he says.

To drive home the point, Vikas uses the example of flying, something he is almost as passionate about as business. 'A good pilot is a safe pilot. Every time you fly you have to land. It's the same with business. Every time you start a venture, you have to finish it.

'So we don't choose debt as an option. Especially, when you are building a company that should last its lifetime, and not your lifetime.'

The lessons learnt during the early days of Oberoi Realty were augmented by advice that Vikas got from some of the biggest titans of the industry, including Michael Kadoorie, one of the wealthiest businessmen in Hong Kong and chairman of the family-owned CLP Holdings. Michael's China Light and Power have an office in Commerz, and through a chance meeting with its India managing director, Vikas got in touch with Michael's office. A meeting was fixed and Vikas flew to Hong Kong to meet the veteran businessman.

The two met over lunch and talked till 4 p.m., after which Vikas caught the flight back to Mumbai. Vikas was intrigued by how Michael's family had managed to remain successful even after more than 100 years of the company's founding. One of Vikas's favourite stories about Michael, illustrates how this was done.

When Michael's company was putting up power plants in India, Michael saw that the costing of the project was much lower than what was usual with the company. Michael asked his senior executive to explain the lower costs. 'Two–three things that are required as standard safety mechanisms in other places are not insisted on by Indian regulations. That helps us save $200 million,' the senior executive told him. Michael wasn't impressed. He said, 'It does not matter whether we are in India or Australia, the value of life is the same. I don't care if the returns fall, but we should have the same safety standards in India too.'

'That is how you build ethics that keep companies afloat over decades,' says Vikas.

His insistence on adherence to governance is as strong as his insistence on listening to the customer. And that begins the moment he starts conceptualizing a project and its flats. 'I like to connect with each apartment that we make. I like to visualize how people would like to live . . . where they would entertain their guests, how they would like their bedrooms to be,' says Vikas.

He has walked the distance to make customers happy. Once when a customer wasn't happy with the pattern of the marble floor, Vikas didn't think twice before telling his people to remove the entire flooring and replacing it with new marble. 'We cannot have a dissatisfied customer. It doesn't matter how much it costs,' he told his people. In another instance, when a customer insisted he wanted to receive his flat keys from Vikas himself, the entrepreneur made himself available.

It is not just that he is willing to meet only happy customers. Saumil says, 'If there is an irate customer, Vikas likes talking to him or her. He has stood in front of customers and said, "I'm Vikas Oberoi, tell me what I can do." In our sector, the last thing developers want to do is to meet customers.' It's not an exaggeration. Many of the real estate promoters in the country move around with a security cordon fit for heads of state.

The focus on customers also means that Vikas is extremely particular about design, something he is most passionate about. Design, he believes, is the backbone of Oberoi Realty. 'The simplicity and the purity of the structure that we build, and how we are able to think it through, sets us apart,' says Vikas. 'Hand on heart, every apartment I have built, irrespective of its cost, I would be happy living in it.'

Like his father, Vikas looks for new inspiration on his travels. When he was in Milan with wife Gayatri, the two spent a whole day at a furniture fair and ended up walking twenty-eight kilometres. 'We love to see new things—new colours, designs, or how a particular shade has been used,' says Gayatri. 'You see it in his work. Aesthetics is a big part of his work and he has picked a lot from his travels. When we go to a restaurant, it's not like we eat and get out. He will examine the fork, check which company had made the plate. He will feel the linen, look at the colours. He comes back from his travels and often changes parts of a project,' she says. So much so that his colleagues often worry what Vikas is going to change the next time he returns from a trip!

When an idea crops up in his mind, Vikas doesn't wait for his architects to draw it on paper. He does it himself. 'Vikas is a hidden architect. He is good with layout and proportions. He can draw as well as a trained architect,' says Gayatri, who shares her husband's passion for design. Even before they had started dating, Gayatri, then a star model, had seen Oberoi Realty's residential project in Khar, Mumbai, and was impressed with it. 'I wanted to buy a flat there. When I met him, I told him that I loved his building in Khar,' she says.

Gayatri is involved in several aspects of the business, including the running of Oberoi school and the design of model flats for residential projects. She says, 'We discuss a lot when a show-apartment is being done. I know his aesthetics and I can expedite the process when he is busy with something else.' If Vikas loves straight lines and clean spaces, Gayatri brings in colour and warmth. 'Everything can't look so plain and straight, I tell him,' she says with twinkling eyes. Vikas's love for classic extends to clothing—grey suits at work, and blue jeans and white shirt for more casual affairs.

Apart from exploring furniture, Vikas loves adventure sports, from bungee jumping and scuba diving to skydiving and waterskiing. 'He likes learning new things. And not just learning, but going deeper and getting technical about everything,' says Gayatri. That includes his new-found love for wine and understanding how grapes mature and from where wines get their flavour. And it extends to cooking, when he prepares Maggi noodles for his children, first sautéing vegetables and then adding herbs to the noodles. 'It's the best Maggi,' says Yuvaan, their nine-year-old son. The older son is Vihaan, eleven.

Nothing though, sets Vikas as free as flying does. 'If not a builder, I would have been happy flying commercial planes. Nine out of ten pilots fly because they love flying and not to make money,' says Vikas. Though he was hooked to flying at a young age (after a friend took him for joyride in a two-seat Cessna 152), his mother had refused to let her only son take to the skies. When the flying licence arrived home in the mail, she tore it up. She finally relented five years ago.

Since then Vikas has used his Sundays to explore the Mumbai skies. He would sometimes fly to Aamby Valley, where he would follow up the flight with a round of golf. When he yearns for street food, he flies to Surat, explores the streets there and flies back. His favourite passengers are his two sons, and he takes them on his favourite route of Mumbai–Goa for the scenery. 'You have the mountains on one side and the blue sea on the other,' he told *Forbes*.[10] In 2015, he flew the Rafale, the French fighter jet, during an aero show. Though fellow-flier Ratan Tata didn't turn up, as was planned, Vikas had an 'out of the world experience'.

To pursue his love of flying, Vikas bought a Cirrus SR22 Turboprop plane. This plane was high on safety, the main reason for his choice. 'I'm too safe a pilot and don't believe in fighting nature. If there are clouds and thunderstorms I won't take the plane out. A good pilot [or CEO] doesn't take undue risks. Just as you never take off before doing all the checks, you should never start a project without thorough due diligence,' he says.

In business, the safety checks come through processes and systems. And by keeping things simple. He once told Saumil, 'A pilot is surrounded by around 100 metres. But he is not looking at all of them. He needs to know the destination, fuel, speed and elevation. The rest is data. That ability to split the data from the noise is extremely important.'

That he does by asking questions. Vikas might say that he hates finance, but when his CFO comes for a meeting, he is ready with his own sets of numbers to check if his maths for a proposed project tallies with his colleague's. 'We often go to him with complicated models and calculations, but he focuses on key indicators . . . he often jokes that it is our excel sheet versus his back-of-the-envelope calculation,' says Saumil.

Vikas keeps a tab on the business in many ways. There is the weekly meeting with every head of department. Oberoi Realty's

---

[10] Naazneen Karmali, 'Flying High', *Forbes*, 24 October 2012, https://www.forbes.com/sites/naazneenkarmali/2012/10/24/flyinghigh-vikas-oberoi-discusses-his-passion-for-planes/#61dd50972625.

departments fall into two buckets. At the front office are the departments of sales, engineering and design. The back-end, or the support function, includes the departments of human resource, finance and liaison.

Apart from these meetings, a whole host of reports is mailed to Vikas every day. This includes mail from the mall with details on footfalls, turnover of stores and even the number of bikes and cars that come in. From the hotel, the mail carries information on occupancy and revenues from room and restaurants. The school mail becomes important during admissions time.

The treasury department sends a mail on how the company's scrip has performed for the day. The sales team sends information on sale of flats, customer walk-ins and a detailed report on customer service, including scores on complaints and those resolved.

These reports are basic, but help Vikas get both a macro and micro view of the company's operations. He may not look at all of them every day, but asks his teams to keep sending him as many mails as they want.

Every year, in February and March, a business plan is prepared, giving a picture of the next one year. There is also planning for the longer term, say, for the next three or four years. Then there are the quarterly board meetings.

'During the meetings, he has this fantastic ability to zoom in, go very micro and get to the last level. And then simultaneously he zooms out and sees things from the 30,000-foot level. So if you are in a spot of bother, you can go to him and he will sit down with you and sort out things,' says Saumil. There is also the weekend review meeting, which was initially held in office, but now gets done over a buffet lunch in a restaurant.

Vikas is smart, 'too smart for all of us in the room put together,' says Saumil. Once, when the sales team was giving an aggressive forecast on sales for a project that was set for a launch, Vikas gave them a different number and said, 'You get me this number [in sales] and I will be happy.' Eventually, when the project was launched, the sales team sold as many flats as Vikas had expected them to. It helps that Vikas continues to have his ear to the ground, talking to developers and brokers, always receptive to a view and an idea, irrespective of whether it is coming from a big or a small broker. After all, years ago it was an unknown broker who led him to his biggest land deal.

If something, or someone, is missing in the organizational structure of Oberoi Realty, then that is a chief executive officer. Vikas 'almost hired' a professional in 2008, but called off the recruitment when the financial crisis broke the industry's back. 'That was a big mistake,' he rues. 'He was expensive, but we had the cash.'

In 2007, Vikas had taken over as the chairman of the company's board. A year later, he added the mantle of managing director to it. His father had handed over the reins of the company to Vikas. Ranvir passed away in 2016.

Vikas is now again looking for a CEO. He needs one because Oberoi Realty is now a big operation, and he needs someone to control the operations. 'My span of attention is that of a creator . . . what interests me is design. I can spend the entire day choosing material. But I'm a reluctant supervisor,' says Vikas.

He is looking for someone who is entrepreneurial. Though he has offered the job to some of his most senior associates, none has accepted. '"Let me be good at what I am doing," they tell me.' Vikas wants the CEO to also take on the mantle of a managing director.

'All the HoDs, heads of departments, will report to him. I will come in only when required, and in matters I am passionate about.'

Over the next few years, Vikas wants to take on the mantle of executive chairman. His strengths lie in conceptualizing and in bringing in the right people—architects and developers— and in thinking out of the box. He wants to make sure the company is going in the right direction, given the national and international context.

He has a vision for the company. In the coming years, Oberoi Realty will fortify its presence in the real estate industry, but in different ways. 'I want to be in the business of real estate—in any business that has a huge component of real estate . . . schools, hotels, hospitals, rental. All of this requires buying land, getting the designs done, getting the buildings done, and then putting in place the operations.'

These are activities the company has now mastered, and the model has already been successfully implemented in the case of Oberoi Garden City, with its school, mall and Westin hotel. 'All I had to do was to build them,' says Vikas.

He has built more real estate than any hospital chain, and will build more than any hotel chain too. At present Oberoi Realty is developing twenty million square feet of real estate. 'Today I have infinite energy to build. If I can build hospitals, residences, offices, malls and schools, why should I not do that,' he says.

As in the case of the mall, each of these segments makes for a good annuity business. As and when REITS (real estate investment trusts) take off in India, Vikas can park this part of the portfolio on the REIT platform, which is modelled after mutual funds. Investors in REITS are promised a regular income stream.

Vikas also broke convention by appointing Samsung C&T Corporation, one of the world's biggest engineering companies, as the general contractor for his company's high-rise project in Worli in 2011. 'It was path-breaking,' says Deepak Parekh. Usually real estate companies will outsource things like lighting, plumbing, design and landscaping for a project to different contractors. But with a general contractor, a single company does all of this. 'There are better safety standards, discipline and timeliness with a general contractor,' says Parekh.

While Oberoi Realty's business model sounds good, analysts have started wondering why land acquisition has dried up at the company, and why it is yet to start a project outside Mumbai. But Vikas is not in a hurry. 'We have plans in the NCR [National Capital Region], but are waiting for the right project and the right partner.'

And there is also the open offer from Deepak Parekh. 'The future of the housing sector is less of luxury and more of affordable homes ... I'm willing to back Vikas if he does affordable housing. We will fund him for land, construction, help in sales and give him loans. We only want him for identification of land and construction.'

Vikas is clearly in no hurry. 'People say greed is good. I don't think so. People say one has to be hungry. I don't think even that is good. Greed can make you do bad things. Hunger can make you desperate. Passion is the only thing that will never force you to cut corners for a result.'

That passion is what has brought him to where he is. And that's why he says, 'If I had to live my life all over again, I would love to do all this all over again.'

* * *

My Learnings

+ Think ahead.

There was no mall here. It would become a natural attraction for people to drive to this location. Even if this area was in the middle of nowhere earlier, now suddenly there would be things happening around the mall.

+ Don't obsess about money.

If you want to make good buildings, money will be a by-product. But if the intention is to make lots of money, then good buildings need not be a by-product.

+ Mistakes are good.

I learnt from those mistakes, that's why I'm here. Had my father, or we, not made those mistakes I would have been never been here.

+ Discipline matters.

I can actually say that I don't have a single project that is a ghost project. I don't have a single project in which I have not given occupation certificates to the customers, or a project which is complete but in which people are unable to stay because of regulatory issues. That was our discipline from the beginning.

+ Keep debt minimal.

So we don't choose debt as an option. Especially when you are building a company that should last its lifetime, and not your lifetime.

+ Live your product.

Hand on heart, every apartment I have built, irrespective of the financial status it reflects, I would be happy living in it.

+ Understand what is important.

A pilot is surrounded by around 100 metres. But he is not looking at all of them. He needs to know the destination, fuel, speed and elevation. The rest is data. That ability to split the data from the noise is extremely important.

+ Follow your passion.

People say greed is good. I don't think so. People say one has to be hungry. I don't think even that is good. Greed can make you do bad things. Hunger can make you desperate. Passion is the only thing that will never force you to cut corners for a result.

7

Priya Paul

There was nothing pleasant about the time Priya Paul joined Apeejay Surrendra Park Hotels, the family's hospitality business run by her father, Surrendra Paul, chairman of the Apeejay Surrendra Group, in 1988. The twenty-one-year-old had recently graduated from Wellesley College in Boston, where she had majored in economics. Priya was geared up to begin her apprenticeship in the financial services arm of the family business group, which also had interests in tea, shipping and real estate, and owned the iconic Flurys restaurant in Kolkata, too. But Surrendra instead asked her to join the Delhi property of Park Hotels as its marketing manager.

It was not the best of times for the hospitality industry. In Delhi, the sector was still reeling from the supply glut after the Asian Games of 1982. Many hotels, including the Centaur, had come up timed for the games. The Park hotel in Delhi was relatively new and had opened in 1987. It was the third property of the company after its flagship one in Kolkata, which opened in 1967, and the second one in Vizag, which opened a year later.

The Delhi Park was ideally located. It stood on Parliament Street, next to the shopping hub of Connaught Place and opposite the historic Jantar Mantar. But the occupancy levels were still low. Even the newness of the property, which had 220 rooms, didn't help. 'Just about seven–eight rooms were occupied the day I joined,' says Priya. 'It was a very challenging time. The first lesson was to go out there and get the business.'

The tariff was brought down to Rs 600—almost half of what it originally was. Still, there were few takers. 'No matter what you did and how much effort you put in, you still didn't have money to pay the bills,' says Priya. She would join the sales team on client meetings and learn how to make pitches. She worked with the public relations team, understanding the effective use of PR for marketing. And she learnt to hold events on a shoestring budget. 'These things helped me a lot later,' says Priya.

It was exactly as her father told her it would be: 'The fact that you've joined the industry when it's down will be your biggest learning. Recessions don't last forever, and neither do booms.'[1]

But the hard days were not going to get over anytime soon. Even as the business was difficult and Priya was beginning to get the hang of things, tragedy struck the family. Her youngest brother, Anand, died in a car crash in 1989. He was seventeen. The family hadn't even started to comprehend the loss, when tragedy struck again.

---

[1] Elizabeth Eapen, 'Priya Paul, the Makeover Artiste', Livemint.com, 20 October 2007, http://www.livemint.com/Leisure/TqbddkeZoOjFWduSGQ6HgI/Priya-Paul--The-makeover-artiste.html.

Surrendra had led the group's investment in tea. On 9 April 1990, he was touring one of the tea estates of his Assam Frontier Tea Ltd (which was later renamed Apeejay Tea) in Tinsukia, about 500 km from Assam's capital, Guwahati. He was on the way back, travelling with his general manager, when suspected militants belonging to the United Liberation Front for Assam, or ULFA, fired at them. Both were injured badly; Surrendra later succumbed to his injuries. He was fifty-four.

'Both were huge shocks,' says Priya. The two events transformed Priya, personally and professionally. She was the eldest of the three children; her sister Priti was just about to graduate, and her brother Karan, the youngest, still had two years of college left. The family rallied around, led by Priya's uncle, Jit Paul. He had always been someone whom everyone in the larger Paul family looked up to.

* * *

The Paul family hailed from Jalandhar, where Surrendra's father had a foundry, making steel buckets and farming equipment.[2] The four brothers—Stya, Jit, Swraj and Surrendra—joined their father in the business after completing their studies. The family later moved to Kolkata in 1951. Here the brothers built the Apeejay Group, which branched out into several businesses. In 1966, Swraj moved to the UK and built the hugely successful Caparo Group. Later, in 1996, he would be appointed a life peer by the Conservative Party.

---

[2] Wikipedia.com, https://en.wikipedia.org/wiki/Swraj_Paul,_Baron_Paul.

In 1987, the brothers agreed to divide the family assets. Jit, who didn't have children, and Surrendra decided to join hands and together drive the Apeejay Surrendra Group. Stya by then had moved to Delhi, where he oversaw the Apeejay Stya Group, best known for its schools.

Surrendra's untimely demise in 1990 was a terrible shock for the whole family. For his wife and her two daughters and son, Jit became the family anchor. Much to the surprise of everyone in the family and the larger business community, Jit made his sister-in-law and Surrendra's wife, Shirin Paul, the chairperson of the business group. It was a signal that the family members were supporting each other in their hour of grief.

It was decided that Priti, Priya's sister, would shift to London after her graduation and handle the shipping business from there. For Karan, the first priority was to complete his studies; that is what their father would have preferred. Jit and Shirin stayed on in Kolkata, keeping an overall eye on the group. Priya, who had been working at the Delhi hotel, was given the responsibility of all three hotels in the group. 'My responsibilities shot up suddenly and I went from handling one hotel to three [Kolkata, Vizag and Delhi]. To top it all, we had huge union problems. Moreover, the Indian economy was not growing significantly, and the hospitality industry hardly existed.'[3]

Clearly, it was a less-than-ideal time to take over the hospitality business, which continued to struggle. A year later, in 1991, the finance minister of the time, Manmohan Singh, backed by Prime Minister Narasimha Rao, would open up the

---

[3] Shradha Agarwal, 'She', *Telegraph*, 8 April 2013, https://www. telegraphindia.com/1130408/jsp/entertainment/story_16759222. jsp.

economy to foreign direct investment (FDI) and bring an end to the 'License Raj'. It was the kind of fillip that the hospitality industry needed, but it would take some years for the impact to show in the form of higher occupancy rates in hotels.

The five-star segment in the hospitality industry was dominated by three brands—the Taj Group, the Oberoi Group and the Kolkata-headquartered ITC Welcome Group. International names included Le Meridian and the Hyatt. While the Taj and ITC Welcome groups had scale, the much smaller Oberoi had made a name for its service and design.

The five-star segment accounted for 30 per cent of the total room availability[4] in the country. And, not surprisingly, the metros, especially Delhi and Mumbai, accounted for nearly 60 per cent of the market.

The Park at that time was a brand that didn't have a strong identity. Its three properties functioned as three separate companies. Functions like marketing, HR or finance were not standardized as there was no corporate headquarters. By 1990, two of the hotels were having problems with trade unions; their staff was ageing and had lost its mojo, so to speak, and the competition shined as more attractive and smarter in comparison.

Surrendra had understood these issues. He was in the middle of putting together a plan to bring all three properties under a single umbrella when he died. He also wanted to revamp Park, Kolkata. 'He had started the process,' says Priya. Now with her

[4] M.R. Dixit and S. Manikutty, The Park, Kolkata, 2001, http://www.theparkhotels.com/sites/default/files/case_study/iimcasestudy-ce5a9ca906f20c0_0.pdf.

father gone, it was Priya's responsibility to complete and execute
the plan Surrendra had envisioned.

The biggest and most important piece of the puzzle was
The Park, Kolkata. It had had a glorious start when it opened
its doors in Kolkata in 1967. While Jit had acquired the land
and conceptualized the hotel, Surrendra later took over the
daily operations of the business, expanding beyond Kolkata to
Vizag and Delhi.

The hotel was located on Park Street, the thoroughfare
popular in the 1970s and 1980s for its nightlife. The place is
home to India's first nightclub, Mocambo, which had opened in
1956. Then there were the popular Moulin Rouge and Trinca's,
clubs that made nightlife in Kolkata hip and colourful.

The Park Hotel made the most of its high-profile location
and its equally popular neighbours. It created a clientele among
the city's corporate honchos. Companies like Hindustan
Motors, the RPG Group, ITC and Bata were headquartered in
Kolkata. Park also found a following among films stars, including
Bollywood legends such as Raj Kapoor and Sanjeev Kumar.

But by the late 1980s the hotel had lost some of its sheen
and glamour.

A case study on the Kolkata hotel by IIM-Ahmedabad
said:[5] 'The standards of service declined. With the increasing
sickness of PSUs and the decline of industrial activities in the
Eastern belt, the business from corporate clients tended to
decline. Coupled with this, the hotel had to contend with aging
staff. New competitors entered, both in the five-star and other

---

[5] M.R. Dixit and S. Manikutty, The Park, Kolkata, 2001,
http://www.theparkhotels.com/sites/default/files/case_study/
iimcasestudy-ce5a9ca906f20c0_0.pdf.

segments, the most formidable among them being Taj Bengal belonging to the Taj Group. The future of the Park chain looked bleak.'

However, Priya had other plans. What worked in Priya's favour, and eventually for the Park, was that she was not a hotelier, because of which she asked questions. 'If you are not from the background and don't have a preconceived idea of what a hotel should be, sometimes you ask questions and the answers evolve. So I asked why hotels have to look the way they look, or behave the way they behave. Why can't we look at hotels in a different way.'

The first task was to get the human resources in order. She roped in Vijay Dewan as the resident manager of the Kolkata hotel. Vijay had completed a diploma in hotel management from the Oberoi School of Hotel Management and had done a seven-year stint in the Oberoi group, including as the food and beverage (F&B) manager in Srinagar and as the front office manager at the Oberoi property in Baghdad, Iraq.

For Delhi and Vizag, Priya made the most of the talent available within the group.

The more problematic HR issue was to do with the unions in Kolkata and Vizag. 'We had situations where we had people *gherao* us. Many things were happening in Kolkata that were not pleasant,' says Priya. The disagreement with unions centred on wages and salaries. Even as Priya, Vijay and the rest of the senior management started a protracted negotiation with the unions, additional steps were taken to make the organization more structured.

'There was no HR manual, no training,' says Priya. 'We were not a super-professionalized company.' While Surrendra had set up some processes and systems in Delhi, it was time to standardize them across the group's properties.

Priya stepped in to fine-tune the organizational structure by introducing new departments, including one for training. People were identified to head these departments. 'The focus was to get professionals who had a background of working with systems and processes so these could be replicated in Park,' says Vijay.

Training was introduced at several levels. New recruits were taken through a training manual; many a time Priya herself led these sessions. She also introduced a management trainee programme in the early 1990s to attract young talent. Young blood was desperately needed to energize the ageing staff in Kolkata and Vizag.

The old-timers were also trained, or rather retrained, especially after a voluntary retirement offer didn't get the response the management hoped for. Now the intention was to make these experienced hands as good at customer service as any of their peers in other contemporary hotels.

Priya frequently visited all the three properties to standardize processes and systems in order to bring in a semblance of a common vision. Many meetings were held between the top executives of the three properties, and manuals were exchanged. Later, these manuals were converted into standardized processes.

By 1994–1995, the union problem was resolved. It was not just that there was agreement on wages and salaries. 'Once we brought in systems and processes, it created an engagement level among employees. The training also helped. Now the employees could see a future for themselves in the company,' says Vijay.

Once a core team was in place in each of the hotels and systems and processes were beginning to get formalized, Priya brought in her first vision statement for the company. As Vijay remarks, it was the 'defining moment for Park Hotels'.

During her travels to New York, Priya developed a fascination for the Royalton Hotel, which had opened in 1898 as a posh residential hotel. In 1988 it reopened and quickly built a reputation for being among the coolest hotels in town. The man behind the revamped Royalton was Ian Schrager, who, a decade earlier, had opened Studio54, the hub of the disco dancing generation of the 1970s. His first hotel, Morgans, opened in 1984, introducing for the first time the concept of a boutique hotel. The Royalton took the concept a step further; it was designed in such a way that it attracted the business class and also the 'cheap chic' of New York.

Looking at the success of the concept in New York, Priya realized it was something she could take inspiration from for India. 'I saw how he was doing hotels in a different manner, and that you didn't have to have a grand hotel . . . And I was very excited by that. It let me be very creative and use high design to set our hotels apart,' she told *HOTELS* magazine.[6]

She had already seen the impact design can have on business when she renovated Zen, the Oriental cuisine restaurant in Park, Kolkata in 1992. It was the first time that a restaurant in the city offered seven different Asian cuisines—Thai, Hong Kong, Singapore, Indonesian, Chinese, Malaysian and Japanese—

6 Adam Kirby, *HOTELS*, http://library.hotelsmag.com/publication/? i=84202&article_id=853082&view=articleBrowser&ver=html5#{"is sue_id":84202,"view":"articleBrowser","article_id":"853082"}

under one roof. 'We[7] gave it a fresh black-and-white Oriental design. Design was used to differentiate our products and services.'

The response to Zen's new look convinced Priya that design was a good differentiator that would set her properties apart from the competition. Her belief was vindicated when she saw the success of the Royalton Hotel in New York. Priya now knew how she wanted Apeejay Surrendra Park Hotels to evolve as a brand.

'Her vision was to create leadership through differentiation. The mission of the company was to establish a collection of boutique hotels and set global standards of service excellence,' says Vijay. 'As we progressed, we created a new focus on design. And design was used by Priya to create this differentiation.'

The focus was also to create experience for customers. 'We did this by using entertainment. We determined that customers come to the hotel not just for business but also to have fun, socialize and meet people. Considering that, we created great entertainment spaces,' says Vijay.

Like Zen, another restaurant at Park, Kolkata, Sujata, which served Indian cuisine, was redone and renamed Saffron. Another addition that soon became a hot favourite among the well-heeled in Kolkata was the Atrium Cafe, touted as the city's 'hottest round-the-clock coffee shop with sky-lift ambience and fountains.'[8] Its collection of coffees of twenty-five different

---

[7] 'She', *Telegraph*, 1 March 2013, https://www.telegraphindia.com/1130301/jsp/entertainment/story_16618033.jsp.

[8] 'Food', Indiatoday.in, 3 December 1993, http://indiatoday.intoday.in/story/the-atrium-cafe-at-park-hotel-in-calcutta-is-worth-a-visit/1/303669.html.

varieties was said to be the largest for any hotel in the country. Curiosity among customers also increased when word spread that the cafe had a plasma TV, the first of its kind, hung on its wall.

The most talked about opening was that of Someplace Else, the British-styled pub that opened in 1994 and immediately became the most sought-after drinking place in the city. While its liquor menu was extensive and helped create a clientele, the pub also focused on entertainment, the cornerstone of any boutique hotel. Over the years, it created a reputation for hosting some of the popular bands of the time such as Parikrama, Indian Ocean, Them Clones and Perestroika. The pub also had open mic sessions, and would later play host to events like Kolkata Autumn Music Festival and Kingfisher Pub Rock Fest.

Later, in 1999, came Tantra. Spread over 5000 square feet on two levels, Tantra became the centre of nightlife in Kolkata. The nightclub had two bars, a dance floor and a hangout area called The Santra Room. While the ground floor was open to the public, the mezzanine level was exclusive for members, the 'mature clubbers' who could choose from a stock of single malts and the finest cigars.

Just like Someplace Else, Tantra too hosted events that brought in the crowd and increased the decibel levels. Fashion shows featuring designers like Prasad Bidappa and Ritu Kumar, and stars like Katrina Kaif and Deepika Padukone were held. The club, designed by renowned American designer Carl Ettensperger, also hosted the likes of Ricky Martin and Melanie Griffith.

While these initiatives made The Park, Kolkata, a favourite hangout for entertainment, Priya also brought in designers to redo the rooms. For the first time for an Indian hotel, rooms in The Park, Kolkata were fitted with fax and Jacuzzi. These facilities were provided in the deluxe suites and rooms that were on an exclusive floor called The Residence. Guests on this floor were also given their own personal music system and video cassette player. Later, these opulent rooms would get computers with high-speed Internet connectivity.

In terms of customer service, the processes were tweaked keeping in mind that the hotel was now promoting itself as a boutique hotel. This meant that the staff was less formal with guests, and that services were customized—features that have now become the norm at most hotels.

'We tackled a lot of things differently,' says Vijay. 'From the time a customer arrives at the hotel and up to the time he checks out, many activities are performed. When you are able to do these more efficiently, we create a cost advantage. If you do these activities differently, then it creates a different kind of advantage.'

The differentiation can sometimes come in very subtle forms. A guest at The Park would go back to his room in the night to find a personalized goodnight note written by the staff. And on his table would also be a bowl of soaked almonds, to be eaten in the morning.

When it came to check-in, the focus was not just on making the whole process a shorter ritual for guests, but also to make it entertaining. 'We started giving guests welcome shots, which could be a cocktail or a mocktail, something interesting,' says Vijay. So while the new processes and systems made checking in smooth and short for guests, the 'shots' brought in the differentiation.

'We had to keep two things in mind. First we had to get the process right and then align the process with a different activity, promoting the company's vision to be a leader by differentiation,' says Vijay, who was elevated to the post of managing director in 2000.

To make customized service a standard process, information technology was employed. The front-end and the back-end were now linked by a software. If a guest was staying at The Park for the first time, all his details—his address, his tastes and preferences regarding food, his wake-up call orders—were saved. The next time the same guest checked in, 'the front desk, housekeeping and room service were alerted about his/ her past history through an "expected arrival report" so that the right questions could be asked confirming the guest's preferences, for example for rooms. This quite often pleasantly surprised the guests. The housemen were also informed about the preferences.'[9]

There were also processes to record complaints, to make sure they were followed up, and to ensure that immediate steps were taken to address them. The management wanted to make sure the same customer didn't face the same problem again in his future visits. The hotel also saved costs by introducing a software for inventory management and to regulate supply for its kitchens. A software by Prologic, which provides solutions for materials management, was used. A software was used to ease online booking too. Later, all the three hotels were integrated into the system.

---

[9] M.R. Dixit and S. Manikutty, The Park, Kolkata, 2001, http://www.theparkhotels.com/sites/default/files/case_study/iimcasestudy-ce5a9ca906f20c0_0.pdf.

Through all these developments and initiatives, there was a continued focus on training. The management trainee programme was scaled up in the 1990s. Aspiring hotel employees were given three years of training and experience in all the critical departments. At the end of this period, the best of them were absorbed by the company.

HR initiatives also included a survey to gauge employee satisfaction. There had been some unhappiness among the staff about the salary structure, following which it was altered. It now matched or was even better than some of the industry peers.

Training was a must for the seniors too. In 1995, Priya encouraged Vijay to go to Cornell·University to do a programme for general managers. Later, in 1997, he went to London School of Business and in 2002 to Harvard to do professional courses. After realizing the importance of these courses in his first educational trip in 1995, Vijay made sure the programme was extended to other colleagues. 'I was sent to the best institute possible. It helps because you are aligned to the latest in hospitality.'

Since 1996, The Park sends five to ten employees—ranging from young executives to heads of departments and general managers—every year to leading overseas institutes, especially Cornell University, to study the latest in hospitality.

'While these courses help to bring them [the employees] in line with what is happening in the world, this also sets them up for success,' says Vijay. 'This is a people industry, and eventually success is created by them. Learning is motivational, and creates a high level of engagement among employees. This translates into engaged customers, which eventually shows in the top line and bottom line of the company.'

The year saw another huge achievement for the hotel. In July 1999, the ministry of tourism upgraded The Park, Kolkata, from five-star to five-star deluxe, bringing it on par with Taj Bengal (of Indian Hotels Company) and Oberoi's property in the city.

A year later, there was international recognition from Small Luxury Hotels of the World, which bestowed membership to The Park. The organization, currently consisting of over 500 hotels, provides its clients an exclusive network of small hotels around the world. By becoming a member here, The Park now could broaden its customer base.

In 2001, two professors from IIM-Ahmedabad, the country's top management institute, authored a case study on the turnaround of The Park, Kolkata. Two years earlier, Prof. S. Manikutty from the institute had attended a seminar hosted at the hotel, and returned impressed with the property, its design and service. He approached the management with a proposal to do a case study on the hotel. After the case study came out in 2001, the turnaround of the hotel became official, validated by a trusted academician.

'We had started the renovation in the post-liberalization era. The economy was doing better and people were beginning to spend. At the Park, we were able to capture this new money, and also the new trend of going out for entertainment,' says Priya. 'We pioneered international concepts and created hotels as entertainment centres. No one was doing that,' she says.

It was a proud achievement for Priya, who, as a child, would wander around the back offices of the hotel in Kolkata, visiting the kitchens, savouring the buffet spread for lunch and following her father to meetings.

In Love with Design

By the time she was ten, Priya knew she wanted to be in business—not necessarily the hotel business, but business in general. There were a few factors that influenced her young, impressionable mind.

One was the Paul family. 'We were a different business family. Dad would not just involve us [the women] in the decision-making, but would also involve us at the managerial level,' says Priya. Her mother, Shirin, who was working before she got married, ran Flurys—the family's legendary breakfast place in Kolkata, a must-visit place for any traveller to the city—for about a decade. 'So it was not that we hadn't seen women in authority,' says Priya.

The young Priya also loved to visit the sites, offices and hotels run by the family. Surrendra would take her to the factories, including the steel plant that he oversaw. She would accompany him to The Park hotel. And many a time after school, Priya would hang around her father's office, watching him at work. During vacations, Surrendra would give her assignments that would turn into her summer internships.

Her uncle, Jit, was also a big influence. He was the head of the family and had founded many businesses for the group, including shipping and real estate. Though not highly educated (he quit school after matriculation), Jit was valued among Kolkata's business community for his advice and foresight. For many, he was the lender at last resort.[10] 'He was a strong person,' says Priya.

---

[10] Manish Basu, 'Three Years after Jit Paul's Death, His Estate May Face a Legal Battle', Livemint.com, 23 July 2012, http://www.livemint.com/Home-Page/ZPIVaE9JadSlBq8qRTkrdL/Three-years-after-Jit-Pauls-death-his-estate-may-face-a-le.html.

Such was the atmosphere at home that Priya, as a young girl, was sure where her future lay. 'I wanted to be in business. I was clear that that was what I wanted to do,' says Priya. The only thing that wasn't clear yet was what type of business.

Priya also had the aptitude to take on responsibilities, and to coordinate their execution. At school she was 'quite an average' student till the seventh grade. But her geography teacher, Vijaya Bisht, saw a spark in her and spurred her on. After the eighth grade, Priya was usually among the top two in class. After completing the tenth grade at Loreto House, where she was head girl, she moved to La Martiniere. She did well there too. Though a new student, she won a medal for good conduct. 'I always had leadership and managerial roles in school,' she says.

Her managerial skills were on display at the drama society. She was the producer in her theatre group, having realized that her skills were not in front of the audience ('I was a hopeless actor,' she says), but behind the wings. She would manage a lot of the work in creating a play, including putting together the costumes, marketing the play, creating brochures and selling tickets. Her friends included Suhel Seth, now a marketing consultant, and Barry O'Brien, the well-known quiz-master. 'We did plays like *The Night of January 16th*, written by Ayn Rand, and Shakespeare's *Richard the Third*.'

Kolkata and its rich heritage in arts also moulded Priya's own interest in sculpture, painting, design and architecture. As a family, the Pauls would explore Santiniketan, home to Visva-Bharati University and synonymous with Rabindranath Tagore. On their visits overseas, Priya would explore the museums with her siblings and parents. 'When you grow up in Kolkata, you get exposed to art,' says Priya.

Her horizons further broadened in the four years she spent at Wellesley College in Boston. 'It was a liberal arts college. I was able to explore varied subjects, from art and archaeology to astronomy and even computer coding. It suited me fine . . . The course was reflective of my varied interests in art,' says Priya. She also spent one semester in Paris, the world's fashion capital, adding one more layer to her love for design.

Years later, in the 1990s, as she worked to turn around The Park, Priya found in her project a natural extension of her love of art. She was playing on her strength when she adopted the boutique hotel concept for her company. No two hotels of The Park would be similar, but they would all reflect a fusion of cutting-edge contemporary design and local art tradition.

While she had used this approach to redo The Park, Kolkata, a bigger opportunity came up in Bengaluru in 2000, when she bought a four-star property with 109 rooms. This was her first buy after taking over The Park, and Priya was uncompromising on design. She appointed Conran and Partners as the designers. The London-based design studio was founded by the legendary Terence Conran, a designer, restaurateur and retailer. His repute grew with his very first restaurant, The Soup Kitchen.

'In Bengaluru we had the opportunity to present the brand in one go and launch the product. And we decided to use international designers,' says Priya. 'We wanted to do a proper contemporary hotel and signal that the brand is out there . . . the Bengaluru hotel was path-breaking,' she says.

Priya, who got introduced to Conran through a family friend, decided to redo the whole hotel. When it was done, the white four-storeyed building was a trendsetting addition to the Indian hospitality industry. Themed after information technology—as it was located in India's IT capital—each of the rooms had an international influence, but with an ethnic touch. The lifts had black leather, and each floor was done in a different tone of colour—the first was aqua, the second was dominated by lime and the third red. The fourth was the most luxurious of all and was done up in silk, wood and leather. The Indian influence was subtle, but added to the ambience; it included the black column in the lobby that had a deep ethnic influence.

'It created a sensation in the market,' says Vijay. And it brought international recognition. The hotel was featured in *Harper's*, and in 2003 was rated among the 101 best hotels in the world by the *Tatler* magazine, which brings out a hotel guide every year. The Park hotel was ranked alongside global brands such as Four Seasons, New York, The Ritz, London, and Park Hyatt, Tokyo.

The success of the new property prompted Priya to hire Conran & Partners for renovation of the Park hotels in New Delhi and Kolkata. The admiration was mutual. 'Priya is a bundle of energy and a detail-maniac. It's good for our designers to work with someone like her as they tend to learn so much more,'[11] says Terence Conran.

One of his architects who worked in all the Park projects was Robert Malcolm. In a book, *The Fundamentals of Design*, he writes, 'There is a Park Hotels spirit which is translated not copied, in each property. Key to this is the vision of Ms Paul, who sends her designers off into new territories, creating challenges

[11] Naazneen Karmali, 'India's Funky Boutique Hotels', *Forbes*, 28 March 2012, https://www.forbes.com/global/2012/0409/feature-life-priya-paul-hotel-education-ian-schrager-indian-style.html.

and questioning received wisdom as to what is and what is not suitable in hotel design.'[12]

Priya's eye for detail was evident again in her next expansion, which was further down south in Chennai. In 2001, she bought what were the erstwhile premises of the famous Gemini Studios which, till the 1980s, had dominated Tamil cinema. Before coming into the Park fold, the premises had two buildings. One, a three-star hotel, was sold to The Park, and the other was later auctioned to Indian Bank. Centrally located, next to the landmark Gemini flyover, Priya made Chennai Park another example of her boutique hotel concept.

Among the designers was a firm from California. After providing the firm a brief, Priya, along with Vijay and another Park official, flew to the US for a presentation by the firm's design team. The presentation didn't go well. In fact, Priya 'got mad'.

'This is not the brief I gave you. I gave you the scope and even sent reference pictures . . . I need it to be more contemporary. I'm sorry, but you have deeply disappointed me,' she told the design team, which was quite shocked. She told them she had planned to stay in California for four days, but after the presentation she was now tempted to fly back the same day.

Chastised, the design team asked for a day's time to come up with another plan. Priya agreed. The three returned the next

---

[12] Robert Malcolm, in a book by Kathryn Best, *The Fundamentals of Design*, https://books.google.co.in/books?id=cFU3DQAAQBAJ&pg=PA160&lpg=PA160&dq=The+Park+bangalore+design+Priya+Paul+conran&source=bl&ots=68FEA4JnSe&sig=KPEkD0Lylc-q1isuC5PNccLwrog&hl=en&sa=X&ved=0ahUKEwjV26n27vHUAhUMLo8KHch8ASs4ChDoAQg9MAc#v=onepage&q=The%20Park%20bangalore%20design%20Priya%20Paul%20conran&f=false.

evening. This time the presentation had some ideas that could be worked on. For the next three days Priya and her team stayed on in the office and worked with the design firm—they didn't even step out for food and just ordered in. By the time Priya caught the flight back to Delhi, 80 per cent of the design work for the Chennai hotel was ready. 'You just couldn't take Priya for granted. She was sharp and knew what she wanted,' says a close associate.

In keeping with its link to the film world, the Park Chennai was modelled around the theme of cinema. Film posters adorned the walls, and an artwork of welcoming lotuses made for a dramatic entrance to the hotel. A spectacle of sound, light and projections transformed the atrium in the night. 'The key element in the rooms was the glass that was used to separate the bath space from the room,' says Vijay. The bathrooms had glass basins and rain/massage showers, a novelty at the time.

While the hotel opened to rave reviews in Chennai, there is also another reason why the property is so close to Priya's heart. She met her husband, Chennai-based businessman Sethu Vaidyanathan, while working on the hotel. The couple married in 2004 and have a son, Surya Vir.

By 2000, the company's revenues were growing steadily. After a workshop in 2001—the company had revenues of about Rs 50 crore at the time—Priya exhorted her top management to double its revenues within two years; The Park Hotels achieved this in 2003–04. Another high came in 2007, when the top line crossed the Rs 300-crore mark. The company reported profits of Rs 150 crore and EBITDA (earnings before interest, tax, depreciation and amortization) of Rs 130 crore.

The hospitality industry was doing well, backed by a fast-growing economy. Indian companies were making billion-dollar acquisitions overseas, and investment from overseas investors was also increasing. These years were marked by the entry of new hotel brands, especially in the budget segment. In 2002, Patu Keswani, a hospitality veteran, founded Lemon Tree Hotels. And Indian Hotels' Ginger opened its first hotel in 2004. The new brands were aggressive, expanded fast across the country and marketed themselves unabashedly.

In 2007, even as Priya was working on her first 'organic hotel' in Hyderabad, she and her brother, Karan Paul, diluted the family's 15 per cent stake in Park Hotels to bring in global financial giant Credit Suisse as investor. Priya said, 'We have run a very successful hospitality business for over forty years and our hotels are industry leaders in innovation and design. This infusion of capital will be a catalyst, enabling us to expand our footprint throughout the region.'[13]

'The Credit Suisse investment helped us to buy land. We acquired property in Pune, and land parcels in Kolkata and Jaipur. Now we are developing these properties,' Vijay added. The investment by the financial giant was worth $55 million.

The opening of The Park, Hyderabad, in 2010 should have been a new high for Priya, despite its delay by about two years. This was the first hotel she had built; all the others were either inherited or bought in shell form. But it was not to be.

---

[13] 'Park Hotels Raises $55m Equity from Credit Suisse', Livemint.com, 10 July 2007, http://www.livemint.com/Money/z2BT8bOfvFrSsnVUy9DLeN/Park-Hotels-raises-55mn-equity-from-Credit-Suisse.html.

The opening was badly timed. The Telangana agitation for a separate state was on and Hyderabad was marred with protests and violence. And it didn't help that the national economy, mirroring the financial crisis globally, was trying hard to keep up its earlier pace of growth. While the GDP grew by over 8 per cent in 2009 and 2010, it slowed down later in 2011, growing only by 6.5 per cent.

The Hyderabad hotel was big and ambitious, by The Park standards. Its six floors had 270 rooms, and Priya didn't leave a single stone unturned in making it a design icon. 'It is the plushest of all Park hotels. Never had so many designers worked on one hotel,' says Ranvir Shah, a Chennai-based businessman, cultural catalyst and Priya's close friend.

Adds Vijay, 'Park Hyderabad is a remarkable contribution to the hospitality business in India. Over a dozen designers were employed. Usually you have one architect also designing, or you have one architect and one designer. Here there was one architect and many designers involved in doing the public spaces and suites. Many local artisans worked alongside. Priya brought all of them together. Local art and culture is dear to Priya.' She used a combination of fashion and textile designers and local artisans to create the product.

The hotel's facade took a leaf out of the metal work found in the Nizam's jewellery collection. The property boasted a three-dimensional pool, 'in which swimmers can enjoy elegant surroundings while diners and club goers beneath can peek into its watery depths through fragmented windows. The hotel has two lobbies. The first one at the entrance is the "street lobby", and the main one is on the third floor. Each of the five floors has a unique "gem" colour. Put together, The Park Hyderabad is, quite simply, an unparalleled luxury destination,'[14] says the website of Design Hotels, a firm that markets an exclusive network of 260 handpicked hotels in over fifty countries and helps these properties in their communications strategy, going beyond traditional tourism marketing. All the Park hotels are part of the Design Hotels network.

The 'lushness' of the hotel made it the obvious choice when it came to hosting the centenary celebration of the Apeejay Surrendra Group in 2010. There were concerts by well-known Indian and overseas stars and heritage walks in Hyderabad led by writer and historian William Dalrymple. Priya was at hand to personally attend to the 600 guests, who were greatly awed by this new hotel.

The main building was done by Australia's Skidmore Owings & Merrill, which had also designed the Burj Khalifa in Dubai. The all-day diner was designed by Conran & Partners; the Andhra restaurant, Aish, had touches of fashion designer Tarun Tahiliani; and his fellow designers like Rohit Bal, Manish Arora, artists Bharati Kher and Subodh Gupta, and textile designer Jean Francois Lesage had worked on the suites.

The grandness of the hotel meant that a lot of money went into building it. And now the weak economy was not helping it meet its costs. The hotel piled up a debt of Rs 400 crore. The investment wasn't followed by the expected level of occupancy, as Hyderabad's reputation as an IT hub and business centre took a beating with the economic downturn.

---

[14] The Park Hyderabad, Design Hotels, https://www.designhotels. com/hotels/india/hyderabad/the-park-hyderabad.

'But the financial aspect is just one way of looking at it. Priya created a new standard. And it highlighted her love and passion for art. The Park hotels, put together, probably have one of the largest collections of art in the country. It is Priya's contribution,' says Vijay.

* * *

Priya's passion for art is best represented by her patronship of The New Festival, which is driven by her friend from Chennai, Ranvir Shah. Ranvir first met Priya when she was building the Chennai property. 'At that time, I was co-running The Other Festival,' says Ranvir. After a chat with him, Priya said she was interested in knowing more and asked Ranvir to meet her in Delhi with a proposal.

The proposal worked, and Priya started supporting (with a Rs 3 lakh annual grant) The Other Festival, which aimed at showcasing new and emerging artists from India and overseas across art forms, including music, dance, drama and painting. Later, when Ranvir separated from his partner in The Other Festival and started The New Festival in 2007, Priya continued to support him.

The festival originated in Chennai, and over the last few years has become a travelling festival, with stops at Kolkata, Hyderabad, Bengaluru, Delhi and Mumbai. In each city, The Park hotel hosts the traveling troupe, the shows and the workshops.

'It is the only private festival that goes national. The festival has come to stay,' says Ranvir. 'Priya gives money [the grant has consistently increased over the years] and doesn't interfere, which is a big thing. Everybody wants to become a part of the festival. But she tells them to contact me "because he takes the decisions". I think for someone who is a patron, it is very easy to want to dabble . . . and have her own agenda. But all these years, she has never done that, never once tried to influence matters,' says Ranvir.

The patronage continued even in difficult years. 'I know that the hotel industry goes through strain. And she does get asked about her support to the festival. But she understands that this builds the company's brand. No amount of advertisement can compare with the exposure the properties get through the festival. She is very clever. And that's her differentiator. She is not doing it because I am a friend,' says Ranvir.

At the end of each edition of the festival, Ranvir meets Priya in Delhi for a review. Priya gets feedback from her staff and close associates, and if something has not worked, conveys it to Ranvir. 'That is the only time when she is involved. Otherwise, she has given me a free hand,' says Ranvir, who runs multiple business, including a restaurant in Chennai.

It will be difficult to say that Priya follows the same style when it comes to managing her hotels. Given the circumstances in which she had to take over at the helm of the company and the subsequent turnaround of its hotels, Priya has been extensively and deeply involved in each of the verticals. This helped her keep a close tab on what's happening even as she added more properties.

Asked[15] if it's true that she chooses every fork bought at The Park, Priya replies: 'Yes it's very true! I am actually involved in all

---

[15] Shradha Agarwal, 'She', *Telegraph*, 08 April 2013, https://www.telegraphindia.com/1130408/jsp/entertainment/story_16759222.jsp.

the decision-making, what goes on in every little bit. I am always on the lookout for new things. And good designs that work are more long-term. For instance, if it's a great set of cutlery we've been using, we are happy to repeat it. So it's true that there is a lot of me in every hotel of ours. I am not a hotelier, artist or designer, but my worlds all intersect at The Park.' In another interview, she admitted that she signed her approval for every bathroom hook.

But this depth of involvement has made her as sharp as anyone when it comes to different parts of the business. In the matter of food, for example, Priya is a self-confessed foodie and a cook, with a degree from Le Cordon Bleu, the world's largest hospitality education institute based in Paris. From her childhood she has been writing and maintaining diaries of recipes and continues to devour cookery books. This passion helps her know the salt and pepper of the food business.

'Once I was with her at The Park, Chennai. And we were waiting for Sethu (Priya's husband),' says Ranvir. 'Sethu got late and we ordered some food. It was pasta. When it arrived Priya instantly knew that there was more meat in it than was required. She inquired with her staff and discussed the dish. She knew the breakdown of the entire recipe by heart, including how many grams of pasta and meat should go into the dish,' Ranvir says.

If she didn't know something, Priya educated herself on it. 'I strongly believe education is a constant thing and you need to renew yourself. I knew nothing about finance so I learnt finance for non-finance managers,' says Priya. She completed the Owner/President Management course in Harvard in 1999. 'That was very useful. I had been working for some time, and had implemented a lot of things, but I needed to know more.

Harvard had great professors and people to talk to. I could validate my business plans, vision and mission statements with them. Till then, I was doing a lot of things by instinct,' says Priya.

She might remain well entrenched in running the business, but with Vijay as the MD of the company, Priya chooses what she wants to focus on. While Vijay handles the day-to-day operations of the company, Priya focuses on new properties, ongoing projects and the company's future path.

She keeps a tab on operations through review meetings and reports that her team mails her daily and monthly. These reports give her the numbers on sales and daily performance of the hotels and their restaurants. Priya conducts a quarterly meeting with the general managers of the hotels. 'I do more project reviews. I also sit in meetings during March–May when we are planning the year ahead. I can drill down to as much detail as I want,' she says. For instance, when the interview for this profile was being done, Priya was debating how a cup of coffee at her restaurants should be priced.

And she continues to ask questions. 'Sometimes you see something and you ask, why are we doing this? For the last three months, as we are renovating our hotels, I have been asking the team—and none has given me an answer—why we need to have three phones in a room. In this day and age, when people don't use fixed line phones, why do we need three phones in a 350-square-foot room?'

Priya has also questioned The Park's business model itself. While some of her peers raced ahead in the numbers game, she was building one hotel a year. 'If you use your own money, it slows you down,' says Priya. While the Credit Suisse investment brought in extra funds, she also had to change the development model. Most of the hotel chains in India and overseas were no longer following the traditional model of building hotels—buying land and then constructing the building. That slowed down expansion. Instead, most of the hotel companies were adopting the management model.

In this model, a hotel chain ties up with an investor (individual businessman or company) who owns a piece of land. The hotel chain helps build the property and then manages the hotel for the investor for an annual fee.

Priya now wanted to do the same. 'She felt that to expand, we needed to get into hotel management, which is the way to grow faster in hospitality,' says Vijay. 'More than that, there was a vacuum in tier 2–tier 3 cities for design-driven, socially engaging products in the market. There were brands, but not inspiring enough for the new India. Priya wanted to fill this gap and create a product aligned to the new India,' he adds.

In 2013, Priya unveiled Zone by The Park, her company's foray into the four-star, mid-market segment. While these hotels are cookie-cutter versions of their five-star Park cousins, Zone hotels haven't completely shed the design component. Zone too has the fusion of modern design and local cultural influences, but the emphasis is more on keeping things smart rather than opulent. Its website says: 'Smart rooms combine new-age technology with distinctive design, smart storage spaces and multifunctional furniture.'

The first Zone opened in Coimbatore in 2015. The fifty-six-room hotel has a customized auto-rickshaw that services coffee and snacks. Priya roped in UK-based architecture firm Project Orange for the Zone property. At present there are Zone hotels in Chennai, Jaipur, Jodhpur and Raipur. 'We are opening three more properties in the next few months,' Priya said in May 2017. 'So that is seven openings in two-and-a-half years. So our speed [of opening new properties] has improved. It's [Zone is] the easier thing to do. If everything is Park, it takes a lot of time and effort. If it's Park, then there is more of me involved with the look and design.'

The management model also means that The Park is not burdened with debt as it increases its development pace. 'We have to grow in a way that we don't over-leverage ourselves,' says Vijay. The hotel company has a debt-equity ratio of 0.6:1. 'We are much better than many of our hospitality peers. In principle, we don't exceed a debt-equity ratio of 0.7:1,' he adds.

Vijay talks about an aggressive growth path for the coming years. 'Overall, we have twelve properties operating. Four, or even five, more will be opening this year,' he says. The new openings include the ambitious Park property in Mumbai. It will be Priya's first hotel in the city. She opened a hotel in Belapur, Navi Mumbai, in 2007.

In 2010, she set a vision of having fifty hotels by 2020. 'We are quite ahead of schedule on that. There are a lot of properties in the pipeline,' says Vijay. The pipeline includes seventeen Zone hotels by 2020. The management model has been extended to the flagship Park brand of hotels too. 'The three upcoming Park hotels—in Mumbai, Indore and Jaipur—will be done through management contracts,' says Priya.

Even as she expands, Priya is continuously renovating her existing properties. Her hotels in Delhi and Kolkata have gone through renovations, and have new designs, new art work and new restaurants. 'The hospitality industry is cyclical. And one needs a lot of capital reinvestment as technology, a big part of the industry, keeps changing,' says the entrepreneur. 'Hotels are full of technology, and you have to keep evolving. You will have a 40-inch TV in your rooms, but then your competition has 50-inch TVs. Where do you stop? Now there are iPads to control room lighting and air-conditioning.' There is the continued investment in machinery for the back-end operations too.

Priya seems to have found a good balance in her business model after venturing into the management mode; so much so that she admits there is a 'lot of scope' in the budget segment of the industry too. 'Budget hotels as a chain hasn't happened enough in India. I don't know about the future . . .' she says, her voice trailing off. But she stresses that budget hotels need a different kind of approach to hospitality, requiring a separate set of teams. Her hotel management school, which she opened in 2007 at the Navi Mumbai hotel, doesn't cater to that segment as of now. But who knows about the future.

On the family front, the Apeejay Surrendra Group has found a leader in Karan, who is now the chairman. Shirin, their mother, has taken the role of chairperson emeritus. Though uncle Jit Paul's demise in 2009 set off a legal tussle over his will (Stya Paul's daughter has challenged it), Priya and her siblings have cemented their relationship by forming a family shareholding agreement. A group management committee, including the three siblings, evaluates the various businesses and decides on investments. There is equal shareholding among the siblings. While Priya sits on the board of the shipping company, Karan is a director in Park Hotels. 'There is a balance between all the businesses,' says Priya. If one business is not doing well and needs capital, then another group business curtails its investment plans.

'She is lucky to have them,' says her husband Sethu of her family. 'She could do what she wanted to.'

A 2015 news report[16] put the group turnover at Rs 6,000 crore. The hotels, vertical, which was valued at half a billion dollars in 2007 when Credit Suisse invested (the company had a top line of Rs 300 crore) has seen its revenues cross the Rs 500-crore mark. With the Zone push and the increasing focus on the management model, the top line and the bottom line are expected to grow faster.

Not surprisingly, Priya, who turned 50 in 2016, has been thinking about retirement. Though the 2012 Padma Shri winner emphasizes that 'retirement is too strong a word', she adds: 'I also think that one shouldn't be doing the same thing for ever. It means reconfiguring my life and my space and how I run the business. And how the business should be run in the next ten years.

'Every business has to evolve, as this has evolved in the last twenty-five years. Businesses are changing, hospitality is changing. You have to start preparing yourself. I will not be around forever. And I don't want to. Don't think that's good for business.' Priya stresses that the business has to be prepared even as the next generation takes over in the next fifteen years.

With a twelve-year-old at home, Priya now works both out of her office in Connaught Place and out of her home office. 'I don't go by hours. The home office helps, if I have to work at night,' she says. 'Her working style is very different from those

---

[16] Elizabeth Kuruvilla, Business Lounge with Priti Paul, Livemint.com, 09 May 2015, http://www.livemint.com/Leisure/hLmCe3jo5Z8ebW06Dt8RoL/Business-Lounge-with-Priti-Paul.html.

of other people I have seen,' says Sethu. 'You meet Priya and you might think she doesn't work,' he adds.

It is evening now, and outside her home on the lawn her son is playing badminton. Even as Priya talks about taking her son for a swim and spending the rest of the day with him, she gets a call and begins chatting about a design presentation that didn't go as well as she had expected. 'I was looking at the design for a new hotel. Finally, after an hour I said it's [the design] beautiful but this is not our hotel, this is not Park. I was blunt . . .'

Surely, retirement doesn't mean that Priya will stop following her passion.

* * *

My Learnings

+   Expect the unexpected.

    The responsibilities shot up suddenly and I went from one hotel to handling three [Kolkata, Vizag and Delhi]. To top it all, we had huge union problems and the Indian economy was not growing significantly and the hospitality industry hardly existed.[17]

+   Ask questions.

    If you are not from the background and don't have a preconceived idea of what a hotel should be, sometimes you ask questions and the answers evolve.

[17] Shradha Agarwal, 'She', *Telegraph*, 08 April 2013, https://www.telegraphindia.com/1130408/jsp/entertainment/story_16759222.jsp.

+ Keep educating yourself.

I strongly believe education is a constant thing and you need to renew yourself. I knew nothing about finance so I learnt finance for non-finance managers.

+ Think ahead.

I also think that one shouldn't be doing the same thing for ever. It means reconfiguring my life and my space and how I run the business. And how the business should be run in the next ten years.

Acknowledgements

I can't thank enough each of the entrepreneurs profiled here for their valuable time and for indulging me. The sessions were long and the questions, innumerable. Thanks for your patience.

My gratitude to their teams for helping me coordinate the meetings.

Over these months, I was fortunate to meet accomplished men and women who shared their thoughts on the seven entrepreneurs. My many thanks to each one of them.

Special thanks to *The Hindu Business Line* editor, R. Srinivasan, who graciously let me explore the author in me. I am grateful to my reporting manager and the senior associate editor at *The Hindu Business Line*, J. Srinivasan.

Most of the travelling and writing for the book happened over weekends, days that are precious for my family. My wife, Sherin, and daughter, Amy, didn't complain once. Yes, Amy did ask for toys every time I returned home. Thanks ladies.

My larger family, including my sister and brother, have always been encouraging with showers of praise. Thanks to each of them.

The book wouldn't have been possible without the initial push of two people. My friends Jinoy Jose and Kanishka Gupta, founder of Writer's Side. Thanks, guys.

At Penguin Random House, thanks to Radhika Marwah for knowing when to push and when to push a little more, and Saloni Mital, who is a delight to work with.

I'm because I believe. Thank god.